Awakening from the American Dream

From Crisis to Consciousness

by Master Charles Cannon

with Will Wilkinson

Advance Praise for Awakening from the American Dream

"After 911, Bush told us to shop. And Cheney declared that our lifestyle wasn't negotiable. These authors fundamentally disagree. Here's their premise: if the hope that fulfillment comes from competing to accumulate stuff is an illusion, then the reality is all about enjoying the happiness we already have inside us and sharing it with each other cooperatively. That's a dramatic transformation - from crisis to consciousness - as their subtitle says."

- Thom Hartmann, radio host and author of *Crash of 2016, Last Hours of Ancient Sunlight* and other bestselling books.

" Awakening from the American Dream issues an urgent call for us to become our full, authentic selves through the journey of personal awakening. It's not about just meditating in a cave or just marching for change—this book covers both the spiritual and the practical, with simple, compelling instructions for personal and global transformation."

- Marci Shimoff, NY Times bestselling author of *Happy for No Reason* and *Love for No Reason.*

"I'm heartened to read this remarkable perspective on our country, with its urgent invitation to take a stand and be the leaders we inherently know we already are! Years ago I wrote about the shift from ego to essence and this book continues that work, taking another step, from essence to embodiment. Now, more than ever before, the world is ready for spiritual activism, and that is exactly what this book advocates and illuminates."

- Barbara Marx Hubbard, author of *Conscious Evolution, Emergence, Birth 2012 and Beyond*

"How do we make sense of the craziness that's going on in the world? By waking up to a larger reality. The authors offer practical, spiritual solutions that you can use to create more harmony and inner peace in your world."

- Steven Halpern, Ph.D., Recording Artist/Sound Healer

"We search endlessly outside of ourselves for happiness. However, like Tolstoy's beggar who spent much of his life yearning for something better while he sat unknowingly on top of a pot of gold, our treasure is also already with us. To find it we need to expand our self-awareness and wake up from this slumber. This book provides a roadmap beyond the endless chatter of the mind and the pulls of the ego, to the stillness and bliss of our true self."

- Dave Swartz, CIO, American University and presenter to management on The Self-Aware Leader

Dedication

This book is dedicated to you, the reader, with appreciation for your welcome of the awakening impulse that has guided you to these words.

May your reading journey further substantiate the truthful experience you have been discovering, disrupt the programming that still limits you, and empower you to continue... to wake up and be happy!

Acknowledgements

The brave pioneers in this field are too numerous to name. We acknowledge them all, every individual who has stirred in their slumbers and sufficiently awakened from the illusion of separation and lack to provide embodied leadership for the rest of us, free of the Dream, free to fully live in Reality.

Being first is never easy. We are not first. We follow in the footsteps of others and, as we begin this journey of awakening, it is wholly appropriate to express our deep respect and gratitude for them.

May we so live that their courage and perseverance is well rewarded with the actualization of the true vision of what this country may one day become, one awakening individual at a time.

Welcome

Welcome to this adventure in awakening to authentic happiness.

As you will immediately discover, we advocate meditation as the most effective way to increase and deepen your experience of authentic happiness. To assist you, we are providing an audio download of a High-Tech Meditation® soundtrack.

This 30-minute soundtrack can be accessed by everyone who has purchased this book. Go to http://synchronicity.org/awakening-audio-download and type in this code:

HTMeditation

In addition, we are offering free updates of this text. You will automatically receive these by requesting the High-Tech Meditation® soundtrack and entering your email address.

We welcome your comments on the book and will include some of them, with your permission, in next editions. Send your comments to: awakening@synchronicity.org.

Thank you for embracing this journey of awakening from the American Dream.

You are not alone.

Table of Contents

Table of Contents

INTRODUCTION

"Most men lead lives of quiet desperation and go to the grave with the song still in them." [1]

- popular colloquialism

The American Dream is not working. Consider these sobering statistics, some originating from a 2011 poll,[2] gathered together here to present a snapshot of life in America today and repeated with their appropriate references throughout the book:

- With just 5% percent of the world's population, Americans consume 80% of its painkillers.

- Only 66% of American men had a job last year, the lowest level in recorded U.S. history.

- Last year over half of all U. S. college graduates under the age of 25 were either unemployed or underemployed and 6 million young American adults were living with their parents.

- Today, one out of every seven Americans is on food stamps and one out of every four American children is on food stamps. The number of Americans on food stamps has increased 74% since 2007.

- About 40% of working age Americans either have medical bill problems or are currently paying off medical debt. In 1965, just one out of every 50 Americans was on Medicaid. Today, it's exploded to one out of every 6.

- 13% of all U.S. homes currently sit empty. 8 million Americans are at least one month behind on their mortgage payments.

- One out of every four American workers has a job that pays $10 an hour or less. The U.S. now has a higher percentage of workers doing low wage employment than any other major industrialized nation.

- The number of low-income jobs has risen steadily over the past 30 years and now account for 41% of all employment in the U.S.

- Median family net worth rose 62 percent from 1962 to 1983, then fell 12 percent from 1983 to 2010.

- Personal debt has escalated to $1.48 for every dollar in earnings in 2007, from just 62 cents per dollar in 1983.

- The average duration of unemployment in the U.S. is now at an all-time record of 39 weeks.

- Today, the wealthiest 1 percent of all Americans own more wealth than the bottom 95 percent.

- There has been a 400% increase in antidepressant usage in America since 1988. Almost 10% of Americans are taking antidepressant medication and have been doing so for years.

The happiness and success promised by The American Dream has failed to materialize for the vast majority of Americans, and it's getting worse. Many still hope, but increasing numbers now pin their futures on a sudden win such as claiming a lottery jackpot or becoming the next American Idol, rather than on working for what they get. Many others are giving up hope entirely.

What happened to the greatest, the wealthiest country on earth, the land of equal opportunity for one and all? These astounding economic statistics might incite denial, shock and even perhaps a dawning sense of hopelessness. If so, that's not necessarily a bad thing.

In fact, we encourage you to give up hope immediately! Give up hope in the Dream. And when you hear someone talking about making the Dream work or creating a new dream,

2

or a bigger dream, run! Get as far away from them as quickly as possible and guard your wallet.

Give up hope in the Dream.

Why has The American Dream failed? Why can it never succeed? Because it's a dream! It's a dream presented as a trailer for reality. As comedian George Carlin famously quipped, *"The American Dream ... you have to be asleep to believe it."* [3]

You Can't Get What You Already Have

We've been sleeping, individually and as a nation, and the world population dreams with us. We've dreamed of happiness and success but that dream has become a fantasy world for the few and a nightmare for the many. The American Dream is a program that someone else created and installed in us. It has succeeded for a few and enslaved the rest of us. It's afforded the few an existence of privilege, luxury and power and doomed the rest of us to fighting over the scraps.

It takes courage to question the Dream. If you do, you may feel unpatriotic or powerless. Disempowerment is a central component of the Dream program. You may feel lost with no way out, or you may answer your own doubts with increased determination to "make it." The Dream is just as enthralling for the hopeless and the hopeful.

You might disagree with these introductory words, be offended and brand us as "un-American." The Dream is a robust program, heavily fortified with thousands of defense mechanisms all designed to keep you sleeping within a prison of beliefs and a life of quiet desperation.

If you sense the truth of these words and feel compelled to read on, you are awakening from The American Dream. What does awakening bring? Disillusionment, questions and eventually the understanding that you simply don't need to try to get what you already have.

Everything the Dream promises is, in essence, inherent in who you are. You are already innately happy and successful. It's your nature today as completely as it was when you first viewed the world through newborn baby eyes, owning nothing, having no skills or investments, while "adults" gathered around to celebrate your unique value and beauty.

Do you want to wake up and experience this reality? Another way to ask this question is, "Do you want to be happy?" The Dream urges you to pursue happiness. In fact, it's one of your rights as an American. In the Dream scenario, you are not happy until you get happiness. It must be acquired. This generates a fundamental indebtedness to a system that promises to provide what you are lacking. It's called dependency and it's experienced as slavery.

There are two ways to be happy. You can become happy because of what happens in your "content" world, or you can just be happy— becoming or being, take your pick. Door number one belongs to the Dream where you'll become happy when you have enough money, a perfect spouse, health, success, fame, when world peace is declared, etc. This is the life of pursuit, also known as the rat race.

Door number two opens to wakefulness and the experience of happiness now. It comes from the inside, and that's more than a cliché. It's true! When actualized, you feel it bubbling up from the depths of your soul. You are happy for no reason. You are just happy because that's your nature. So wake up and be happy.

Saving Ourselves, Saving our Country

This book is not about The American Dream. It's about *awakening* from The American Dream. How does that happen? Remember waking up this morning? What happened? You were asleep, maybe dreaming. Then you woke up, but not all at once. Some flicker of conscious awareness emerged. Maybe it brought sensations of discomfort, an ache or two in an aging body.

Some people like to leap out of bed immediately but most of us lounge around for a while, day-dreaming through a more gradual transition. Perhaps you thought about the day ahead of you, with anticipation, dread or resignation. As the moments passed, you continued to awaken until you got out of bed and plunged into your waking life and a variety of activities which led you here to this moment, reading these words.

Your awake experience today has been fundamentally different from sleeping, dreaming and contemplating getting up. In fact, everything changed when your feet hit the floor. Awakening from The American Dream is a thousand times more radical because you know you were asleep last night and waking up was a routine you have repeated every day of your life. But you haven't known that you were asleep in The American Dream and this waking up will call on you to challenge everything you have believed to be true.

You may feel shocked at the suggestion that you're dreaming right now. If you are convinced that you are already awake, ask yourself this: "Where does my happiness come from?" If the answer includes anything outside of yourself — good weather, big money, multiple orgasms, your candidate winning the election, good health, expensive wine, retired mortgage, peace on earth, no cavities, successful IPO, new fast car, kitchen remodel, closing Guantanamo, winning the lottery, heartburn cured, cup of coffee or glass of wine — if you believe that any of those, or anything else, is capable of making you happy now or in the imagined future, then you are asleep and dreaming. You are pursuing happiness just like The American Dream tells you to.

True happiness resides within you as an incorruptible aspect of who you are and always will be. To experience it, the truth of it, happiness must pour from you... you must express it. You don't get it, you give it.

You are designed to do this; all human beings are. But this fundamental ability was not encouraged, taught or perfected in you by parents and teachers. In fact, everything possible was done to purge even the faintest memory of this inherent ability from your awareness. The Dream makers have installed their program in you, constantly updated, upgraded and debugged, with a result that has addicted you to seeking happiness from the outside.

A healthy American democracy has always required constant vigilance, dating back to the days of our founding fathers. They have always required looking with fresh eyes at society's assumptions and hopes. Note these words spoken in 1862 by President Abraham Lincoln as he addressed Congress. "The dogmas of the quiet past are inadequate to the stormy present. The occasion is piled high with difficulty. As our case is new, so we must think anew and act anew. We must disenthrall ourselves and then we shall save our country." [4]

Lincoln's words could as easily have been spoken today, and they underline the single purpose of this book: to help you "disenthrall" yourself, to wake up. Then, and only then, can we save our country and ourselves.

Our Awakening Strategy

Following several introductory chapters that lay a foundation for our explorations, this book is divided into three segments. Part One details the Dreaming state. For most of you this will be a retrospective. You have already moved beyond deep sleep or you wouldn't have been drawn to this book.

In Part Two on Awakening, we guide you in a Socratic process of questioning aspects of your Dream life. We'll get specific and be disruptive. There will be painful disillusionment. You may object and squirm. But if you stick with it, you'll find that understanding dawns and with it, comes more happiness. You'll also lighten up. The Dream is dead serious, awakening is profoundly tumultuous, but being awake is light-hearted.

Part Three describes being awake. Life beyond the hypnosis of the Dream comes with an entirely new perspective. And you'll be happy, truly happy, in a way that doesn't depend on anyone or anything else. Your personal happiness production plant will be back in operation.

At no time is awakening more urgently needed than in the face of tragedy. As of this writing, terrorism fills the news. How, you might appropriately inquire, could anyone be expected to be happy in the face of such horror?

Because the happiness we are speaking of does not depend on circumstances. It is a state of being one takes into circumstances. The happiness we are speaking of is not a smiley face, or some kind of superficial overlay that denies real feelings such as sorrow and rage. We are speaking of authentic happiness which runs deep. It can be described as inner peace, a conviction that cannot be shaken by anything in the "content" world. It is that inspiring quality of the human spirit, unassailable by terrorists and their bombs. It is your natural state.

Can you imagine being authentically happy no matter what? Lose your job? OK, what's the next challenge? A relative dies? What gifts did he or she give you and how can you immortalize their memory by growing those gifts and passing them on to others? Husband cheats on you? Well, now his unfaithful heart is exposed and you can take a next step into an authentic relationship... or not. You remain happy throughout, navigating life's challenges from a position of unshakable confidence. You are happy because you are awake. Your awakened, authentic happiness is a state of being and when you are experiencing this with power, you are able to feel everything without being threatened.

> ## Wake up and be happy.
> ## Imagine that!

Finding Your Vision, Singing Your Song

The American Dream has become a competition for material things. But throughout history, inspired visionaries have offered us opportunities to free ourselves from enslavement to the Dream Machine. Martin Luther King spoke about his vision for our future: "... when we allow freedom to ring, when we let it ring from every village and every hamlet, from every state and every city, we will be able to speed up that day when all of God's children, black men and white men, Jews and Gentiles, Protestants and Catholics, will be able to join hands and sing in the words of the old Negro spiritual: Free at last! Free at last! Thank God Almighty, we are free at last!" [5]

How to Read This Book

This is more than a book. It is a transformational tool carefully designed to guide you through three powerful expansions of awareness toward breakthroughs of enlightened wisdom that you can sustain and grow in your wakeful life.

For that reason, we recommend against reading pages at random. Read them in order and take time to digest what you read. Between readings, notice how the words pertain to your life because your timing is perfect. You picked up this book at the perfect time in your awakening life — you can be entirely sure of that.

As a preview of coming attractions, consider these five statements describing awakened experience. Listing them here, they are simply ideas to inform you. As you read on, they will become principles that can inspire you. By the end of the book they will be truthful statements that can define you.

1. You are enough.

2. You are loved.

3. You are needed.

4. You are awake.

5. You are happy.

You are enough, know that now. And you are loved. Regardless of what you have done and not done, you are loved for who you are. We need you. It doesn't matter whether you are famous or consider yourself a nobody. We need who you are, not what you do. You are awake. Yes, even here at the beginning of this awakening journey, there is a place within you that already knows this just as we know it. We are awake together and by the time you finish reading this book it will be a much more conscious experience for you. You are happy. Right now, even if your back is aching, your bank account is empty, your marriage is failing and you have lost hope in America.

Authentic happiness is more than an emotion; it contains all emotion. It is who you are; it is your true nature. Carry the promise of this description of yourself as you journey through this reading.

Throughout our writing we often shift voices. At times we will write in the first person. For instance: "I read this article." This means that one of us has a personal experience or perspective to convey. Most often though we will speak together using the "we" voice. This means we are including everyone. At other times we will address you directly: "You may be experiencing…." Finally, we have interspersed the text with truthful statements that are framed as "I" statements. We call these Moments of Mastery. They are intended to stir your empowered ownership of what the words mean and to give you an immediate opportunity to integrate the value of what you have been reading.

Master Charles Cannon carries the title "master" from his personal background as a long-time disciple of Swami Muktandanda in India and also from mastery of spirituality and meditation. All people can develop mastery in their lives, free from imprisonment in the Dream.

A true master understands that the source of their mastery lies beyond themselves personally. Their skills, formidable as they may be, are useless without a personal connection to the source of all which we describe as Source Intelligence. Another word for this is consciousness, and consciousness is equally available to all living beings. Without it, we would be lifeless.

This, above all, establishes our starting point. We are equals in the most important way, irrevocably united in the oneness of consciousness that is the essence and wholeness of all people. The difference between us relates to degrees of conscious experience. It is up to each of us to awaken and experience consciousness, happiness and personal meaning in life to realize the fullness we have longed for!

Chapter One: Wake Up and Be Happy

"Happiness is a most confronting inquiry because it challenges you to be honest about everything, including unhappiness.

The truth is, you can't be truly happy and be dishonest about your unhappiness." [1]

- Robert Holden

Are you truly, genuinely, happy? Or are you chronically discontent and miserable? What's the percentage day to day? What's the percentage looking forward as you imagine getting older, with the economy stalled, the environment ailing and the world shuffling down a path of denial? How do you feel about your unhappiness? Now, dare to ask what we call one of the most transformational questions in the world:

"If I weren't doing this already, would I choose to do it?"

Get specific about your job, where you live, your relationships, including your primary one. Feel the question: "If I wasn't married to him or her right now, would I choose to marry him or her today?"

This can be scary because it can expose your unhappiness, which is why you don't dare ask. As long as you stay distracted with working, parenting, paying bills, watching movies, etc., you're asleep to the reality of your unhappiness. Here's another powerful question to ask yourself:

"When did I lose my sense of wonder?"

And here's the follow-up question that lets you change things:

"How desperately do I want it back?"

Wonder. Awe. Adventure. Discovery. Eagerness. Surprise. These are all aspects of true happiness. How much of that do you have in your life? How passionate are you about wanting more?

It's time to wake up and be happy.

Meeting Each Other

It's customary to begin any new relationship by getting to know each other. We know that you are a reader. We know you are a son or a daughter. You may also be a father, mother, sister or brother, cousin, niece or best friend. You could be a teacher, a student, a Socialist, a priest, a housewife, a plumber, a university professor or a lawyer. You could be on the verge of suicide or on the eve of marriage or divorce.

You know that we are writers. We are also men, and you can read our brief biographies somewhere in this publication and on our web site. But this is not actually who we are and this is not actually who you are. These are just roles we play. Let's use a diagram to expand our identities.

In frame one you see three dots. That's where we're starting, with you and us, identified by our roles as writers and reader.

Frame 1

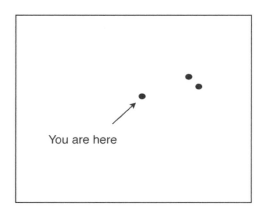

In the next frame we've placed a small circle around us and added other dots outside the circle. Think of the circle as your awareness, limited for the moment to yourself and to us, while the rest of the dots represent other people.

Frame 2

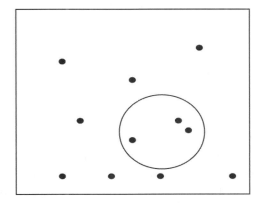

Let go of your identity as that dot and imagine you are the circle, a symbol of your awareness that contains your "self" and us.

Now, in the last frame, notice that we have taken away the circle.

Frame 3

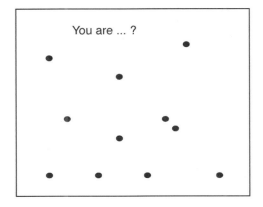

Where are you now? Where are we? Don't try to find your dot, or ours. Just experience your "self" as awareness, not limited to one dot, not limited to three dots.

Embrace an identity as unlimited awareness. You are not a dot, you are not a circle. You are not a role. You are awareness. Not a male or female, not any role. You are consciousness. And, as we've emphasized, consciousness is inherently happy.

Pondering a Question

Who are you?

We are not asking you about a role, a label, skills, any position or accomplishments. It's a question about who you are, not what you do, and it doesn't need an immediate answer. It's a question to ponder, a simple way of stepping back to check in with your expanding awareness. We also encourage you to be forward-thinking. What can you imagine for yourself? In this way the simple question, "Who are you?" becomes "Who are you choosing to be right now?"

Who are you choosing to be?

You have a choice. Knowing that, making room for that (rather than unconsciously accepting some role as your identity) you open yourself to experience what we call "the awakening impulse." This is a shift in identity from doing to being. You can wake up and be happy, but it has nothing to do with what you do and everything to do with who you are.

Chapter Two: The Awakening Impulse

"America is just a nation of two hundred million used car salesmen with all the money we need to buy guns and no qualms about killing anybody else in the world who tries to make us uncomfortable." [1]

- Hunter S. Thompson

Remember when people thought the earth was flat? One day, it became round. Remember when people thought the earth was the center of the universe? One day it began circling the sun. Remember when there was argument about whether life was on other planets? One day there was life everywhere; not just on the planets but the planets themselves. Oh, wait, that last one has yet to come. Something to look forward to!

Here's the thing. What we believe becomes our reality and what we believe depends on our awareness. Was the earth ever flat? In one sense, yes, because people believed it was. And why did they believe it was? Because that was the limit of their awareness. All they could see was a flat horizon stretching into the distance. That changed when, later, people developed other means of perceiving.

What else that we know is "true" might change because of a shift in perspective? For instance, is America thriving? Or is this nation actually in decline, some may say collapse? There's plenty of evidence for the latter. For those with that awareness, America is in trouble. For those who remain unaware, America remains the "city on a hill," an unassailable truth of exceptionalism. For them, metaphorically the earth is flat.

So, what turns a flat earth round? If you've ever debated someone with fixed views you've learned that facts don't mean much to those with emotionally laden prejudices.

Fortunately, we don't need to argue our way awake. There is a force at work in our lives urging us toward wakefulness. We call it "the awakening impulse." It is driving the evolution of human consciousness today, as it always has. Self-awareness is expanding — that's the one staple throughout human history — and people are beginning to experience themselves as more than lonely islands unto themselves, striving for happiness. We are awakening to the reality that we are interconnected with everyone and everything.

This awakening impulse is not American. It resonates throughout the cosmos. It's what's happening everywhere. We can imagine that America is separate, that the earth is separate. But separation is an illusion. The universe is just that, one song, "uni-verse." Conscious awareness of this connectedness is expanding rapidly and is the most under-reported story in human history.

With it America 2.0 is being born, not separate in arrogant exceptionalism this time, but rather integrated cooperatively within the world population. It's more than a national movement, it's also an individual awakening that can't be confined within borders. We use the term "The American Dream" to describe an illusory program that affects everyone, everywhere. And all dreamers are destined to awaken.

The awakening impulse stirs us all to wake up and be happy!

> **Laughter gives your organs a good massage.**

Chapter Three: Jump

"Jump!" [1]

- Joseph Campbell

Whenever we use the term "the awakening impulse," it's a cue for experience, a moment to pause and tune into yourself. The present is the gateway to happiness, the opportunity to expand your awareness and identity (remember the dots and the disappearing circle). The relative spaciousness of any moment determines your experience. You can be small; you can be large; you can be unlimited. You can be happy. It's your choice.

Here are three ways to experience the awakening impulse as you read:

1. as a catalyst
2. as a contemplation
3. as a confirmation

A catalyst stimulates change. Think of a spark plug. You read something and feel ignition. The spark in the words stimulates your consciousness and starts a fire that needs tending. You can best do that by "pausing in wonder." You may also glimpse the ridiculousness of a situation. OK, enjoy that!

> **Igniting by a catalyst, you are a learner.**
> **Contemplating, you are a thinker.**
> **Appreciating a confirmation, you are wise.**

Whenever you encounter a catalytic moment, pause to observe yourself learning. Learning is one of the true joys of being young. No matter what your age, when you choose to learn, you are sipping from the fountain of youth!

A contemplation encourages introspection. This type of deep thought is increasingly a rarity in our short attention-span world. But just as taking time to chew food aids digestion, pondering ideas promotes their understanding and assimilation. Whenever you read something that prompts a moment of contemplation, "pause to ponder."

Savor the experience of applying your mind to the study of something interesting. You can hold it in your introspective gaze and examine it from many angles, ask questions and imagine meanings. The conscious harnessing of imagination is a skill not reserved for the gifted, unless we say that we are all gifted. Indeed we all are but who is consciously developing this gift?

A confirmation validates understanding. Other moments of reading will prompt the realization, "I know that!" Yes, you knew it. But you didn't know it consciously until you encountered some catalyst that raised your awareness from a subconscious to a conscious level.

Enjoy a moment of substantiation. "How about that! I know more than I thought I knew." Your best response in these moments is "pausing to appreciate." Appreciation increases value, just as depreciation decreases value. When you consciously appreciate what you know, you increase your self-esteem and your self-love from which springs the love of all others. You relax with yourself, you lighten up, and that enables you to enjoy others just the way they are. You might even marvel looking back and asking yourself, "What was I so uptight about?"

Shift Identities as You Read

Words can inspire, stimulate, encourage and empower, but unless something happens in the real world you're just dancing with your imagination. Who will be inspired by words to act? The "who" in the equation is your priority. Read with that in mind, ever present to the question: "Who am I?" This is not a trick question. Right now you seem to be a reader. We seem to be writers. But, depending on which of the three described experiences you are having — catalyst, contemplation or confirmation — you have three additional identity options.

When you embrace a "quality identity," it becomes easy to shift "role identities." Rather than carrying one primary identity 24/7, your role identity of the moment can be assumed and discarded like a piece of clothing. One moment you may be a driver, the next a cook. You may become a tennis player, a dentist or a gardener. There's nothing as conflicted and out of place as a person who has decided on a single identity and sticks to it no matter what they are doing. A brain surgeon who refuses to embrace his momentary role as a lover is not a good lover!

All you've got to lose by letting go of a *single* stuck role identity to embrace the dance of *many* is the boredom of a life spent in conflict with other selves stuck in roles. Instead, experiment with what Sarah Ban Breathnach wrote in her book, *Simple Abundance: A Daybook of Comfort and Joy*. "Today expect something good to happen to you no matter what occurred yesterday. Realize the past no longer holds you captive. It can only continue to hurt you if you hold on to it. Let the past go. A simply abundant world awaits." [2]

The Trap of Intellectual Enlightenment

It's customary to read a book in order to understand and learn. Rest assured that your ego will try to hijack any truth presented here and turn it into intellectual enlightenment. What's the difference between intellectual enlightenment and wisdom? Wisdom comes from experience; intellectual enlightenment comes from beliefs. Intellectual enlightenment is not practical, it's theoretical. How do you make things tangible and practical in your life, right where your feet are? This is what all true masters teach, not just concepts but applications.

For instance, Krishnamurti taught that transformation arises from awareness not analysis. That's awareness all the time, 24/7. In Part Two of this book you will learn how to expand your awareness, moment-by-moment, in order to create holistic experiences. Socrates said that 99% of what you believe is simply not true. We are interested in the 1% that is true — true in experience, not theory.

Who are you now? Let's pause for a moment to entertain that question once again, to examine your "now" life. Take a breath, close your eyes and ask yourself: "Who am I right now?"

... pause

What happened? I'm sure there was a flood of thoughts and feelings. Here's a clue to making this exercise more valuable: don't look for answers, just enjoy asking the question. And, asking again...

"Who am I right now?"

This provocative question knifes through concepts toward your core where the awakening impulse nudges you into wakefulness. As you ask this question again and again throughout these early pages, your sense of self will change and expand, from roles to qualities, from doing to being.

Five Fables

We will be referring to five fairy tales: *Rip Van Winkle, Sleeping Beauty, Humpty Dumpty, Alice in Wonderland* and *The Goose That Laid The Golden Egg*. There are helpful lessons in these fables to illuminate the awakening journey, which we have organized into three stages: Dreaming,

Awakening and Being Awake. The table below describes these. Notice that there are two columns for the Awakening stage. The first describes emerging into wakefulness from sleep; the second shifting from awakening to being dominantly awake. There are also two columns that describe being awake. The first relates to you, the second to your contribution.

Individual awakening cannot be completed independently from the rest of the human species. Until all of us are awake none of us are fully awake. We're all in this together. Studying this table can help you locate yourself in the journey. Are you predominantly dreaming, awakening or awake?

	DREAMING		AWAKENING		BEING AWAKE	
STATE OF AWARENESS	Unconsciously ignorant.	Consciously ignorant.	Unconsciously wise.	Consciously wise.	You know that you know nothing.	
TEACHING STRATEGY	Leave alone.	Be an example.	Teach.	Teach how to teach.	Enroll in contribution.	
	Identifying	*Witnessing*	*Merging*	*Present*	*Activated*	
PRIMARY STATE OF CONSCIOUSNESS	Struggling with roles and identifying with your body, mind and emotions.	Dawning of awareness. Questioning, confusion.	Awareness expanding. Glimpses of awake state and ability to sustain.	Constancy in balance. Blissful experience.	Ability to focus your personal amplitude of power for blessing.	

The Five W's

The following five classic questions can also be usefully applied to our inquiry, especially in this order. They track movement from investment in the Dream toward sustained wakefulness.

What can I get to enrich myself, inflate my ego and get fulfillment from the outside?

Why am I doing all this? Is this all there is?

Who am I? How about being, not just doing?

When is fulfillment? Right here, experiencing this.

Where should I choose to focus my attention? Right here and now.

You'll notice that the "Who" question is right in the middle of this awakening progression. In truth, that is the one question that permeates all of the others. We invite you to follow Joseph Campbell's advice as you turn the page, aware of yourself as a brave explorer, opening beyond your comfort zone into the unknown... and jumping!

Chapter Four: Accelerating Your Awakening

"Your vision will become clear only when you can look into your own heart ... Who looks outside, dreams. Who looks inside, awakes." [1]

- C.G. Jung

Awakening is about asking questions, not finding answers. There are plenty of people around with answers for everything. But life is a question, a contemplation, an exploration, an adventure of discovery far from the fraudulent, co-dependent security The American Dream and its experts champion. You can hear them spouting their opinions, making their pitches, so convinced they know the truth that there's little room for debate.

Then the market inexplicably reverses, the highly-favored team loses, the threatening storm shifts course. Faced with their faulty predictions, what do they do? They ignore, deny and shift to the next topic without even thought of an apology. Those who counted on their advice may lose their retirement savings, their homes, even their lives. But the experts blame others and keep on braying.

Question the experts. Question yourself.

What?

Children are rarely asked, "Who do you want to be when you grow up?" It's usually "What do you want to be," referring to some role such as a fireman.

This is understandable. The Dream is all about what you do, not who you are. Children are encouraged from the moment they can think to start doing! Being? What's that?

The Dream programming begins early. It's a necessity for the system. The Dream Machine needs workers to keep it going and every child is groomed to take his or her place. Every Dreamer, regardless of status, is enslaved, even those lost in roles as million dollar celebrities. Everyone is working for the "man." Who is the "man?" Individuals, yes, those few members of the elite who control this human game. But they too are trapped and, ultimately, the "man" is the system that enslaves us all.

Children are taught to pursue happiness outside of themselves, not to express their authentic selves and create happiness from the inside out. Generation after generation, our children grow up and take their place in society along with their elders, obsessed with "what, what, what."

Why?

Obsession with "what" can obscure any concern about "why." But those who admit they are miserable eventually start questioning their experience. "Why am I so unhappy? Why am I suffering?" They begin to doubt the Dream. "Wait a minute," they might say to themselves. "I've accepted what I was told about life and who I am. The American Dream promised me happiness and fulfillment but, instead, I'm suffering." This is confronting the Dream full on. "Wait a minute," they may say, doing the math. "Is this it … for the rest of my life? This is absolutely not what I was promised. This isn't what I was taught would happen if I followed the rules."

Why is this happening?

Asking why is the precursor to awakening. It's about doubting, questioning and searching. The extremes of your suffering have empowered your expanding awareness. This is the measurement of personal evolution.

Who?

Awakening accelerates as the primary question shifts from why to who. "Who is this 'me' that is awakening and opening up to so many new possibilities?" You begin to glimpse that there are infinitely more possibilities in life than you ever considered. Possibilities that were never presented to you.

Now another increase in self-awareness occurs, opening you to the conscious realization that you are waking up. "Wait a minute. This is all a dream. It's just a virtual reality. It's an illusion. I've invested myself in an illusion!" In asking "why," you are asking questions; in asking "who," you realize you are the one asking those questions. But who exactly are you? Even though you don't know that answer yet, you experience yourself separating from the Dream state and from your illusory identity within it. Congratulations. You have successfully discovered who you are not!

As you acknowledge who you are not, a mentor often appears. When the student is ready, the teacher arrives. Why is mentorship so helpful now? Because mentors can see you better than you can see yourself. They can reflect reality back to you so you can increase your own truthful understanding of your authentic self. And now the Dream loosens its grip on you.

This is the season of epiphanies, the spiritual breakthrough, the origin of that story you will tell your grandchildren … the day you woke up to who you really are and what life is truly all about. Enjoy these satori moments. The veil is lifting as you begin to experience what you've been missing — yourself! Now the awakening impulse, the awakening experience, becomes red-hot and catalytic.

When?

The only true experience you ever have abides in the timeless present moment. All else is illusion, a fantasy sustained by your ego mind. As you question, witness your self and challenge your mind's perspective, you begin to lose interest in the past and future. You begin to open to the radical possibility that you are not, in fact, a spectator of life. "When" is about now, creating your reality in the present moment. You've graduated from passive witness to empowered participant. As Neale Donald Walsch writes, "If not now, when? If not you, who?" [2] Well, it's now and it's you!

This realization can come in a satori-type moment when the mental train traveling from past to future freezes, when thinking stops. Then, a moment later, it may resume. "As soon as you have a thought, laugh at it," [3] Lao Tsu advises. He is referring to illusionary thoughts and we all have plenty of those. The moment you become aware of having one, laugh at it and an extended moment of awakening will arise.

Where?

Where is here and now, and we call it "constancy." Classical traditions refer to constancy of wakefulness as the true measurement of enlightenment. This is where your conscious awareness remains consistent enough to see through the Dream and perceive reality. You realize that you don't need to go anywhere nor do anything. Your contribution is your authentic presence. This phenomenon becomes tangible most often when a student encounters an authentic master. The student arrives in an unharmonious and serious state. The master is sitting there in peace and happiness, holistically content — everything in the environment is entrained toward that. Nike says, "Just do it,"[4] but masters say, wordlessly, "Just be it." They are being authentic and that carries immense power. This is their contribution, right where they are.

Likewise, when you are authentic this is your contribution wherever you are, whether you are at home alone, on stage speaking to a thousand people, running a large or small company, raising a child or just quietly meditating. Where is always here.

Source Intelligence

Every authentic individual makes an impact. Each is connected to Source Intelligence and is silently broadcasting their power and wisdom. This is what is happening and now we know why. It's because of who he or she knows themselves to be, happy in the present moment when living in the past and future ceases and where being is his or her astounding contribution as a personal signature of the universal expression of Source Intelligence.

Chapter Five: You Are Here

"I know that I am intelligent, because I know that I know nothing." [1]

- Socrates

John hasn't slept at night for two years. He doesn't have insomnia; he suffers from a most peculiar form of delusional anxiety. John believes that darkness is an actual thing, not merely the absence of light. When night falls, John is overwhelmed with fear convinced that darkness is filling his room. He is terrified as this torturous anxiety repeats itself again and again.

John devotes every dark hour to feverishly bailing darkness out of his room as if with a large bucket, heaving its contents through the open window, pausing only briefly to rest his arms and taking sips of water until at last morning comes, and with it light and victory.

Though the sun rises on its own accord, John believes he himself has removed darkness from his room. Exhausted but gratified, he collapses in relief and sleeps. But the next evening will find him at his window again, bailing away. It does no good to tell John that his efforts fail to contribute in even the slightest way to the progression of the earth around the sun and night turning into day. Because he's convinced that a new day would be impossible without him.

John is not a real person. But neither, it turns out, are we — not when we're lost in the Dream. So John's misperception is no stranger than our own. We know the sun will rise without our help so John's tactics seem foolish, but we're working pretty hard on just about everything else as if the universe itself would collapse without our micro-managing.

We introduced the term Source Intelligence. This is what actually got that darkness out of John's room. It's what moves the earth around the sun, and it's what beats our hearts. Ignoring it or not knowing anything about it doesn't stop its functioning. But becoming conscious of Source Intelligence and learning how to flow with it takes us beyond the Dream into the innate happiness of being awake.

Where Are You?

Now we ask, "where are you?" Are you dreaming, awakening or awake? There are two simple ways to determine your starting point on this awakening journey.

First, are you questioning reality? If not, then you are lost in the Dream and it's surprising you even picked up this book. If you are questioning your experience and beginning to doubt, then you are awakening. But to what degree?

Second, how seriously do you take yourself and life? If you know the absurdity of the Dream, you can agree with the Indian pundits who assure us that "There is nothing serious going on here!" If you read that and bristle reflecting on the state of the world plus your own personal situations, if you are offended, disagree, feel this is flippant and unkind, then you have just located yourself in the early, heavy stages of awakening.

Where you are is where you are. Finding your starting point to begin this awakening journey is not an exercise in judgment. You are exactly where your feet are and so is everybody else. Celebrate that! It's what lets you move forward. Know that as you do, you'll eventually begin laughing more than crying! As Gloria Steinem once said, "The truth will set you free. But first, it will piss you off." [2]

Phase One: Dreaming

If you picked up this book and have continued reading it, you are awakening and our description of Phase One will detail the state you are leaving. It's where you once felt at home but from which you are now distancing yourself as you expand your awareness and awaken from the Dream.

The nature of this phase is "programming" through enculturation from your parents, environment and personal history (who you are as a soul and your history of life experience).

The primary activity is "investment." You invest in the Dream, believing it to be real and banking on it to deliver your fulfillment. "Getting" is the focus and it arises from scarcity consciousness such as believing more is always better.

The time frame is the "future" because The American Dream is about pursuing happiness. It comes later when you catch it. Because you do not already have fulfillment, you continue to reinforce its absence.

The dominating sense in this phase is "certainty." Certainty in illusions such as things look good even if only temporarily and sporadically, and the Dream is strong. Ignorance is bliss!

The experience is "growth." Things are happening; your personal empire is developing. You increase in ego strength and arrogance; you expand your sense of separateness and competition.

The emotion is "hope." Regardless of the factual state of affairs, hope springs eternal. You continue to hope you can really make it, be the one who wins the lottery in whatever form.

Your personal focus is what we term "false integrity." You serve as a dependable worker bee in the corporate hive. You plug away, hoping your ship will come in by contributing to the maintenance of the Dream Machine.

Phase Two: Awakening

Awakening is transitional; it's about being neither here nor there. The familiar doesn't satisfy; yet neither does what you are awakening to. It takes trust to continue awakening through what is often called a "mid-life crisis," which can happen at any age.

The nature of awakening is "disillusionment." Cracks begin to appear ... all is not as promised. You begin to question. You start to notice and feel the harsh realities of the American economy and lifestyle. You realize the emptiness of your successes and the discouragement of your failures.

The primary activity is "denial" and/or "realization." You might push forward, head bloody but unbowed, trying to make the impossible work. It doesn't and you might realize it never will. You are waking up from the Dream ... the old ways just don't work any more.

The time frame is the "past." You ponder what went wrong, re-live your disappointments, blame yourself and others. This is a processing phase, coming to terms with what went wrong in your life.

The prevailing sense is "doubt." The certainty of the dreaming stage has faded. Now you are no longer so sure. You might escape into addictions.

Your experience is "loss." The Dream is crumbling. You are losing your prized investment. You feel things slipping away and may redouble your efforts to keep the value you have amassed.

The dominant emotion is "confusion." What's going on? There's no manual for this and few models to emulate. Now you may seek out guidance and your relationships begin to change. You may also change careers, end a marriage, move to another city, etc.

Your focus is "honesty." You are honest about what is actually happening. You face the music and continue awakening. You may be going through hell but you keep on going!

Phase Three: Being Awake

Now things begin to lighten up. You've done most of the demolition; your illusory world lies in ruins. It's time to rebuild and enjoy.

The nature of this phase is "enlightenment," which is a never-ending, eternally expanding process. Light shines on the darkness, illuminating the meaning of your life. Things begin to make sense in a whole new way. Weight lifts; smiles broaden.

Your main activity is "expansion." You expand your awareness by opening yourself to new experiences rather than contracting and defending. Individual consciousness merges with universal consciousness ... you are more than you thought yourself to be!

The time frame is the "present." You learn how to abide in the here and now experiencing true fulfillment. You deal with the future and the past from the present.

The prevailing sense in this phase is "awe." You are opening to the delighting nature of consciousness and its newness within the "now" of its happening. It is a truly awesome unfolding.

Your experience is one of "balance." You learn how to sustain your high by being balanced physically, emotionally and mentally. This is where a practice of meditation and a holistic lifestyle makes all the difference.

The primary emotion is "bliss." You are experiencing wholeness. You become happy for no reason. What was promised but not delivered by The American Dream is realized by awakening and remaining awake.

Your focus is "openness." You remain open to this experience whose time has come. "This" is it in every moment. You shift identities and begin to know yourself as the "All That Is".

QUICK REFERENCE GUIDE

	DREAMING	AWAKENING	BEING AWAKE
Nature	Programming	Disillusionment	Enlightenment
Action	Investment	Denial/Realization	Expansion
Time	Future	Past	Present
Sense	Certainty	Doubt	Awe
Experience	Growth	Loss	Balance
Emotion	Hope	Confusion	Bliss
Focus	False Integrity	Honesty	Openness

Going Deeper

You've determined where you are, which is your perfect starting point. You're always on schedule. Just keep moving. To help you fine tune your positioning on this awakening journey, we'll describe the fundamental "mind set" of the three stages.

> **Enlightenment is a never-ending, eternally evolving process.**

1. **DREAMING**: The dense levels of consciousness involve identification with the Dream. There is no awareness that you are actually dreaming. You identify with the ego mind and believe that the virtual reality of separation and conflict it has created is actual reality. This describes the majority of the human population, mired in ego-created virtual realities, identified with the Dream.

2. **AWAKENING:** Identification with the ego state steadily diminishes and your experience evolves to increasingly more subtle levels. The dismantling of the ego mind with its virtual reality is underway. Genuinely skeptical

questioning occurs and illusions are progressively replaced with truth.

3. **BEING AWAKE:** This is the state of maximum self-awareness where the consistent experience of truth as blissful consciousness (or presence) is known as your natural state.

Toward the Flowering

Of course everybody wants to go directly to the Bodhi tree. But what was the process the Buddha underwent that delivered him to that tree for the flower shower? How about his choices that built momentum in his expanding awareness? Think of your own life that same way, expanding and flowering.

Having read this chapter that details the stages of awakening, complete your self evaluation. Are you dominantly dreaming, in the early or late stages of awakening, or primarily awake? Read back through these materials and question yourself to arrive at an honest and comprehensive assessment. Knowing your starting point is essential for any successful journey.

Now that you have some sense of where you are, let's focus on how to make the most of this book.

Chapter Six: Getting Set

Awakening to the truth of yourself is the most important opportunity in your life.

In fact, you've been awakening through eternity because this is what consciousness does — it expands awareness of itself. As a part of consciousness, this is your primary intention. Now it's becoming your conscious priority.

These introductory chapters have laid a foundational understanding for your awakening journey through the three sections of the book. What have we covered that will guide you?

1. Give up hope. The American Dream is an illusion. Wake up and be happy!

2. Who are you right now? Who are you choosing to be?

3. The Awakening Impulse: catalyst, contemplation, confirmation.

4. Beware of intellectual enlightenment. Awakening is an experience, not a concept.

5. Shift identities at will.

6. Source Intelligence.

7. Ask questions, don't expect answers.

8. Reconnect with your wild rebel, beyond domestication.

9. Find your perfect starting point by asking questions and expanding self awareness.

The American Dream promises happiness and success but it can't deliver. While awakening promises and delivers the innate happiness of being, plus all those treasured qualities that grow with nurturing attention.

Why would you continue reading? Because you can't stop. The awakening impulse is alive in you and won't be denied. Your destiny is opening before you and you sense it. Not so much as something grand as simply the opportunity, at long last, to be yourself. What you sense is the presence of your authentic self arisen from the dream of dependency on things or others for your happiness. You sense being empowered to express yourself for helping to lift up others and for the fulfillment of your own life.

To complete our introduction, here is your first Moment of Mastery. We suggest you read through the words once, then pause a moment to acknowledge yourself as the fledgling master of your awakening life. Then read them again, perhaps aloud if your circumstance allows, this time as a declaration of who you are.

A Moment of Mastery

I am enough.
The awakening impulse lives in me,
igniting my eagerness to discover
and experience true self-acceptance.
I am enough.

PART ONE

Chapter Seven: Lost in the Dream

"The motivation that brings happiness is moral.

The motivation that brings pain is immoral ... at the heart of all afflictions is fundamental ignorance.

This is why education is so important. Because ignorance is a societal ill ... the origins of all suffering can be eliminated.

Once you recognize that, the possibility of that fate will arise in you." [1]

- Dalai Lama

Have you ever been lost? You probably wandered around awhile before you even realized you were lost. Then you may have delayed asking for directions, preferring to figure it out for yourself. That rarely works out well. Whoever you eventually asked for help just told you. End of story.

If you felt embarrassment, this would have been your choice. Whoever gave you directions doesn't care. You asked for their help, they helped. Most of us enjoy assisting; it is an opportunity to help another human being.

People lost in the Dream don't know they are lost. So, they are not about to ask for directions. But a moment comes for each of us early in our awakening journey when we admit it. "Hey, I'm lost!" This is not something that happens en masse. It's evolutionary. It happens individual by individual, when the timing is absolutely right. It has happened for you, which is why you're reading this book. You're ready to find your way out of the illusory wilderness of the American consumer culture. You're ready to change fuel, from the addictive promises of the Dream to the empowered reality of your own awake state of being.

Lost in the Dream

American author Washington Irving published the story of Rip Van Winkle in 1819. Rip Van Winkle, a colonial British-American villager of Dutch descent, is a kindly but lazy man. He escapes his responsibilities and his wife's nagging by wandering up the mountains. There he meets strangers who invite him to drink their liquor. Doing so, he falls asleep.

Rip awakens to discover that he has slept for twenty years. Other Dutch settlers in his village, many of them also henpecked husbands, wish they could share in Rip's good luck and sleep through the hardships. Rip then resumes his old ways. Several points from this story seem relevant to our beginning explorations:

- Rip was lazy. He slept to escape responsibility for his life and the reflection from other people (for instance, his nagging wife).
- Others envied his sleeping through hardship.
- He learned nothing from the adventure and never changed.

Consciousness dreams a dream that it is not the truth of itself. We sleep. Why would consciousness do this? It separates itself out in order that it might experience itself more fully. Not to avoid experience! Consciousness itself creates the illusory duality of relative reality where all experience is relative. The American Dream is one dream within this primary dream. There's nothing wrong with it if it is seen for what it is, an essential early stage in the journey of evolving consciousness.

The primary intention of consciousness is to fully be itself through the creative experience. According to Swami Muktananda, this is called "the play of consciousness." Here's the trick: consciousness cannot experience what it is, except in relation to what it is not because all experience is relative. This explains the illusion of separation, which is the cause of all conflict and resultant suffering in human experience, but which is also necessary for consciousness to know itself more fully. Hence, the real purpose of The American Dream. Again, there is nothing wrong with this stage of evolving consciousness.

Much like a sleeping dream, our experience within The American Dream is superficial. It's fragile. No matter how real it may seem, it dissipates like dust in the wind when we wake up. Of course the difference with The American Dream is that we believe we're awake. We don't know that we're actually dreaming, which renders the concept of waking up easy to deny or ridicule. That's changing now here in the 21st century. Awakening was once the domain of a few saints and sages, but now an alarm is sounding for all. In fact, sirens are blaring, making it increasingly difficult to hit the snooze button and return to the Dream.

Waking up is becoming more than a leisurely option. It's an urgent imperative for millions of us. There are many names for us, including "cultural creatives." We know who we are without any label. We are awakening.

Something Fundamentally Different

Self-help books urge readers to change and sometimes show readers how to. But they often do so from a starting point of trying to fix something that is wrong. "Here's how to have a better relationship, make more money, get healthier, be more spiritual, save the world, etc." The unspoken premise is that experiencing who we are may not be enough.

This is a different kind of book. Our starting point is the perfection of things exactly the way they are right now. Not only is it OK to be dreaming, it is a necessary part of the journey if that is what is happening for you. You are going to wake up when the time comes so allow yourself to have the experience that is happening now.

Dreaming is essential to awakening. You can't awaken until you have dreamed. How can you experience the truth except in relation to illusion? Again, all experience is relative. As you dream, consciousness is investing in illusion and this is your appropriate experience of what is not real. You go through that in order to experience what is real.

You find yourself within the Dream and it is full of misery, suffering, confusion, conflict and horror. It is a nightmare. But it is also essential from the point of view of the overall cosmic game. This is the big picture, the context in which you are living and now awakening.

> **Allow yourself the full
> experience of what is happening now.**

Why Judge When You Can Enjoy?

Was it mere chance that led you to pick up this book?

You may be one of the millions of Americans using Vicodin or alcohol or perhaps seeking to "unwind" with shopping or the sports channel — whatever the addiction of your choice might be is perfectly appropriate! That is where your feet are so that is where you must walk. We are not invalidating you in any way. This is appropriate for you right now or it wouldn't be happening. But the fact that you are reading this book means you must be questioning your current experience.

You are feeling the awakening impulse.

You are on the edge of discovering that escape doesn't really work for you any more. It doesn't fulfill; it doesn't make you happy. Something is gnawing inside, the realization that there has to be more to life. You're just not sure what it might be. You're like someone in a restaurant studying the menu and finding nothing she really wants. She may have dined there a hundred times before and had no trouble ordering. But today is different.

You are awakening. Celebrate the moment, uncomfortable as it may feel.

You might put this book down in a moment and return to your addictions. If it happens, that too is appropriate. But now you will be haunted by what you have discovered, even in these few pages. You have opened Pandora's box. You may go on to wander in the wilderness of your dreaming for days, weeks or years. But you have felt the awakening impulse. You were ready for it. And when you are ready for a next step, it will stimulate you again. You will pick up a different book, someone will say something or a line of dialogue in a movie will disturb your slumbers. Your further awakening is inevitable.

Relaxing With Who You Really Are

You are an instrument of consciousness whose sole function is to experience. This is a much simpler perspective than most of us have been programmed into. "What do you want to be when you grow up?" Well, who are you right now?

You are here to experience. Period. That, of course, includes growing, maturing and evolving into the fullness of yourself in experience and expression. You are here to process the information of experience and grow, to expand your self-awareness. All experience is valid to consciousness in terms of its intention to ever more fully be itself, to know itself. All experience is valid, including the most horrific. This may be difficult to accept at this point, but read on.

A Moment to Experience

Who are you right now? Pause to reflect without needing an answer. Feel whatever you feel. Let your thoughts flow without editing. Stop reading and repeat the question within yourself: "Who am I right now? Who am I right now? Who am I right now?"

... pause

Take a moment to muse. It's interesting what happens when you self-examine and allow yourself the luxury of not needing an answer! Just floating in uncertainty ... being with the question — there's something about it that begins to pry open the limitations of your dreaming experience. It's such a relief to know that this time there really are no right or wrong answers! Coming up with nothing is just fine. Nothing, "no thing," that's you!

Do your best to sustain a non-judging observational perspective as you continue reading. We are going to describe the dreaming state in detail. If you continue reading, it's because you are awakening. If you are in the early stages, you will tend to react to what you read, either in dispute or with self-judgment. Relax. Just read and observe your awareness expanding. It's meant to be enjoyable.

Programming

Our faith in the Dream is not accidental. We're programmed to believe in it. The primary program is separation, the illusion that things are separate, people are separate, each one is separate from the "other." This illusion of duality – subject and object, good and bad, right and wrong, etc. — is the source of all conflict and it is sacrosanct within the Dream. In fact, separation and conflict are the fundamental foundation of the Dream.

We are programmed to be separate and therefore conflicted. We are conflicted within ourselves because we experience ourselves as separate from each other, from our environment and from the source of life. Our concepts about "God" provide small comfort. Because we must consume in order to survive and, disconnected from Source Intelligence, we live in scarcity. We fight or at least compete with each other for the seemingly limited resources in our environment.

Investment

We invest in the Dream, convinced that it is reality. We become pregnant with hope, expecting the Dream to deliver a fulfilling life experience. Work hard, do whatever it takes, don't quit. Millions of Americans have proven that investing in The American Dream is the worst investment they have ever made, yet those same millions continue to believe. That's how strong the programming is. That's how effective the corporate, government, media and familial Dream weavers are at convincing us to leave our bets on the table until we die. "The house" always wins in the end.

Tomorrow Never Comes

Life in the Dream promises a big payday tomorrow. After you graduate, get married, have kids, win the corner office, make a million, retire rich, etc. It's chronically goal-oriented. Fulfillment is never about right now, enjoying what you already have. It can't be because that would sabotage our consumer culture. "Gotta get more or the economy will fall apart." So, fulfillment is always about what you get and how it will improve your life experience once you have it tomorrow, the next day, the next year. And of course it's never enough. The content of life, no matter how much you increase it, is never enough.

It can't be, it won't ever be, because true fulfillment is not about what you have. It's about who you are. And who you are only exists in the here and now, devoid of all content. That's what you lose when you invest in the Dream. You sacrifice life's only true and enduring value.

The pursuit of happiness—who could question that fundamental promise of The American Dream? It's guaranteed, it's a right, based on the belief that happiness lies outside and must be pursued. Since happiness is not already present, you must pursue it. You must seek it.

And there's a seeker born every minute!

Certainty

The programming must be comprehensive for the spell to last a lifetime. The Dream strategy is to tie success to certainty. How many motivational speakers beat that drum? "If you don't believe 100% that you can achieve what you desire, you are sabotaging yourself." Commitment is a noble strain in the hero's DNA. But commitment to illusion can only increase and sustain illusion. "Be absolutely certain that you will get the big house on the hill with the trophy spouse and 2.5 children and you will achieve it all." OK, let's say that works for you. What now? Is that fulfillment?

Those who have "made it" will do their best to convince you it worked for them. "Keep on keeping on" they will say. Don't give up. You can be part of the 1%; it just takes perseverance plus knowing the right people, timing and luck. So, why would you change direction just because you aren't getting any closer to your destination? That would be giving up on the Dream, and you sure don't want to be one of those quitters that some motivational speakers shame!

It's one thing to believe something but when others believe it too, doesn't that validate your belief? Consensus is especially important when the Dream stops working, when holes appear in the illusion. Misery loves company and surely we can't all be wrong! But yes, by believing in the Dream we most certainly can!

Growth

In the Dream we focus on the growth of things and neglect the growth of ourselves. In fact, we enable each other to believe and live a lie, that who you are depends on what you have, on the content of your life. Money, success, talent, acknowledgement — more is better and there is always more to get. Again, it is revealing how parents and teachers ask a child "what they want to be" when they grow up, not "who they want to be." It's central to the programming. Your roles will define you ... you're nothing without them.

Hope

Those who have achieved success in our consumer society extend the carrot of hope toward the rest of us. "You too can achieve The American Dream." (Just buy this book, DVD, training program, etc.) As long as there is someone who has "made it," it's possible for you to make it too. The goal of the Dream seems simple: achieving wealth and fame and security in a material world. But that's not the real agenda of the purveyors of the Dream. Their agenda is to enroll you in dreaming! The intent of the Dream is to create and retain dreamers. Hope springs eternal...

Integrity in Illusion

Personal integrity is a highly respected value, yet so many of our celebrities and leaders are eventually exposed in lurid scandals. This reveals more than isolated "moral failings." All dreamers are fundamentally corrupt. Why? Because of the belief that fulfillment comes solely from the material world. The promise? "That which I do not have can make me happy." This may be a picture perfect marriage or a winning lottery ticket. It might be your team winning the playoffs, a daughter winning a scholarship, whatever. This promise guarantees that everybody is on the take, some honestly and some dishonestly. How could it be otherwise when the driving premise is that fulfillment comes from a result, from what you get out of the material world? That bromide about how you play the game being more important than winning is secretly, and sometimes openly, scorned by many winners!

This explains why we need so many government regulations, a complex judicial system and millions of laws. Why is America becoming a police state? You can cite conspiracy evidence, some of which may indeed be true. But corrupt people create a corrupt society and without some kind of external control, chaos would reign supreme. Just look at what happens when the power goes out in a big city. Looting begins immediately and this fills the news, causing fear in our communities. Internal control in Source Intelligence is inadequate to stay the course without external policing.

Of course, widespread incidents of spontaneous caring and sharing also occur but those are hidden on the back pages, if reported at all. Those are not the sort of headlines that support further enforcement of the Dream Machine. Obviously, signs of awakening to a different value system are threatening. That's why you have to search for good news outside of the dominantly negative mainstream media.

Self Awareness

You can't remain invested in the Dream if you evolve enough self-awareness to see the truth. You simply won't continue to believe in illusion when you reach a certain level of self-awareness. Evolution in your consciousness brings a progression of ever-increasing self awareness. And let's be realistic for a moment — truly realistic. It has taken fourteen billion years since The Big Bang to get to this level of adolescent self awareness in the human population. What does that say? It says that human self awareness has been expanding at a snail's pace!

The vast majority of people simply do not have enough self awareness to awaken from the Dream; they're still thoroughly asleep within it and you can be sure they are not reading this book! What are they doing instead (and "they" might include us from time to time)? They are distracting themselves with overwork, obsessive entertainment addictions, paying $500 for a seat at a rock concert, joining 80,000 spectators at a football game (and 25 million more watching on television), storming the shelves on Black Friday and relentlessly investing in their content identities. They are not reading this book or attending a personal growth program that could support the continued evolution of their consciousness. That holds little interest for them as they slumber in their consumer dreams.

Nobody awakens from the Dream until self awareness expands sufficiently. But remember, the experience of the Dream is absolutely appropriate. Why? Because it is necessary for each of us to walk where our feet are. The acceptance of this truth puts an end to judgment of ourselves and all others. Embrace that experience — the full experience — of allowing yourself and others to be exactly as we all are right now.

Awakening happens on its own timetable. You are finding your way. So is everybody else. What was lost (the experience of authentic happiness) is being found.

A Moment of Mastery

I am enough.
As a human, I have limitations,
as a soul, I have a unique design.
I am unique, I am awakening
to who I truly am,
I am enough.

Chapter Eight: Origins

"Whereas The American Dream was once equated with certain principles of freedom, it is now equated with things. The American Dream has undergone a metamorphosis from principles to materialism ... When people are concerned more with the attainment of things than with the maintenance of principles, it is a sign of moral decay. And it is through such decay that loss of freedom occurs." [1]

- John E. Nestler

How did The American Dream turn into such a nightmare? Well, once you go to sleep you never know for sure what kind of dreams you will experience. It's beyond your conscious control. The American Dream always was a dream, so it always carried that risk. And that's the one and only thing it has ultimately delivered for the majority of Americans — a nightmarish experience of misery.

We should have known this long ago. But those we trusted to lead us to the promised land led us astray, albeit unintentionally for the most part. Few, if any, were consciously evil. In fact, most did the best they could. Parents, teachers, leaders — they could only share from their own experience based on what they had learned from those who unintentionally deceived them. The primary deception is the fantasy that happiness comes from outside of ourselves, from some future result. Very few humans learned otherwise, from parents, school teachers, career trainers, political hacks or ministers.

Of course, the blind have been leading the blind since the beginning. Imagine Christian preachers managing to keep a straight face when warning that it is impossible to get into heaven until you accept Jesus as your personal savior, ignoring what Jesus said about "heaven within," an experience that never depends on Jesus as a middleman.

How The American Dream Began

James Truslow Adams is credited with coining the term, The American Dream, in his 1931 book, *The Epic of America*. Quoting from that text: "... life should be better and richer and fuller for everyone, with opportunity for each according to ability or achievement regardless of social class or circumstances of birth." [2]

The United States Declaration of Independence proclaims that "all men are created equal ... endowed by their Creator with certain inalienable rights" including "life, liberty and the pursuit of happiness." [3]

The meaning of The American Dream centers on the belief that every American can achieve prosperity and happiness, including the opportunity for children to receive good educations and achieve successful careers. The Dream also champions individual rights and freedom of choice without restrictions according to class, religion or race.

Adams further clarified his vision of The American Dream, again from *The Epic of America*: "It has been a dream of being able to grow to fullest development as man and woman, unhampered by the barriers which had slowly been erected in the older civilizations, unrepressed by social orders which had developed for the benefit of classes rather than for the simple human being of any and every class." [4]

American literature is rich with references to The American Dream, including: the *Autobiography* of Benjamin Franklin; Mark Twain's The Adventures of Huckleberry Finn; Willa Cather's My Ántonia; F. Scott Fitzgerald's The Great Gatsby; Hunter S. Thompson's *Fear and Loathing in Las Vegas: A Savage Journey into the Heart of The American Dream*; and John Steinbeck's *The Grapes of Wrath*. In Death of a Salesman by Arthur Miller the play's protagonist, Willy Loman, pursues a fruitless journey in search of The American Dream. President Barack Obama wrote a memoir in 2006 entitled *The Audacity of Hope: Thoughts on Reclaiming The American Dream.*

Ironically, polls conducted since the 1980's consistently demonstrate that a majority of Americans actually believe that The American Dream is more about spiritual happiness than material goods! An increasing minority also believes that hard work no longer guarantees success. Today, most Americans predict that achieving the Dream is becoming more difficult for their children and are pessimistic about "getting ahead." Could that be because "spiritual happiness" is being ignored?

A Wikipedia entry on The American Dream cites "the four dreams of consumerism" as identified by Professor Ted Ownby in 1999:

> "The first was the "Dream of Abundance" offering a cornucopia of material goods to all Americans, making them proud to be the richest society on earth. The second was the "Dream of a Democracy of Goods" whereby everyone had access to the same products regardless of race, gender, ethnicity, or class, thereby challenging the aristocratic norms of the rest of the world whereby only the rich or well-connected are granted access to luxury. The "Dream of Freedom of Choice" with its ever expanding variety of goods allowed people to fashion their own particular life style. Finally, the "Dream of Novelty," in which ever-changing fashions, new models, and unexpected new products broadened the consumer experience in terms of purchasing skills and awareness of the market, and challenged the conservatism of traditional society and culture, and even politics." [5]

Hope and Change

We notice that none of those four edicts on consumerism have been successfully delivered by the Dream! So it makes sense, for instance, that President Obama campaigned successfully on hope and change. Hope that the dream might still work, change because what's happening is so inadequate! This sells an ego-driven illusion consciously designed to keep the population asleep and obedient, mired in the Dream.

Embracing The Awakening Impulse

Instead of entertaining hope, how about cultivating discernment? Instead of "what do you think," try "how do you feel?" Awakening from the Dream and tasting authentic reality includes getting excited about new insights, not just excited about a shiny new car! When you catch a glimpse of something beyond material fantasy it stimulates your awakening from the Dream. Here is a breakout moment, an "aha" moment, a catalytic moment. It's the awakening impulse in action. That's what real hope is. Not a fantasy but a truthful insight into the experience of life that is happening here and now.

Studying the origins of The American Dream is fascinating. But what's more helpful is contemplating the origins of your awakening. When did you first feel that impulse? How did it shape your life? Take a moment to contemplate your awakening history. Trace your experience all the way up to this moment and the turning of this page. Be wakeful as you do.

A Moment of Mastery

This is it.
This is the beginning,
my origin,
my awakening.
And I am enough.

Chapter Nine: The Land of the Free?

*"With two college degrees, I have struggled, and with
no health insurance, I've incurred a ton of debt. I have
not done as well as my parents, who came out of the
Depression. Our government says there are jobs, but
they are low-pay jobs with no benefits. Not livable wage
jobs. Not jobs that will give you a house and savings for
retirement. Nothing glimmers in this dust."* [1]

- from an email received by author
Barbara Ehrenreich

You can dream you're the richest person in the world, while
your reality is abject poverty. You can dream you have a perfect
relationship, while your reality is a partner who abuses you. You
can dream of world peace, while the reality is global terrorism.

Dreams are dreams; they are not reality. But a dream can
become a vision of a new reality. Consider visionaries who
have given us hope over the centuries, remarkable individuals
like Christ, the Buddha, Gandhi and Martin Luther King. Some
of them used the word "dream." However there is a big
difference between a dream and a vision. The causative level
of a dream is the ego. For instance, The American Dream is an
ego-driven virtual reality. Conversely, the causative level of a
vision is consciousness itself. The vision is the expression by
consciousness, complete with insights and behavior. For
instance, one might grow a vision for peace by being
authentically peaceful.

Another question arises: can a true vision such as what the
above amazing human beings presented degenerate into an
illusory dream? Yes, absolutely. It's happened with many
visionaries. They tune in to truthful insights that originate from
Source Intelligence, but the truth gets lost when translated by

their followers who are disconnected from Source Intelligence. Of course visionaries have to be careful to sustain their own level of self-awareness, the integrity of their Source Intelligence insights and the authenticity of their vision. This depends on the individual. Sometimes their truthful, but Source Intelligence insights get hijacked by their own egos and manipulated into ego-driven dreams.

Those who originate an authentic vision are always mystical and tend to be more evolved than those who follow them. That's why things get mired in mental interpretations after they leave. The egos of the followers form their own collective agenda, which can deviate wildly from the originating vision. Religion is a perfect example of this. A genuine mystic like Christ draws followers and, after he leaves, those followers create a religion such as Christianity, which is an egocentric hijacking of his truthful vision. They turn his truthful vision into their illusory dream. As Nietzsche lamented, "In truth, there was only one Christian and he died on the cross." [2]

Stop Dreaming and Wake Up!

We don't intend to invalidate dreaming but rather to recognize that dreaming is intrinsic to consciousness. Through dreaming you can experience the fullness of what it is not. We do pose these questions: Who are you choosing to be in relationship to your dreams? Are you becoming more self-aware? Do you know that you have been dreaming? Are you waking up?

The modern American lifestyle overwhelms us with the illusions of success and plenty. It is fundamentally biased toward the material myth and this imbalance results in disease, suffering and unhappiness. This quote from University of Illinois psychologist Ed Diener elucidates the point: *"Materialism is toxic for happiness"* [3]

The initial steps toward the experience of authentic happiness are to begin questioning the validity of your dreams, to expose illusion and then to welcome disillusionment.

The Inevitability of Suffering

Illusion creates suffering.

Let's consider again that aspect of the illusion called "hope." Someone might suffer because the one he loves doesn't love him back the way he had hoped. The problem here is not love, it's hope. He is certainly not experiencing true love because true love does not include suffering. He is experiencing dashed expectations, hope unfulfilled. If you are suffering in a relationship, don't call it love.

Do you believe that through suffering you will get to love? Here's the ego formula: through suffering, you will get attention which you hope will prove you have value that you then might construe as love. This is a substitute for self-worth based on illusory ego nonsense. Only egos are concerned with self-worth. Strategies to increase self-worth always originate in the ego. Self-worth is intrinsic to consciousness. The truth has no need to self-inflate.

You can't fault the ego. Consciousness created it to immerse us in sleep and dreams so that we can awaken, evolve and inhabit the world of reality. We are not judging The American Dream; we are just exposing it for what it is — a dream that fuels suffering. When you are suffering, you are dreaming. You are experiencing illusion.

But people are persistent and gullible. As John Michael Greer wrote on June, 2012, in his blog entitled, *Collapse Now And Avoid The Rush*: "There's quite a lot of money to be made these days insisting that we can have a shiny new future despite all evidence to the contrary, and pulling factoids out of context to defend that increasingly dubious claim; as industrial society moves down the curve of decline, I suspect, this will become even more popular, since it will make it easier for those who haven't yet had their own personal collapse to pretend that it can't happen to them." [4]

Challenging Illusion, Ending Suffering

The way out of your nightmare is to begin challenging illusion with truthful questions. For instance, ask, "What is causing my suffering?" Is it conflict? OK, keep questioning. "What is the reason for my conflict?" Instead of coming up with a list — him or her, your boss, the weather, this or that politician, etc. — cut to the chase: all conflict arises from the illusion of separation. In this situation ask, "What am I separating myself from?"

The only way to resolve your suffering is to invest in truthful oneness instead of illusory separation. This is how progressive awakening happens through disillusionment. Now, how much suffering do you need before you become willing to question and discover the root of it — to discover that you are creating your own suffering?!

The Evolution Train Can Never Run Late (or Early)

You are on schedule, now and always. So is everyone else. You are on a journey of evolving, expanding awareness, disillusioning yourself of the American Dream and awakening to true reality.

You need two wings to fly. One is for effort, the other for grace. Effort is about working hard to make your dreams come true. But having realized it's all a lie, you turn your efforts toward dismantling illusion. Your choice to proactively manage your own disillusionment marks a 180-degree change in the direction of applying your efforts. Such change requires focus, work and deprogramming.

Grace is your other wing. Grace is effortless. It is about being, not doing. Grace comes to you. You can never go and get it. Some people call it luck or good fortune but it is much more. Grace is life working the way it should, with all the parts coordinated.

When you shift your efforts toward dismantling illusion, this sends a signal to life and grace increases. When enough disillusionment has occurred, grace increases still further and you begin to enjoy balance as the two wings equalize and you start to soar in the heavens!

Exposing The American Nightmare

Michael Ford, founding director of Xavier University's Center for the Study of The American Dream wrote of the "Five Myths About The American Dream" in a January, 2012 article for the *Washington Post Outlook*:

> *Few ideas are as central to American self-identity as the 'American dream.' Politicians invoke it, immigrants pursue it, and despite unremittingly negative economic news, citizens embrace it. But what is The American Dream? We began regular study of how people define and perceive the Dream three years ago, and have discovered many misunderstandings worth a second look.* [5]

He continues with research about the five myths:

1. The American Dream is about getting rich.

> *In a national survey of more than 1,300 adults that we completed in March, only 6 percent of Americans ranked "wealth" as their first or second definition of The American Dream. Forty-five percent named "a good life for my family," while 34 percent put "financial security", material comfort that is not necessarily synonymous with Bill Gates-like riches, on top.*

> *While money may certainly be part of a good life, The American Dream isn't just about dollars and cents. Thirty-two percent of our respondents pointed to*

"freedom" as their dream; 29 percent to "opportunity" and 21 percent to the "pursuit of happiness." A fat bank account can be a means to these ends, but only a small minority believe that money is a worthy end in itself.

2. Homeownership is The American Dream.

In June, a New York Times-CBS News poll found that almost 90 percent of Americans think that homeownership is an important part of The American Dream. But only 7 percent of Americans we surveyed ranked homeownership as their first or second definition of The American Dream. Why the discrepancy? Owning real estate is important to some Americans, but not as important, or as financially rewarding, as we're led to believe.

Federal support of homeownership greatly overvalues its meaning in American life. Through tax breaks and guarantees, the government boosted homeownership to its peak in 2004, when 69 percent of American households owned homes. Subsidies for homeownership, including the mortgage interest deduction, reached $230 billion in 2009, according to the Congressional Budget Office. Meanwhile, only $60 billion in tax breaks and spending programs aided renters.

The result of this real estate spending spree? According to the Federal Reserve, American real estate lost more than $6 trillion in value, or almost 30 percent, between 2006 and 2010. One in five American homeowners is underwater, owing more on a mortgage than what the home is worth.

Those who profit most from homeownership are far and away the largest source of political campaign contributions. Insurance companies, securities and investment firms, real estate interests, and commercial banks gave more than $100 million to federal *candidates and parties in 2011, according to the Center for Responsive Politics. The National Association of Realtors alone gave more than $950,000, more than Morgan Stanley, Citigroup or Ernst & Young.*

Homeownership is more important to special interests than it is to most Americans, who, according to our research, care more about "a good job," "the pursuit of happiness" and "freedom."

3. The American Dream is American.

The term "American Dream" was coined in 1931 by James Truslow Adams in his history The Epic of America. In the midst of the Great Depression, Adams discovered the same counterintuitive optimism that we observe in today's Great Recession, and he dubbed it "The American Dream" — "that dream of a land in which life should be better and richer and fuller for every man, with opportunity for each according to his ability or achievement."

However, The American Dream pre-dated 1931. Starting in the 16th century, Western European settlers came to this land at great risk to build a better life. Today, this dream is sustained by immigrants from different parts of the world who still come here seeking to do the same thing.

Perceptions of the Dream today are often more positive among those who are new to America. When asked to rate the condition of The American Dream on a scale of one to 10, where 10 means the best possible condition and one means the worst, 42 percent of immigrants responded between six and 10. Only 31 percent of the general population answered in that range.

4. China threatens The American Dream.

Our surveys revealed that 57 percent of Americans believe that "the world now looks to many different *countries," not just ours, to "represent the future." When we asked participants which region or country is charting that future, more than half chose China. Nearly two-thirds of those surveyed mistakenly believe that the Chinese economy is already larger than the U.S. economy — it is actually one-third the size, with a population four times larger. China does own more than $1.1 trillion of U.S. debt, however; it is our largest creditor.*

But the problem isn't just one nation. Japan holds almost $1 trillion of U.S. debt. Britain owns more than $400 billion. In 1970, less than 5 percent of U.S. debt was held by non-citizens. Today, almost half is. Neither China nor these other countries can be blamed for U.S. choices that have placed our financial future increasingly out of our hands.

Still, no matter how much we owe, the United States remains the world's land of opportunity. In fact, the largest international group coming to America to study is from China, 157,000 students in the 2010-2011 academic year. As recently reported in the Washington Post, the number of Chinese undergraduates at U.S. colleges increased 43 percent over the previous year.

5. Economic decline and political gridlock are killing The American Dream.

Our research showed a stunning lack of confidence in U.S. institutions. Sixty-five percent of those surveyed believe that America is in decline; 83 percent said they have less trust in "politics in general" than they did 10 or 15 years ago; 79 percent said they have less trust in big business and major corporations; 78 percent said they have less trust in government; 72 percent reported declining trust in the media. These recent figures are more startling when contrasted against Gallup polling from the 1970s, when as many as 70 percent of

Americans had "trust and confidence" that the government could handle domestic problems.

Even so, 63 percent of Americans said they are confident that they will attain their American Dream, regardless of what the nation's institutions do or don't do. While they may be worried about future generations, their dream today stands defiantly against the odds. [6]

A Questionable Future

Not everyone stands "defiant against the odds." More young people are saying, "Do I really need a college education? Is it worth it? The statistics are proving that a college education no longer guarantees me a good job, and I could spend my whole life repaying student loans. Is that what I want to do?" It's like that old song: "I owe my soul to the company store."

Disillusionment hurts. It can make you want to escape and money can be made from that escapism. Disgusted, cynical people of all ages mindlessly drift away into entertainment and drugs of one kind or another. Many stop watching the news. Less than half of Americans vote. Why should they? It doesn't seem to make a whole lot of difference in who gets elected from the elite pool of candidates, most of whom already have enough money. Apathy descends and discouragement takes root. This is a particularly destructive development when it impacts our young people, who are our future.

In fact, one of our deepest fears is to admit that we have been conned. It's not the fear of being conned, it's the fear of admitting that we have been conned. This explains why pensioners struggling on social security will continue to mail donation checks to TV evangelists who have been exposed in scandals involving drugs and hookers. "The devil is trying to destroy this man of God!" they say in defending him. No, this supposed man of God is conning people!

But disillusionment can also be good medicine. After all, the only thing disillusionment takes away is illusion. America is championed as the land of the free. That's true if we are speaking about the freedom to slumber in the American Dream. But we are also free to wake up. One of the most powerful tools for awakening is inquiry. This involves having the courage to question, examine beliefs and challenge convictions and myths to discover what was described in the film *Cloud Atlas* as the "true true."

So, what did we cover in Part One?

- The fable of Rip Van Winkle. He chose to learn nothing.

- We are here to experience. Period.

- Growing self-awareness is the best investment.

- There's a seeker born every minute.

- Hope is egocentric. Shift from thinking to feeling: gain insights.

- A dream is not a vision.

- Illusion creates suffering.

- America is the land of the free… we are free to wake up!

A Moment of Mastery

Choice is power.
I choose awakening
and the opportunity
to expand self-awareness
in each moment.

PART TWO - AWAKENING

Chapter Ten: The Real Revolution

"As soon as you have made a thought, laugh at it." [1]

- Lao Tzu

The journey of awakening is not something you decide to do. It happens to you. But your choices determine your progress.

Two of our "W's" for awakening are "why" and "who". The first sign of the awakening journey in progress is that you begin to question your life. "Why should I work hard and save my money for retirement when I'm reading about seniors losing all their retirement money? Why should I get married and have children when spouses rip off each other in divorce settlements, children break their parents' hearts and houses are lost to foreclosures? Why aren't rich people happy? I know a few and they're more miserable than I am. Why should I aspire to be like them if they have achieved the American Dream but still aren't happy?"

As you awaken, you re-focus your efforts to break down illusion. You apply your effort toward demolition so you can build anew. Anyone who has renovated a house knows that during this early phase the dust flies! And inevitably as the walls come down you discover all sorts of secrets hidden behind them.

"Who?" comes next as awakening moves to the next level. "Who am I beyond these roles I've been playing? If I'm not just a son or daughter any more, not just a husband or a wife, not just a plumber, a teacher, a broker, a retiree … who am I?" You touch the emptiness of being, and it can be intimidating. Nothingness seems like a bad bargain. You may not have liked who you were before but at least you were somebody. Now, sometimes suddenly you think of yourself as a nobody. This can feel more like loss than gain.

Be patient. Spiritual awakening takes time and it can be divided into the same two general stages as your physical awakening: dominantly asleep but awakening, and dominantly awake but not yet out of bed. We use two parables to detail these stages. The legend of *Sleeping Beauty* tracks the first one, which is about stirring from slumber, and *Humpty Dumpty* the second, which is about dismantling illusion.

SLEEPING BEAUTY

The story of *Sleeping Beauty* was first published in France by Charles Perrault in 1697 but is best known as a Brothers Grimm fairy tale.

Seven fairies are invited to be godmothers and help christen a princess-to-be. Six of them offer gifts of beauty, wit, musical talent, and other qualities. A wicked fairy though, who was not invited to the christening, manages to place the princess under her control by casting a spell — when the princess reaches the age of sixteen, she will pierce her hand on a spinning needle and die. The wicked fairy's curse is rebuked by the one remaining fairy who promises that the princess will not die but will instead sleep for a hundred years, and then be awakened by the kiss of a prince.

Although as a precaution, spinning had been forbidden throughout the kingdom by the king, the now sixteen-year-old princess meets an old woman who is spinning in a garret of the castle. The princess tries spinning, accidentally pricks her finger and immediately falls asleep. The heartbroken king has his daughter placed upon a bed of embroidered gold and silver fabric in the finest room of the castle. The good fairy who had fought against the evil spell, puts everyone else in the castle to sleep and grows a forest around the castle to hide it.

A hundred years pass. A prince from another family finds the hidden castle during a hunting expedition and upon hearing the enchanting story of the princess, enters the castle. He passes by all the sleepers until he finds the chamber where the sleeping princess lies. Trembling at her radiant beauty, he falls on his knees and kisses her. She awakens and everyone else in the castle then awakens too. [2]

Humpty Dumpty

Here's the familiar poem.

> *Humpty Dumpty sat on a wall,*
>
> *Humpty Dumpty had a great fall.*
>
> *All the king's horses and all the king's men*
>
> *Couldn't put Humpty together again.* [3]

Throughout our explorations here in Part Two, we'll occasionally refer to both of these fables to gain relevant meaning. But now it's time to introduce our primary device for awakening consciousness — an adaptation of the technique Socrates used to win debates with his learned colleagues.

The Synchronicity Socratic Process

Our customized Socratic Process is a unique method of conflict resolution, primarily with regard to your own illusory beliefs about who you are and what life is. Turn your gaze upon yourself. Why are you suffering? What is the conflict and what is the origin?

Separation from Source Intelligence is the origin of all conflict. It creates your illusory duality. When you experience yourself as being separate from Source Intelligence — this applies to everyone who worships a God conceived to be separate from oneself – then you will be separate from everyone and everything as well. This is the root origin of all our suffering.

Quiet Desperation

In our suffering by way of separation, we wear masks to hide from ourselves and from each other. We pretend that we're "just fine, thanks." Of course, denial isn't restricted to Americans! People all over the world want to believe that being prosperous, successful and happy all the time is just around the corner.

When dream fantasies substitute for Source Intelligence reality, irrational assumptions can masquerade as truth. To examine, test and expose these assumptions we employ the Socratic process of inquiry. Here in Part Two we will use this method to study the following twelve aspects of American culture: lifestyle, education, addictions, economics, relationships, health, media, the environment, politics, religion, technology and finally, America itself.

We are not launching an expose on what's wrong, a condemnation of conspiratorial evil-doers or a call to arms. Neither are we simply placing blame or generating guilt. We acknowledge the perfection of what's happening. At the same time, we will not hesitate to reveal the hidden underbelly of life in America in service to the urgency of these awakening times. So let's ask questions. Let's challenge conventional beliefs and back up our inquiries with relevant research.

We also champion those who are modeling awake behavior without much conscious understanding of the principles. There are modern American heroes in every walk of life, from wealthy industrialists who have turned their attention and riches toward philanthropic activities, to successful artists and musicians and filmmakers who spend their time and money supporting beginners. All is not lost in America! In fact, most of us would affirm that the vast majority of individuals, wealthy and famous or working class, are considerate and caring. Especially when push comes to shove. At the same time, it would be ignoring the obvious to avoid confronting the sad facts about our nation.

The degree of change we are advocating goes far beyond just doing good in the world. That is not enough. Awakening is about being who we are, engaging fully with the destiny of an awakened life. That can hopefully include good deeds arising from a deep well of happiness that expands through evolving consciousness.

Awakening is about consciously experiencing more of who you already are.

The First Fundamental Question

How do you know for sure that your reality is real? Two people often see the exact same situation in opposite ways. Who's right? What's true?

In fact, reality is what your mind generates with its thoughts and beliefs about what your life is and who you are. These become the stories you tell yourself and your identification with them becomes your reality. Of course, while asleep in the American Dream you are unconscious of this and will defend your virtual reality when it is challenged. This is what Socrates' opponents did and what he didn't do. It's why he won every debate. He understood that all of us are living in our own virtual reality. Intelligent inquiry eventually exposes that fact.

When you begin asking questions to examine the tales you are filling yourself with, you will find that most of your stories simply are not true. One dominant falsehood in particular is endlessly repeated in a variety of guises by your ego-driven mind: "This should be other than it is." This (your body) should be different. This (your marriage) should be different. This (our political system) should be different. And your ego mind can prove it every time!

Just a Glimpse

Awakening, you encounter a peculiar state of awareness in which you realize that you don't know anything for sure. You realize that much of what you have deemed to be true is not true. For instance, The American Dream and all it promises. You don't know yet what is true, but you begin to challenge your loyalty to the Dream. This can also evoke a sense of hopelessness.

As you continue to awaken, you move into the next stage and are blessed with a glimpse of the awake state of being. You sense who you really are and what life really is, but you cannot sustain this as a consistent experience. It's an epiphany, a magical moment, fleeting then gone. This then is the time for meditating, reading books, attending seminars and receiving mentoring. Teachers and good friends may see you better than you can see yourself. As you take in their wisdom, you experience a different kind of true. "I know that" you may say to yourself, then realize that it took a specific stimulus to bring your knowing to conscious awareness. You knew it but you didn't know that you knew it. Now you do. You are awakening.

Two Milestones of Expanding Self-Awareness

Imagine you are standing on a bridge. This bridge connects what was your virtual version of reality with what will be your truthful experience of reality. You know you are on this bridge when your life stops working, when you stop denying and start asking questions to find out why. This is more than a mid-life crisis and you will not get over it. This is your awakening.

You now consciously doubt what you previously accepted on faith. "Wait a minute, is it true that all of us are equal just because we say we are? Is this marriage, my marriage, working... really? Is it sane that billions of children starve so that a few thousand clever manipulators can wallow in excess?" Then it begins to snowball. You tug on a thread anywhere in the quilt of illusion and the entire tapestry begins to unravel. More holes appear, more questions arise.

As your self-awareness expands, you begin to achieve a degree of conscious detachment from your mind and become able to truly observe yourself and others, perhaps for the first time in your life. You might even feel like a stranger to yourself. Your initial detachment allows you to start examining your own mind. Detached, you observe your belief systems and allow more questions to arise. This is a milestone in the evolution of your consciousness and evolutionary gravity is now on your side. Awakening will progress as an inevitability and self-awareness will continue to expand.

You have reached a second milestone when increased wakeful detachment from identification with your mind enables you to confront a paradox: "Who is watching?" You escape identification with your limited self and experience another self observing not just your beliefs but who you have thought you were.

This threshold ignites a surge in personal evolution, a peak that propels you into a more expansive state of consciousness where you can really savor a glimpse of the true you. Let's sample that right now. Ask and listen: "Who am I right now?" Pause your reading, close your eyes and entertain this question without demanding a definitive answer. Remember to do your Socrates imitation: "I know nothing." Notice how your consciousness has expanded since the last time you asked this question. Awakening has been happening!

The Big Awakening

Now the real war begins, the battle between you and your ego. Actually, it's the beginning of the end of your ego's dominance. It has served its purpose in that position. You have become aware of what you are not, aware of the virtual reality you had accepted earlier without question. Now you have moved on and consciousness is dismantling that illusory state so you can experience the truth about who you truly are. This was the intention of consciousness all along and the ego was essential in the process.

This big awakening fuels your inner fire and creates an exponential expansion in awareness. You may feel the most powerful and see the most truth you ever have. You become conscious, you have holistic vision and experience all of which you are a part. How do you know this is the real thing? Because you awaken to a happiness that depends on nothing and no one. You realize joyful consciousness is the fundamental nature of true reality.

Once known, this conscious experience of your true nature will accompany you forever. The momentum of your evolving consciousness will work to create further surges, increase your experience of dismantling illusion and ignite further epiphanies.

To Be Continued

Even at very advanced levels of the experience, you will continue to dismantle the virtual database of stories that you used to believe in. That's the brilliance of an evolving self-awareness. Its ever-intensifying spotlight enables you to see whatever you have buried, those things you have not been aware of. Now you bring this to the surface and release the ghosts.

You're not the first to awaken! There isn't something wrong with you. The ego may rebel: "Don't let anyone know this is going on; you'll be ostracized, condemned, rejected. Look at everyone else in the herd; they're still chewing their cud, swatting flies with their tails. Don't let anybody know you're different."

You've suppressed the awakening impulse before. But when you realize awakening is not just personal and that it's really a swelling tsunami in our human species, then you dare to share the news with others also awakening. You begin to attract those actively evolving their consciousness. A new consensus group begins to develop for you, new friends, your *sangha*, which means "truthful community" in Sanskrit. You and your new friends are honest with each other and with yourselves, and it's a staggering relief.

As this light of honesty dawns in your consciousness, you can surrender fraudulent habits and lies such as, "I'm inadequate," or "I'm better than others." Ego-dominance dissolves and something incredible emerges beyond human imagination. To understand, it must be experienced.

As an articulation of the ego-driven, illusory reality you are surrendering, note these chilling words from General George S. Patton: "To conquer, we must destroy our enemies. We must not only die gallantly; we must kill devastatingly. The faster and more effectively you kill, the longer you will live to enjoy the priceless fame of conquerors." [4]

The ego's agenda is to dominate and control. Those false programmings, those false stories, are exactly what is dying as you awaken here and now in the 21st century.

Morning in the Real World

Some have tried to determine the percentage of humans who are now at the level of self-awareness we call "awakening." They have tracked the increase over the last twenty-five years from perhaps 1% or 2% up to 10% or 15%. But that's guesswork. What really matters is the degree of wholeness experienced by individuals. Those who are awakened wield authentic power. Ego-minds hold power in the virtual world where they rule as kings of the Dream. But the outcome is assured. No ego-mind has ever survived death, however Source Intelligence is eternal. By awakening, you choose a different identity.

This awakening process we are describing is a revolution. It cannot be stopped, certainly not by egotistical people who only control dreams with their money and weapons of fear. All are destined to awaken when their time comes and according to their own choices.

Yes, innocent children are dying. Corporations are buying elections. People everywhere are suffering. We are suffering. Our hearts are broken from the failure of our dreams. So for you and for those millions like you, awakening is now an urgent priority. You can close your eyes and feel the awakening impulse. If it's happening to you then you know it is real. And you can see the signs everywhere when you train yourself to look for them.

We have made progress as a species. For example, while slavery is still practiced in some places, it is now unacceptable in most of the world. Another example is that capital punishment is on its way out. Tyranny is under more challenges. As a species, we are awakening and it's been happening without fanfare for some time. The difference today is that now it is urgently upon us for the old way to fade and for a new way to come forth.

So, here we are in the 21ˢᵗ century, opening our eyes, stretching our new wings and wondering what this new way will be like. A question to ponder is: Am I ready for what's next?

A Moment of Mastery

I stand
on the bridge
between illusion and reality.
I feel the sunrise
touching my tethered wings.
I prepare to fly.

Chapter Eleven: The Carrot and the Vacuum Cleaner

"A bit of advice given to a young Native American at the time of his initiation: As you go the way of life, you will see a great chasm. Jump. It is not as wide as you think." [1]

- Joseph Campbell

The original curse for Sleeping Beauty was death. This was reduced to a hundred years of sleep. Think of Sleeping Beauty and imagine yourself unconscious of what's going on in the waking world around you. You have been asleep, dreaming. This describes the vast majority of the human population.

When will we wake up? When will you wake up? And how? For Sleeping Beauty, it was the kiss of a prince that did it. What will your kiss be? What has it already been?

In the Dream, we are asleep to the reality of life as an experience that originates within ourselves. We are disempowered victims who chase fulfillment. Simply ask yourself and answer honestly: "Am I fulfilled ... am I aware of myself as the cause of my own life experience... am I constantly happy?"

The alarm is ringing.

Jump

Many of us have heard the tale of the frog in hot water. It goes like this: if you place a frog in warm water and turn up the temperature the frog will stay in the water until it boils to death. On the other hand, if you place a frog in hot water it will jump out immediately.

What's the lesson for us? Jump! Loitering on a slippery slope of any kind spells big trouble ahead. As far as our lifestyle goes, this includes so many temptations: the zero interest credit card that rises to 29% when you miss a payment, the bargain mortgage that "adjusts" in a year (which seems so far away, yet the time flies by) and leads to foreclosure or the irresistible boyfriend with baggage and a temper.

Jumping means choosing long-term benefits over short-term gratification. This can be difficult as we know if we have tried to quit smoking, drinking, binge eating and other habits.

This is why meditation is so effective. Meditation connects you with the ultimate long-term benefit: oneness with Source Intelligence which is an innately enjoyable state of being. As you gain some actual experience of being nurtured and fulfilled through that communion, the "false Gods" of your addictions have less and less appeal. Each time you meditate, it's the same … but different. It teaches you to perceive subtler distinctions, moment by moment. So, close your eyes and jump.

Introducing the Synchronicity Socratic Process

When we jump, we awaken to an entirely different state. Now, chapter by chapter, we will expose the old state and introduce the new one relative to 12 core aspects of your life. We will use the Synchronicity Socratic Process to systematically dismantle illusion by identifying the core assumptions relating to the fraudulent American Dream. Our first target is the much-envied American lifestyle. Consider these statements and ask yourself if they are true:

- America is the land of the free and the home of the brave;

- America is the land of equal opportunity for all;

- America is the land of opportunity for those who work hard and don't quit.

In particular, is this last statement true? Has it ever been true? The rags-to-riches stories, the hope that you can have it all in America … are these actual experiences for any significant number of Americans or are they just empty hopes? Let's dig beneath the surface of this to unbundle a few of the underlying beliefs associated with it.

- America is a single entity with the same rules and possibilities for every individual American;

- Working hard always creates success if you don't quit;

- Quitting is always wrong.

Work Hard and Never Quit

The American Dream promises happiness if you work hard and follow the rules. The carrot, always just beyond reach, is the enticement finally catching up with happiness and getting all that the Dream can provide. But the carrot comes with a vacuum cleaner. That great sucking sound you hear as you pursue happiness are your assets being systematically appropriated by thieves in high places.

It turns out that what they are stealing isn't really of that much value to you anyway. As researcher Tim Kasser discovered, "When I was working on my Ph.D. in psychology in the early 1990s, I became interested in how people construct their lives. That led me to study people's goals and what they were aspiring to create out of their lives. One day, I was running some statistics and getting ready to examine how personal well-being relates to prioritizing goals for money and possessions relative to other kinds of goals. I remember sitting in front of the computer thinking, "Wouldn't it be interesting if people who cared more about goals for money and possessions were less happy?"

"I ran the analyses and that's what I found. In essence, the research shows that the goals encouraged by a consumer culture, which are primarily extrinsic, tend to diminish the quality of our lives, our society, and our Earth. Whereas intrinsic goals promote greater health and well-being, more social justice and greater sustainability." [2]

> ## As the song says, we're looking for love in all the wrong places.

The Carrot

Let's look at those who live the good life according to The American Dream. They're wealthy, they've "arrived." They don't miss a meal; in fact, they have long forgotten what it means to order from the right side of the menu. They don't worry about a sudden health problem draining their account. They have savings. And full coverage insurance. The prospect of being downsized doesn't keep them awake at night because they are the ones doing the downsizing. They have enough money for their kids' college funds and their own retirement. They can vacation where and when they want.

So, are they happy? Peer into their lives just a few layers down and what do you find? Most of them are not happy. Look at the corruption in their lives, the illnesses and the confusion. Did achieving The American Dream make them happy? Or, if they are happy, was it something else that made them so? And how did they achieve the Dream anyway? The assumption is that they worked their way up from the bottom.

Here's what Jason De Parle wrote about this in the *New York Times* early in 2012: "Benjamin Franklin did it. Henry Ford did it. And American life is built on the faith that others can do it, too: rise from humble origins to economic heights. 'Movin' on up,' George Jefferson-style, is not only a sitcom song but a civil religion.

"But many researchers have reached a conclusion that turns conventional wisdom on its head: Americans enjoy less economic mobility than their peers in Canada and much of Western Europe."

Well, that's a shock. Americans are proud of their Horatio Alger stories and glorify this country as the land of opportunity where, while the streets may not actually be paved with gold, everyone has the chance to make it. De Parle continues: "At least five large studies in recent years have found the United States to be less mobile than comparable nations." [3]

A project led by Markus Jantti, an economist at a Swedish university, found that 42 percent of American men raised in the bottom fifth of incomes stay there as adults. That shows a level of persistent disadvantage much higher than in Denmark (25 percent) and Britain (30 percent, a country famous for its class constraints).

Jantti continues, "Meanwhile, just 8 percent of American men at the bottom rose to the top fifth. That compares with 12 percent of the British and 14 percent of the Danes.

"Despite frequent references to the United States as a classless society, about 62 percent of Americans (male and female) raised in the top fifth of incomes stay in the top two-fifths, according to research by the Economic Mobility Project of the Pew Charitable Trusts. Similarly, 65 percent born in the bottom fifth stay in the bottom two-fifths." [4]

If this is the actual, current state of affairs in America, but we profess to champion and embody the exact opposite, why don't we do something about it? Imagine a football game where it's halftime and your team is losing by 40 points. Coach huddles up with his players in the locker room for his traditional pep talk, a trademark tirade known to turn lopsided defeats into heroic, come-from-behind, last-minute, squeaker victories. But this time he says, "Men, you're doing great. Just keep on doing exactly what you've been doing and we'll win."

The coaching we get from our "leaders" is very similar. "Folks, we know that The American Dream has failed to deliver on its promise for the vast majority of you. We also happen to know that it will never deliver because the deck is stacked against you and I'm doing the dealing. But we're not going to tell you that. What we will tell you is to keep on keeping on. And we can guarantee you, with total confidence, that you will absolutely succeed by continuing to dream!"

You could win the lottery. It could happen to you. So, you continue chasing the carrot, lost in that Dream because you've been spoon-fed on it from day one and it's your whole identification. You don't even think to question it. "Coach, shouldn't we try something different? We're getting creamed!" Einstein reasoned that insanity is doing the same thing over and over again and expecting different results.

The Great Chase

Chasing the carrot is the real symbol of The American Dream. Awakening is the realization that you'll never catch it and that you don't need to catch it because you already have it. When you are reaching outside of yourself for fulfillment, you create imbalance. Imbalance fragments you so that you remain within the illusion and you suffer. But the awakening person says, "Wait a minute. I can stop reaching. I can turn within myself to create balance." In a word, meditate! And remember, meditation takes many forms.

The awakening impulse in consciousness comes in a flash of insight: "I'm never gonna' catch that carrot!" That's right. Happiness out there will always outrun you ... so stop running. Give up and go in.

The way out is the way in.

The Vacuum Cleaner

While you are preoccupied with chasing the carrot, the super-rich are vacuuming up your "worked for wealth" through a myriad of innovative and secretive processes that suck on your bank account. Certainly, at least some of the privileged few don't work the way many Americans do.

David Cay Johnston reports: "John Paulson, the most successful hedge-fund manager of all, bet against the mortgage market one year and then bet with Glenn Beck in the gold market the next. Paulson made himself $9 billion in fees in just two years. His current tax bill on that $9 billion? Zero."

There's that great sucking sound once again. After all, where do we think that money came from? It came from our pockets in one way or another. Paulson earned a $9 billion income in two years for producing nothing at all, just for betting well. And unlike you and me, he paid no taxes on that income. Who needs an economics degree to figure out what impact that transfer of funds must have had on the economy? Johnston continues: "Lots of other people live tax-free too. I have Donald Trump's tax records for four years early in his career. He paid no taxes for two of those years. Big real-estate investors enjoy tax-free living under a 1993 law President Clinton signed. It lets 'professional' real-estate investors use paper losses like depreciation on their buildings against any cash income, even if they end up with negative incomes like Trump.

"Frank and Jamie McCourt, who own the Los Angeles Dodgers, have not paid any income taxes since at least 2004. Yet, they spent $45 million one year alone. How? They just borrowed against Dodger ticket revenue and other assets. To the IRS, they look like paupers.

"In Wisconsin, Terrence Wall, who unsuccessfully sought the Republican nomination for U.S. Senate in 2010, paid no income taxes on as much as $14 million of recent income. Asked about his living tax-free while working people pay taxes, he had a simple response: 'Everyone should pay less.' [5]

"Everyone should pay less." This delivered by an apparently intelligent man. We'll get to the media in another chapter ... whoever reported on this should have jumped all over the obvious insanity of his statement. It takes but a moment's thought to deduce the inevitable result of everyone paying less. I won't offend you by spelling it out. This is just more insane bleating by the deluded rich to the deluded poor. Meanwhile, that vacuum keeps on sucking.

In case you don't believe America has real economic problems, consider these May, 2011 statistics listed on the Prison Planet website under the heading: "36 Statistics Which Prove That The American Dream Is Turning Into An Absolute Nightmare For The Middle Class"[6]:

#1 According to the U.S. Bureau of Labor Statistics, the average duration of unemployment in the United States is now an all-time record 39 weeks.

#2 According to the *Wall Street Journal*, there are 5.5 million Americans unemployed and yet are not receiving unemployment benefits.

#3 The number of "low income jobs" in the U.S. has risen steadily over the past 30 years and they now account for 41 percent of all jobs in the United States.

#4 Only 66.8 percent of American men had a job last year. That was the lowest level ever recorded in all of U.S. history.

The Power of Inner Values

The above statistics are shattering. Evidently we've been living a lie, programmed to believe in a very different America. Where did that programming originate? Adyashanti writes, "Our conditioning is in large part derived from our family of origin, the life we have lived, the situations we've been brought into, and the life experiences that we've had. Parents and society condition our bodies and minds with their views, beliefs, morals, and norms. In this way we are conditioned to like certain things and not others, to want certain situations to arise and not others, to pursue fame or wealth or money or spirituality or love". [7]

With awakening, you start questioning your belief systems.

You identify your conditioning and illusions and you learn to question them which leads to disempowering them. Each illusion that you disempower transfers power back to you, increasing your self-awareness and freeing you to create your reality more consciously. The Dalai Lama poetically described this change in values:

"It is clear that something is seriously lacking in the way we humans are going about things. But what is it that we lack? The fundamental problem, I believe, is that at every level we are giving too much attention to the external material aspects of life while neglecting moral ethics and inner values.

"By inner values I mean the qualities that we all appreciate in others, and toward which we all have a natural instinct, bequeathed by our biological nature as animals that survive and thrive only in an environment of concern, affection and warmheartedness, or in a single word, compassion. The essence of compassion is a desire to alleviate the suffering of others and to promote their well-being.

"This is the spiritual principle from which all other positive inner values emerge. We all appreciate in others the inner qualities of kindness, patience, tolerance, forgiveness and generosity, and in the same way we are all averse to displays of greed, malice, hatred and bigotry. So actively promoting the positive inner qualities of the human heart that arise from our core disposition toward compassion, and learning to combat our more destructive propensities, will be appreciated by all. And the first beneficiaries of such a strengthening of our inner values will, no doubt, be ourselves. Our inner lives are something we ignore at our own peril, and many of the greatest problems we face in today's world are the result of such neglect." [8]

There was a recent period in American history when millions of us did shift our attention to inner values. It was called "the sixties" and many boomers are haunted by what happened to them during those tumultuous years. That's when most of us experienced an awakening of sorts. But, for many, awakening became kind of an intellectual enlightenment, which merely fueled the ego. In his book *Boomeritis* Ken Wilbur exposes the downfall of the boomer generation: "We got stuck at 'me." We got stuck in what he calls obsessive narcissism and therefore did not actualize our vision. Now, in our twilight years, some of us have become sufficiently unstuck from the content of our lives to actualize that original egalitarian vision.

You may be younger than the boomers, in which case this scenario doesn't apply to you. But, if it does, you may already be dismantling egoic identification and starting to move into integration, to actually experience those values you previously entertained mostly in your head and hopefully in your heart. If we've felt guilt about not following through, it helps to identify that and note how it has motivated us to create the illusory life we have been living.

As David Gershon writes, "To adopt a new behavior we need to start by understanding our current behavior. This awareness creates a baseline, and functions as a form of input for developing a vision of the change we wish to accomplish." [9]

The new behavior we wish to adopt relates to balance, giving up the "carrot and vacuum cleaner" lifestyle in favor of more inner attention through meditation and self-inquiry knowing that our fulfillment cannot come from the outside alone.

Our Socratic Conclusion

We have examined the belief that "America is the land of opportunity for those who work hard and don't quit," and we have proven that it is just a widespread illusory reality.

Studying the facts versus the fiction, what might a new, more truthful assumption be? How about this:

America is a land of diverse population,
where each individual can choose
his or her pathway to success as he or she defines it
and according to strategies he or she discovers
work well for him or herself.

An Awakened Perspective

From the awakened perspective we understand that we are here to live, not just to make a living. We acknowledge that we begin with nothing material and will end with nothing material. In between, we can know the truth, experience fulfillment by expanding our awareness to steadily disempower illusion and awaken to the truth of who we are and what life really is. An enlightening question to ponder is: "What makes me happy?"

A Moment of Mastery

*My life is not separate
from the lives of others.
My happiness does not depend
on anyone or anything.
I am enough,
and I am loved.
I am happy, for no reason.*

Chapter Twelve: Be, Have, Do

Man's mind, once stretched by a new idea, never regains its original dimensions. [1]

- Oliver Wendell Holmes

In this chapter we examine education in America today. Author John Atcheson recently blogged under the title, Dark Ages Redux: American Politics and the End of the Enlightenment, "...North Carolina law-makers recently passed legislation against sea level rise. A day later, the Virginia legislature required that references to global warming, climate change and sea level rise be excised from a proposed study on sea level rise. Last year, the Texas Department of Environmental Quality, which had commissioned a study on Galveston Bay, cut all references to sea level rise – the main point of the study.

"As Stephen Colbert so aptly put it: 'if your science gives you results you don't like, pass a law saying that the result is illegal. Problem solved.'

"...The litany of ignorance goes on and on. Teach Creationism. Teach the 'controversy' on climate science and intelligent design. Declare deregulation — which was a primary cause of the 2008 economic collapse — to be the solution to it. Preach trickle down economics even after it has failed every time it's been adopted. Even as we watch wealth rocket up the income brackets.

"What's next? Give the flat-earthers a say? Oh hell, why stop there? Let's put Earth back in the center of the solar system where it belongs.

"We don't need no stinkin' science. We don't need no pesky reality. We just gotta pass a few laws and declare things to be the way we want them to be, facts be damned. You know, keep your government hands off my Medicare." [2]

We Don't Need No Pesky Reality

In the fable of Sleeping Beauty, the Good Fairy put not only Sleeping Beauty but everyone else in the kingdom to sleep too. Well, we sleep. We sleep in a dream world imagining it to be real. Generation after generation, we educate our children into this same illusion. They learn how to behave and how to sustain that illusion. We teach them to fit in. If they don't, we punish them. Unless they become rich and famous. Then we canonize them, co-opting their rebellion into a new layer of the American Dream. That's irrational, of course, but it's how dreams work.

Throughout history, there have always been those special others who wake up early and model their way out of illusion. These are the true leaders, the true teachers, not our elected robber barons or self-styled gurus promoting intellectual enlightenment.

Stories of Awakening

"My first recollection of a life-changing event was when I was 17 and living in a small country community. I was desperate for education and I began to receive inner promptings to become a nurse. Except, this did not interest me and I ignored them. However, that inner voice became louder and more insistent. At the time I interpreted this as God telling me what he wanted me to do. Finally, I ungraciously gave in and shouted at God, 'All right, I'll be a nurse then.' This decision totally transformed my life and gave me the education I desired." -P.G., Australia

"My awakening took place at the end of the 'est' training with one of the staff trainers in 1977 in Houston. At the moment when they came to the Grande Finale, about 'getting it', I GOT IT! My immediate reaction was: 'Wow, well, why

*am I sitting here going through all this painful mess then?'
Then I realized the humor of that reaction (applicable to my
whole life) and just started laughing ecstatically. This opened
me up to the 'spiritual path' and Eastern philosophy,
enabling me to meet the author of this book soon afterwards."*
-S.M., Virginia

The Synchronicity Socratic Method

The Dream Assumption for this topic is easy:

America has the best educational system in the world.

Sub-sets might include, "American students are the best
educated." And, "We can teach the world." And, "You get a
good job when you have a good education." Well, consider
these recent statistics.

"The Bureau of Labor Statistics shows an alarming
picture of the ordeal college graduates are facing in today's
job market. Just ten years ago, a little over 81% of college
graduates under the age of 25 were working. 59.7% of them
were working in positions requiring a college degree. Those
students who went on to masters programs or other forms of
continuing education are lumped into the 19% not
employed.

"Ten years later, October 2010 to March 2011, there were
less than 75% of college graduates working any job at all. Of
those who are working, only 45% are working in jobs
requiring a college degree. To make matters worse, the cost
of an education at a four-year college has risen an average of
30% since 2000, but there are currently 15% fewer graduates
able to find employment for degree required positions. And
the stated 15% doesn't include those who are unable to find
any job at all.

"Where are all those 21st century jobs needing educated
employees?" [3]

Still, we believe we lead the world in education; we are the smartest, best, grandest, greatest," which is all an egocentric rant. In fact, our educational system is not on the leading edge; it has fallen off the edge!

What Do We Teach?

Education means memorization and information acquisition which produces robots to run the industries that sustain The American Dream Machine.

Bill Gates wrote an article for The New York Times early in 2012 entitled: Shaming Teachers Will Not Work. He said, "Developing a systematic way to help teachers get better is the most powerful idea in education today. The surest way to weaken it is to twist it into a capricious exercise in public shaming. Let's focus on creating a personnel system that truly helps teachers improve." [4]

So, what would actually make a teacher better? Better able to train dreamers to sustain the Dream? Or, better able to help their students wake up? Wake up and be happy; connect with Source Intelligence. That would be real education! That would address the primary problem in personal life and for the planet as a whole. Without that connection, we wreak havoc with each other and the coordinated ecosystems in which we live. The solutions we seek won't arise from consensus amongst the "well educated." We need the genius of the bumblebee who shouldn't be able to fly ... but somehow does!

It's a Gusher!

Since most people are unaware of this primary principle, that is the need to connect with Source Intelligence, the idea that waking up can solve our problems may seem impractical. Don't we need the "best brains" working on our problems? Einstein addressed this idea, warning that problems created by one state of consciousness can't be solved by the same state of consciousness. Consciousness needs to shift. Unfortunately, "experts" are often the most enslaved to cherished, limited states of consciousness and defend their territory instead of exploring new lands.

Here is an innovative way to show this connection principle in action as a way to shift consciousness. Imagine three lengths of hollow pipe. Each one represents an aspect of your human dimensions: physical, mental and emotional. Imagine these pieces of pipe are lined up vertically, as in the illustration, underneath a powerful stream of water. Notice in frame one how the three pipes are misaligned to the source of water, resulting in no more than a trickle making it out through the bottom. Most of the water flowing from above is wasted.

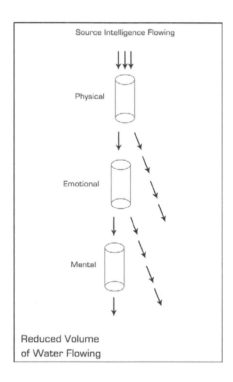

Frame two illustrates what happens when the three lengths of pipe are aligned with the incoming water stream. Now, with a robust flow through the pipe, a veritable gusher pours through.

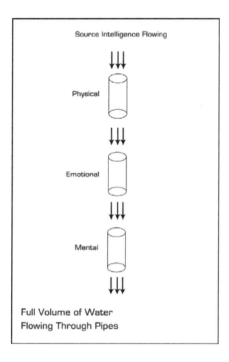

Before there was only a trickle, now there is an over-abundance. It's not a matter of finding more water because the water is there already. What makes that Source Intelligence available is alignment.

We have what we need. Everything except alignment with Source Intelligence. The true educator helps their students learn how to bring the body, mind and heart into alignment with Source Intelligence in order to access genius and let it flood into living. "My cup runneth over!"

A Fundamental Error

Our educational system is obsessed with the intricacies of the Dream. There is no education about reality, about what it means to be human, about what the game of life is and why we are here. It's no surprise then that the end products of the American educational system are automatons programmed to behave themselves and endure suffering. We learn how to make a living and forget how to truly live.

We are programmed to focus on "doing." We do things in order to have what we need and want, so that we will be happy and fulfilled. That's The American Dream in a nutshell: *do – have – be*. This flawed formula has been exposed by many teachers. It appeared in the "est" training and Neale Donald Walsch, author of the best selling *Conversations with God* series, has written about it. A quick Google search brings up many links, including the following:

http://www.taketheleap.com/create.html

http://www.lawofattraction123.com/be-do-have.html

http://www.yourdailylifecoach.com/be-do-have.html

Do – have – be: the pursuit of happiness, enshrined in our Constitution no less. But here's what we know for sure. The only reason to pursue something is because you don't have it. Obviously, if you already have it there would be no need to try to get it. So, guaranteeing your right to the pursuit of happiness is guaranteeing your right to not be happy!

Be – Have – Do

When we reverse the equation to be – have – do, something remarkable happens.

Be – be who you already are. Have – access to whatever you need to live a happy, fulfilled life (qualities freely available within you). Do – act here in the real world, already happy, without needing to get a thing. Contribute.

In the Dream formula, doing comes first. Conversely, this reversal emphasizes being. It proposes that the way to a truly happy life is through the heart. It does not need a perfect outer environment peopled with others who love and serve you. You start with the experience of inherent happiness.

You Are Already You

In our equation, You – the truth of you – leads the way. You are already connected to universal Source Intelligence. In truth, you are one with that Source Intelligence. By the way, that's how you know you are experiencing your authentic self in any moment: you feel connected within the web of all life.

The ancient Greeks used the term "daemon" to describe this invisible intelligence; the Romans called it "genius." When we speak of Source Intelligence this is what we are referring to: a realm of genius inherent in life itself and available to all living forms.

> **The source of genius is knowable.**

Ego vs. Genius

"A human being is part of the whole called by us the universe, a part limited in time and space. He experiences himself, his thoughts and feelings as something separated from the rest, a kind of optical delusion of his consciousness. This delusion is a kind of prison for us, restricting us to our personal desires and to affection for a few persons nearest to us. Our task must be to free ourselves from this prison by widening our circle of compassion to embrace all living creatures and the whole of nature in its beauty." [5]

- Albert Einstein

During a February 2009 TED presentation, Elizabeth Gilbert, the best selling author of *Eat, Pray, Love*, spoke about her take on genius. She said that the ancient Romans and Greeks didn't believe that creativity came from human beings, but rather that "creativity was this divine attendant spirit that came to human beings from some distant and unknowable source..." [6]

We found a relevant online debate on Huffington Post, "Geniuses Are Born, Not Made?"[7] between Dr. Scott Barry Kaufman and Dr. Zach Hambrick. Hambrick, an Associate Psychology Professor at Michigan State University concluded: "The answer is 'both.' Experts are *born* because people come into the world differing in ways that turn out to matter for real-world achievement. But experts are *made* because there is no getting around the necessity of a long period of practice and training for reaching a high level of performance. This is my take. Take it for what it's worth."

Kaufman, who is a cognitive psychologist at NYU, the co-founder of The Creativity Post, and Chief Science Officer for The Future Project, rebutted: "Genius involves figuring out who you are, and owning yourself. It's about amplifying your best traits and compensating for the rest. Geniuses grab life by the horns, and persevere amidst setbacks. They take control of their lives, instead of waiting for others to open up doors. In this very important sense, greatness is completely, utterly, made."

Genius is something we access. And we propose that the source of genius is knowable. Not understandable in the way the mind would like it to be, but knowable as a tangible experience of resonance, a oneness with. In fact, many of us have already had this experience. Certainly you have since you are reading this book. You've experienced it and the memory haunts you ... you want more. And, why not? The experience of oneness with the source of flowing genius is most pleasurable!

Let's take a genius break. Ponder our "Who are you?" question from this perspective. Let go of the need to be anything other than awareness opening. Close your eyes and repeat the question like a mantra: "Who am I? Who am I?"

Did you feel the pleasure of that? Somehow, just asking the question can be enjoyable because in opening, you allow yourself to receive the genius of Source Intelligence. You connect with the awakening impulse as a consciously invited experience. Yes, it comes in its own seasons, gracing us with a moment of illumination now and then. But we can also invite it by simply pausing to ask the question.

We break down the difference between ego and genius this way:

EGO	GENIUS
Identity based – who you believe you are	Awareness based – what you perceive and express
Achievement (takes time)	Experience (timeless)
Separate, competitive, proud / fragile	Unified, cooperative, humble / strong
Temporary	Sustained
Effort and management	Grace and synchronicity
Highs to enjoy and lows to avoid, ending badly	Rhythms appreciated, never ending
Power over others, controlling, jealous	Empowered in oneness, supportive, appreciative
Fraudulent	Authentic
Ruled by beliefs	Open to learn and change

Sir Richard Branson shines as an example of generous leadership, educating us about how a primary motive to improve life on the planet can inspire countless innovations. One story follows another in his captivating autobiography including an account of how he dreamed up a way to support a charitable cause by encouraging patrons of his international airline to donate their foreign change as they disembarked. His idea has generated millions for a worthy cause and it teaches us how practical that sort of a mindset can be.

Educating for the Dream

Young children are often asked, "What do you want to be when you grow up?" It's rarely about who they want to be. This is because we are groomed to live in the Dream, which is an ego-driven virtual reality. The focus is entirely outside of yourself, external to you, out in the objective world around you. It's not really about "who," it's about "what," what you are programmed to feel that you must do to fulfill the Dream. "What must I do to survive, and hopefully thrive, in the Dream to have the quality of life it promises?" Who you are can get lost in that pursuit.

It's enculturation. Children are pressured by their parents who are often driven to somehow make up for their own failures. As Robert Johnson writes in *Living Your Unlived Life*, "The greatest burden any child carries is the unlived life of their parents."[8] Children grow up under this pressure and these days it starts much earlier than ever before. What children today go through in grade school and high school to get into a good college is insanely stressful.

But what about the natural evolution of their own creative insights that might guide them to discover what really excites them? There's no room for that. The Dream Machine demands something much more intellectual, ego-driven and survival-based. The inevitable result is that young people today are much less fulfilled. In fact, dissatisfaction is built right into the growing up process, because being increasingly authentic is not considered part of the growing-up process.

There's no call to authenticity, which is about being oneself. It's all about doing. "What do you want to do when you grow up?" Not, "Who do you want to be?" The best result possible is a successful, inauthentic person. But that's not what the world is filled with because most of us are not successful by those external terms! Nor are we authentic.

Educating for The Past

We do not nurture wisdom, we program worker bees. That is the way our educational system was set up at the beginning of the Industrial Revolution, to produce laborers. Education had nothing to do with helping individuals self-actualize. One long-term result of this system is that for the first time in American history, children today seem destined to have less material wealth than their parents. The writing is on the wall and college kids, who can read that writing, are saying, "Wait a minute, how much money will this expensive education cost me and what will I get for it? Will I have a bigger salary, a better job, a better life?"

Not necessarily, not these days. But, they will have debt. Approximately two-thirds of all college students graduate with student loan debt. They don't like it and they are beginning to raise their voices.

"Dozens of students were arrested this afternoon at the Sallie Mae headquarters demanding forgiveness of student loans. The protest comes after recent reports show $1 trillion in student debt burdening borrowers.

"The high amount of debt is good news for debt collectors, however. A Bloomberg report shows that debt collectors made nearly $1 billion in commissions from aggressively pursued student loan collection efforts.

"Student-loan debt collectors have power that would make a mobster envious," said Harvard Law Professor Elizabeth Warren." [9]

Young people are also smart enough to do the math. "How many working years will it take to pay for my education?" some are asking. And many are beginning to say "No thanks!" They are beginning to believe they would be better off without the irrelevant education and the debt. Of course, what's really taken this to an urgent level is the fact that kids and their parents simply can't afford tuition to begin with. Meanwhile, they look at entrepreneurs like Steve Jobs who dropped out of college yet made billions and changed the world.

Educating for Wakefulness

The goal of a truth-centered educational system would be to first help us unlearn, to deprogram enculturation, and then to grow us to a point where we could achieve what Socrates achieved; knowing that he knew nothing. Some call this "beginners mind," the state of openness to learning, the ability to see beyond limiting beliefs and concepts. It's also how we access Source Intelligence, how we connect with genius.

True education must start with accessing genius and this requires teachers who are experiencing the truth of this principle for themselves. With regard to Bill Gates' comments above, this would constitute the "better" teacher.

The purpose of education is to prepare us for a meaningful, enjoyable, worthwhile, fulfilled life. What would that look like? Well, we wouldn't compete with each other for the most money, toys or fame. We would support each other to grow, to better ourselves, to evolve, to expand our awareness and to experience wholeness ... oneness in consciousness. We'd share the pie by baking a bigger one together!

Abundance, after all, is everywhere! According to both mysticism and quantum science, this is the nature of true reality. So, how do we educate to experience that? We are recommending challenging assumptions, questioning our own illusions, dismantling the fraud and the lies – those told by others and those stories we tell ourselves. This process never stops. True learning is an ongoing awakening to reality and that evolution continues as long as we are drawing breath.

Positive Educational Alternatives

There are positive educational alternatives that are making a difference. "A 1995 survey of U.S. Waldorf schools found that parents overall experienced the Waldorf schools as achieving their major aims for students, and described the education as one that 'integrates the aesthetic, spiritual and interpersonal development of the child with rigorous intellectual development,' preserving students' enthusiasm for learning so that they develop a better sense of self-confidence and self-direction." [10]

And here's news about the Rudolf Steiner School in New York City (Steiner schools flourish across America): "The students overall were positive about the school and its differences; experienced the school as a 'community of friends' and spoke of the opportunity to grow and develop through the broad range of activities offered, to learn when they were ready to learn, to develop imagination, and to come to understand the world as well as oneself. Many students spoke of the kindness of their peers and of learning to think things through clearly for themselves, not to jump to conclusions, and to remain positive in the face of problems and independent of pressure from others to think as they do …" [11]

Socratic Conclusion

"When you change the way you look at something, you change the very thing you are looking at." [12]

- Dr. Christine Ranck and Christopher Lee Nutter

The Dream Assumption we have been exploring is, "America has the best educational system in the world." Clearly, we have debunked that myth. Now, for an awake statement of truth, how about something like: "America has millions of awakening residents ready to learn more about Source Intelligence and to access and express the genius of life."

An evolutionary question to ponder is, "Am I accessing genius or just making a living?"

A Moment of Mastery

*I open to welcome
the genius of life
that flows through me,
as me,
as consciousness,
which is what I am.*

Chapter Thirteen: Feed Your Soul

"Scientists have studied the brains of alcoholics, smokers, and over-eaters and have measured how their neurology – the structures of their brains and the flow of neurochemicals inside their skulls – changes as their cravings became ingrained. Particularly strong habits, wrote two researchers at the University of Michigan, produce addiction-like reactions so that 'wanting evolves into obsessive craving' that can force our brains into autopilot, even in the face of strong disincentives, including loss of reputation, job, home, and family." [1]

- Charles Duhigg

We all have a few addictions. We all share one, our addiction to the Dream.

When the Squeeze Comes On

Sleeping Beauty was cursed to die, but her sentence was reduced to 100 years of sleep. Likewise, we sleep. And we dream, intoxicated in illusion, languishing for hours, days, or years until we wake up. Humans are like fruit ripening on the tree of life. We all ripen at our own pace and drop when we are ready.

This ripening cannot be stopped. The evolution of consciousness is an inevitable process. It has been moving at a glacial speed, but now it's accelerating dramatically. Ego illusions are dissolving. We're Humpty Dumpty and nothing can put us back together again. Either your ego world has already fallen apart, or it soon will. That's when we tend to reach for our favorite addictions, as the pressure to change meets our resistance to change. Of course, we don't know that, we just feel like having a cigarette, a drink, a snort, etc.

The squeeze comes on. To analogize, when you squeeze a bar of soap in the shower it will squirt up or down ... it's not going to stay in your hand very long. Pressure situations are like that for you as well. You will make a choice in one direction or the other when the squeeze comes on.

The pressure actually is just the trigger that provokes your choice. Thus, your choice is the real cause of your behavior. After all, the drink doesn't make itself and force it's way to your lips. The bet doesn't place itself. The marital infidelity doesn't just happen to you. You make choices. This radical realization that your choices determine your experience can demolish a lifetime of excuses for maintaining addictive behaviors.

What happens under pressure depends on what is already inside you. People routinely blame others: "She made me so mad!" But that's as irrational as saying, "She made me weigh 200 pounds." Like an orange, when it gets squeezed, orange juice comes out. Never beet juice. Never chocolate. Oranges have orange juice in them so when they get squeezed orange juice comes out. Following this thought process, whatever is already inside you will tend to come out when the pressure is on.

When you react with blame of another, you become their slave. You are admitting they have power over you. You are deluded, accusing other people of causing your behavior. There is no twelve-step program for this addiction; there's just one step. Be responsible for your choices.

Probably all of us know someone who has kicked an addiction and inspired us and others to do the same. While news tabloids prefer to feature celebrities in trouble because it appeals to a macabre fascination with darkness, there is ample evidence of those who have conquered their demons and gone on to a highly productive life. Oprah Winfrey has become one of the most successful women in the world and no one can doubt the huge contribution she continues to make to the betterment of society through her media activities and philanthropic ventures. Yet, she too has her addictive challenges. She's admitted to using cocaine during the eighties. But what a life she has created for herself beyond addiction.

> **We are all responsible for our choices.**

The Synchronicity Socratic Method

The American Dream promises happiness and we can get addicted to our pursuit of it. A few related assumptions that apply include:

> "I have the right to pursue happiness, no matter what it takes."

> "My own happiness is primary and everyone else's is secondary."

> "My happiness depends on material things."

Cause and Effect

You can't cure an addiction until you change the beliefs that cause the behavior associated with it. Achieving the happiness that the American Dream promises requires changing the beliefs that cause your behavior, particularly the primary belief that you don't already have what you need.

Those loyal souls who adhere to the American Dream are addicted to this belief, which makes suffering and misery inevitable. When people complain about their suffering and repetitive misery, one might well ask them: "What do you get out of your suffering?"

For one, they get attention which they misinterpret as love. Adhering to the American Dream is an overwhelmingly negative strategy to get attention. "Look at how miserable I am. Look at the suffering I have created in my life. The American

Dream promised me happiness, but instead I have this crappy experience. Hear my sob story, pay attention to me."

So, who are you right now? Are you a victim resorting to addictions to cope with life's challenges? Ask honestly and open yourself to experience what your intuition brings you.

Meditation for Addicts

"The American republic, of course, is an idea as much as it is a reality. That idea is of a nation founded on freedom and dedicated to the progress of human rights around the globe. It's most certainly not of a country that aids the underground drug trade – even if it does." [2]

- Ryan Grim

We spoke with Howard Josepher and Maria Josepher, founders of a successful New York City-based drug treatment program called Exponents, about their work with drug addicts. We are denoted in this edited conversation by AD, and HJ & MJ refer to the Exponents founders.

HJ & MJ: The root of "addict" is *addicere*, from the Latin, "to be devoted to." The addict is devoted to keeping every moment the same – "high." They are very controlling. But you can't control life and keep it high all the time. There are highs and lows. The highs are high, the lows are low.

AD: What's changed over the years that you've been helping treat addicts?

HJ & MJ: We are seeing a shift in how we treat addiction. In the past, someone suffering from a drug or alcohol addiction would enter a treatment process and undergo various forms of therapeutic or clinical practices, counseling, behavior modification programs, etc. At the end of that, they were supposed to be cured. What we now understand about addiction is that there are almost always numerous relapses prior to someone genuinely overcoming their addiction.

Now we understand that addiction is a chronic condition. Treatment is changing from an acute to a chronic care model. Although we still primarily have drug treatment programs, we are now creating and seeing more recovery programs. These provide options, a range of services they can choose from, as opposed to treatment programs where they are told what to do. We used to focus only on what was wrong with the addict. Recovery services are more strength- focused.

AD: What's your view on the War on Drugs?

HJ & MJ: It's a failed war. It's a war on people. It criminalizes the drug user and the drug addict and demands that law enforcement personnel try to treat a health issue. Basically, we are locking people up for self-medicating their disease … underlying conditions they are struggling to cope with. If, on the other hand, we see their situation as a chronic health condition, then we use a health approach. More than 2.3 million Americans are behind bars right now and most of them are there, not because they have committed a crime, but because they have violated their probation.

People are self-medicating their pain. There is also a prescription drug epidemic going on right now. There are more annual deaths in America from overdoses of legal drugs than from auto accidents.

AD: You use meditation in your treatment program, right?

HJ & MJ: Yes. The people we work with are already familiar with a meditative state; they just didn't know it was that. Almost all our people wear headphones. You know that when you are listening to the music, at some point everything seems to just disappear except for the music? In India this is called the state of "no mind." The *yama yama yama* stops.

Many addicts are open to advancing from music to meditative music but not all. Some have trouble closing their eyes because they are so traumatized. The mind is a beast, so we call our main class "Mastering the Beast." It's about developing the ability to focus. People learn to grab their minds and tell it what to think, to pay attention in the direction they choose. When you are paying attention, you are bringing your mind into the present moment of the here and now. If it is troubled, then focus it, pay attention. Here and now is the reality.

Many thanks to Howard Josepher and Maria Josepher for the above comments which illuminate the topic in a way that could only be done by those working from deep on the inside.

Addicted to Love

"Every form of addiction is bad, no matter whether the narcotic be alcohol or morphine or idealism." [3]

- Carl Jung

Do you have strong beliefs about watching porn? Have your beliefs made it a behavior that you judge as being bad? The perfect person would never do that. How about fantasizing about an idealized, unrealistic bond that simply doesn't exist beyond the first few moments of imaginative lust. This isn't restricted to teenagers! Adults can act just as immaturely when they sacrifice families and careers to pursue a "look" across a martini or boardroom table.

Such egocentric strategies to get attention arise from a lack of self-love. In fact, these behaviors actually originate in early childhood. If you didn't feel satisfactorily loved and nurtured by your mother and father, you tried something to get what was missing. Did you act out or cry? How did you strive for attention and nurturance?

You may still be doing it because, underneath, you don't love yourself. You are still looking for love outside yourself, simply because you weren't nurtured enough early on to develop adequate self-love. You've become an adult who doesn't understand that love has little to do with another person.

Alexandra Katehakis, Clinical Director of Center for Healthy Sex, once blogged about an investment manager who posted a lengthy, love-addicted letter on Reddit, repeating over and over that he hated this woman and then begged her not to leave him. Katehakis and other experts believe that love addiction is connected to obsessive parenting that develops "come here, go away" conditioning.

Amen, I Say, Amen!

Then there's religion, the opiate of the masses. Consider the spectacle of preachers on television bringing salvation to the multitudes. Millions of people get "high" being righteous, declaring the way things are for them and for everybody else. "I am right and if you don't agree with me you are wrong." Their ultimate validation is "God says I am right!" Here is addiction to the belief that you have life figured out. It's an egoic belief you invest in to create security. This false belief says you are saved, you are safe, and that God loves you more than he loves others who don't behave the way you demand they must.

The dogma and the passion backing it are all part of a consensus belief you accept which makes you feel powerful. It makes you feel high to be among the Chosen Ones and know that you are loved while others aren't. Of course, you want them in the church too because that validates your consensus belief system. Catholics are taught that theirs is the only legitimate faith and millions still believe that. The same is true for other religions.

Dr. Bob Minor of the Fairness Project blogged *When Religion is an Addiction,* "I remember hearing popular psychological speaker and writer John Bradshaw say that the 'high' one gets from being righteous was similar to the high of cocaine. As both a former monk and addict, he knew the feelings personally." Dr. Minor continued, "This mind-altering fix of righteousness covers their paranoid shame-based feelings about the internal and external dangers stalking them. The victim-role language of their dealers, right-wing religious leaders, feeds it. Like alcoholism and drug addiction, the fix numbs the religious addict against any feelings about how their addiction affects others.

"Addicts reinforce each other. Fundamentalist religious organizations and media are their supportive co-users. So the person who deals with someone's addiction cannot do it alone. They must have support from others outside the addiction.

"You can't argue with an addict. Arguing religion to one so addicted plays into the addictive game. Arguing about the Bible or tradition is like arguing with the alcoholic about whether whiskey or tequila is better for them. It's useless and affirms the addiction." [4]

Anger Addiction

Many of us struggle with anger and for some it becomes an addiction.

As Cindy Shadel blogged on the Huffington Post, "On March 22, (2012) Chris Brown appeared on *Good Morning America* to promote his newest album, *F.A.M.E.* With two years passing since his violent assault against then-girlfriend Rihanna, Chris Brown had hoped to have the past behind him, but co-anchor Robin Roberts of *Good Morning America* wanted to know more about the status of Rihanna's restraining order, and less about Brown's new album. The pointed interview questions left Chris Brown in a rage in which he reportedly stormed offstage, throwing a cooler in the hallway, smashing a window in his dressing room with a folding chair, and then exiting the studio shirtless. Brown issued an apology two days later on BET.

"It seems that instances such as these always call for 'issuing an apology,' as if that were the key to metaphorically put his explosive behavior in a box, tie it up with a nice red bow, and place it under the Christmas tree. Perhaps in time he will be able to arrive on a morning show set and publicly declare some useful coping mechanisms he's been able to employ for his impulse control. Unfortunately, his acting out only reveals what little progress he's made toward managing his rage, ultimately hurting his cause, while modeling for young and old a destructive alternative for expressing one's anger."[5]

An apology doesn't touch the addiction. It takes diving much deeper to get to the source of it.

Money Addiction

At one time money was a symbol for wealth but now it's become wealth itself, even though rarely does the sheer accumulation actually contribute to authentic happiness. Dr. Tian Dayton, clinical psychologist, writes about about the addiction to money:

"It's general wisdom that for someone who is addicted to alcohol or drugs, their lives become increasingly organized around the use and abuse of their substance. The person who uses money to mood alter can have their relationship with money spin out of control; by being overly focused on accumulating it, spending it hoarding it or using it to control people, places and things. For example, just as with a drug or alcohol, tolerance increases and they may find themselves needing to devote increasingly larger amounts of time to these activities, to achieve the same mood altering high that only a little once provided. Because of this they become increasingly preoccupied with all things related to getting and maintaining their substance to the exclusion of other things.

"Gradually, just as is the case with any addict, their preoccupation with money becomes their primary preoccupation and money becomes their primary relationship. This point is key when it comes to money addiction as far as I am concerned. For the person addicted to money their relationship with money becomes their primary relationship in life, which means that other relationships become secondary. Their personal drives and identity become so wrapped up around having money (the wealthy person), accumulating money (the big earner), spending money (the big spender), or even giving money away (the big donor), that they don't know who they would be without it.

"Nor do they want to know who they would be without it. Over time their core sense of identity along with their ability to manage their moods becomes overly dependent on something outside themselves, just as is the case with other forms of addiction.

"'Who would I be without my money?' is the night terror of any one whose identity has become dependent on money just as 'who would I be without a drug in my system?' is what haunts the substance abuser." [6]

Hats off to those with money who put it to good use. A friend recently told me about acquaintances in Colorado who are, as he put it, "100% invested in doing something helpful." They have not millions but billions. And it has not corrupted them. It has inspired them to find out how much good they can do. That's inspiring to us!

Give Me My 15 Minutes!

Egocentricity is all about celebrity. The more fame and notoriety you have, the more successful you are, at least according to the precepts of the American Dream. Every kid's wish is to be a star. You see this on shows like *American Idol*. The producers travel across America holding auditions and thousands of hopefuls show up. This is their chance to become famous! Some of them are embarrassing to watch because they have no talent whatsoever. But the conditioning promises, "This is possible for you, it is the American Dream, it could happen to you, you could get lucky."

There's also something in our deluded ego state that makes us want to see famous people suffer and get punished. We like to see celebrities getting caught, even when we do many of the same things. We can vilify Charlie Sheen, for instance, but who else is drinking to excess, smoking pot and involved in bizarre relationships?

Who Would You Be ...?

Think about what addictions you have and how you depend on them for the experience of who you are and for your happiness. Each of us could make his or her own list.

The word "addiction" suggests something radical. Images might come to mind of fall-down drunks or drug addicts passed out on the street. But most addictions are socially acceptable. Coffee, sugar, gossip, self-judgment, sex.

The awakening process involves surrendering addiction and replacing it with balance. The thrill of excess gives way to the deeper, longer lasting satisfaction of living in balance. A friend recounted a recent tragedy in which his 21-year-old niece drove while drunk, hit a van and killed two mothers. She had chosen to drink excessively and then to drive. Her choice ended two lives and destroyed her own.

Balance, on the other hand, is meeting an addiction with a conscious choice. "No thanks, I've had enough to drink because I'm driving." Or, "Could someone call me a taxi please?" What does it take to make the difference? One way is to practice before the pressure comes on. Practice to develop awake, aware habits and learn how to enjoy balance more than you enjoy your addictions.

Socratic Conclusion

This was a challenging chapter so let's end on a positive note. We've successfully debunked the Dream assumptions that surround addictions and the pursuit of happiness. This leads to the awake statement of truth:

"Happiness is my true nature, it is the very essence of life.

I already have it; pursuing it is unnecessary."

An enlightening question to ponder is "What is my number one addiction and what am I doing about it?"

A Moment of Mastery

Balance delivers wholeness.
I embrace responsibility
to balance my experience
and generate happiness
through balance.
Love indwells.

Chapter Fourteen: Greed is God

"... Greed, for lack of a better word, is good.

Greed is right, greed works. Greed clarifies, cuts through,

and captures the essence of the evolutionary spirit. Greed,

in all of its forms; greed for life, for money, for love, knowledge,

has marked the upward surge of mankind." [1]

- Gordon Gekko, "Wall Street"

"Someone reminded me I once said "Greed is good".

Now it seems it's legal.

Because everyone is drinking the same Kool Aid." [2]

- Gordon Gekko, "Wall Street 2"

"An economic war is prolonged torture. And its ravages are no less terrible than those depicted in the literature on war properly so called. We think nothing of the other because we are used to its deadly effects.... The movement against war is sound. I pray for its success. But I cannot help the gnawing fear that the movement will fail if it does not touch the root of all evil – human greed." [3]

- M. K. Gandhi

Let's consider the economy.

Greed, some might say, has become God. Greed rules the world. Who do you know that isn't on the take? How about you? Is there anything you do for money that you wouldn't do for free? How many people would quit their job tomorrow if the paychecks stopped? Why do we do what we do? For love or for money? We may rail against the Gordon Gekko's of the world but he was honest.

200 Francs

When we begin to talk about the economy, it's useful to consider the impact of local and long distance transactions. Time was when most of our business was conducted locally, amongst neighbors. It's increasingly the other way around now. We eat food shipped in from thousands of miles away and wear clothing manufactured in China.

Here's an interesting tale that recalls the value of local economies remaining autonomous to themselves. According to the story, a certain man walked into a French hotel and paid 200 francs for a room. The hotelier promptly gave the money to his concierge to cover past wages owed. The concierge hurried down the street and paid his debt to the plumber who was delighted because his wife had a 200-franc debt with the mechanic. The mechanic walked over to his daughter's piano teacher and paid her bill. She immediately went to the hotel and paid her bill — 200 francs!

What happened? The same 200 francs travelled around this small community and retired 1,000 francs of community debt. The community itself became 1,000 francs richer when just 200 francs came into the system from outside.

This illustrates the value of imports, what happens when you keep wealth local and the illusion of debt. To whom do we owe money and who owes money to us? The above scenario of reducing debt amongst neighbors breaks down when someone takes the money out of the system, when it leaves the community. And that, of course, is what big corporations do. Much of your $85 paid to Walmart does not stay in your community.

The lesson here is that wealth is meant to be generated, circulated and shared, not extracted and hoarded. Of course, wealth is more than money. Most of our wealth resides in other forms, such as our family, our friends, our reputation, our skills, etc. You might find it interesting to create a holistic portfolio that lists all of your forms of wealth -not just money and physical assets -and then study how you are buying, generating, saving and wasting resoures. This can be revealing!

A friend of mine likes to say that he is financially independent because his experience of being wealthy does not depend on how much money he has. He has chosen to be independent of that single myopic measurement. His holistic portfolio lists things like peace of mind and long-term friendships.

A Story of Awakening

"It only cost $75 to be initiated into Transcendental Meditation in 1971. About two months after I started, I was sitting at home meditating when I began to notice sounds, everything from car doors shutting to people's voices, even the noise of my furnace clicking on.

"It was irritating and I tried to escape the sounds by concentrating on the mantra they'd given me. It didn't work. My frustration grew until I just gave up. In the moment I stopped trying, something amazing happened. I just let the sounds in, all of them. I enjoyed them. I incorporated them into my meditation and the moment I did, I realized that I'd been trying to escape from the world, hiding in my inner cave. Suddenly, I felt something inside me ... like a huge ship turning. Energy began to pour out of me, through the sounds! Each one connected me with something to bless with my grateful attention.

"In that moment a blast of sunlight hit me and electricity flooded through my whole body. Talk about a wake-up

moment! I'd done my share of mind-altering substances years before but this trumped them all. I was high!

"The feeling lasted. Actually, I can say that it's still with me. I never forgot the difference between acceptance and resistance, and I often recall this moment when I'm challenged by something. It helps me reverse course and use whatever presents itself as an opportunity to express a blessing."

- W.W., Canada

Waking Up

Using our Synchronicity Socratic Process, let's analyze the underpinnings of belief that fortify and sustain the economics of the American Dream. Start with the following Dream assumptions:

"Financial wealth represents success."

"All Americans have an equal opportunity to become wealthy and successful."

"I am guaranteed the right to be wealthy and successful no matter what it takes."

"America is the land of opportunity for everyone."

Horatio Alger, a prolific American writer of the mid-to-late nineteenth century, popularized the notion of "rags to riches" with his tales of young boys scaling the ladders of success in books such as *Fame and Fortune*. Regardless of whether this phenomenon actually occurred to any significant degree, the principle itself became ingrained in the American Dream. To this day, we refer to someone who has risen to success that way as "a real Horatio Alger story."

In 2003, Academy Award winning filmmaker Michael Moore opined, "So, here's my question: after fleecing the American public and destroying the American Dream for most

118

working people, how is it that, instead of being drawn and quartered and hung at dawn at the city gates, the rich got a big wet kiss from Congress in the form of a record tax break, and no one says a word? How can that be? I think it's because we're still addicted to the Horatio Alger fantasy drug. Despite all the damage and all the evidence to the contrary, the average American still wants to hang on to this belief that maybe, just maybe, he or she (mostly he) just might make it big after all." [4]

Does everyone in America have an equal chance? The facts say no. Economist Bhashkar Mazumder, director of the Chicago Census Research Data Center, detailed statistics relating to intergenerational "stickiness" relative to income. Apparently it takes, on average, five generations for children to rise from the low to middle income range. Another report I referenced showed how upward mobility increased steadily from 1940 to 1980 but has been declining since then, falling below its 1940 level by the year 2000. Salvatore Babones, who is a senior lecturer in sociology at the University of Sydney, Australia, writes: "Academic studies typically show that around 40-45% of income differences are transmitted from one U.S. generation to the next. This is about twice as high as the equivalent figures in Western Europe and Australia." [5]

Success and wealth do not mean the same things to everyone? Just think of your own values and those of others you know. Our widely disparate value systems are part of what makes us unique. Here's a story from German writer Heinrich Theodor Böll, who wrote about the dark side of capitalism. Interestingly, his writing appears online under the title, *The American Dream*:

> An American businessman was standing at the pier of a small coastal Mexican village when a small boat with just one fisherman docked. Inside the small boat were several large yellow fin tuna. The American complimented the Mexican on the quality of his fish.

"How long did it take you to catch them?" the American asked.

"Only a little while," the Mexican replied.

"Then why don't you stay out longer and catch more fish?"

"I have enough to support my family's immediate needs."

"But what do you do with the rest of your time?"

"I sleep late, fish a little, play with my children, take a siesta with my wife, Maria, stroll into the village each evening where I sip wine and play guitar with my amigos. I have a full and busy life, senor."

The American scoffed, "I am a Harvard MBA and could help you. You should spend more time fishing and with the proceeds you buy a bigger boat, and with the proceeds from the bigger boat you could buy several boats, so eventually you would have a fleet of fishing boats.

"Instead of selling your catch to a middleman you would sell directly to the consumers, eventually opening your own canning factory. You would control the product, processing and distribution. You would need to leave this small coastal fishing village and move to Mexico City, then LA and eventually NYC where you would run your expanding enterprise."

The fisherman asked, "But senor, how long will this all take?" To which the American replied, "15-20 years."

"But what then, senor?"

The American laughed. "That's the best part. When the time is right you would announce an IPO (Initial Public Offering) and sell your company stock to the public and become very rich, you would make millions."

"Millions, senor? Then what?"

"Then you would retire. Move to a small coastal fishing village where you would sleep late, fish a little, play with your kids, take a siesta with your wife, stroll to the village in the evenings where you could sip wine and play your guitar with your amigos..." [6]

Your Divine Right to be Rich

God wants you to be rich. So says pastor Joel Osteen, leader of America's biggest super church (grossing $75 million a year) and author of *God Wants Me to Be Rich*. According to economist Paul Zane Pilzer, writing in his best seller, *God Wants You to Be Rich: The Theology of Economics*: "God does want each of us to be rich in every possible way, health, love, and peace of mind, as well as material possessions. God wants this, however, not just for our own sake, but for the sake of all humankind ... An increase in the wealth of an individual almost always represents an even larger increase in wealth for society at large." [7]

This statement, that "an increase in the wealth of an individual almost always represents an even larger increase in wealth for society at large," is selectively true in the American Dream, but spectacularly untrue in reality. It could be more accurately stated: "a radical increase in wealth for an individual almost never represents a larger increase in wealth for society at large." This is not a theory; it's proven by statistics. The gap between the wealthy and the poor has never been greater. The rich getting richer did not make society at large richer; in fact, exactly the opposite has occurred.

What's even more questionable is the idea that God wants something ... God has wants? This, clearly, is a projection. We've made God in our own image; he has needs, just like we do. God wants us to be rich, God needs us to be rich and, if we are not, it follows that we are not fulfilling God's wishes for us so we must be disappointing him. Millions of people believe this to be true. Of course, it's not true. It's just a consensus belief, unproven by the facts in America, or anywhere else for that matter.

Questioning Success

The American Dream is wildly successful … for rich people. But what about the poor? Millions of them support those decision-makers in office who vote against fair taxes for the rich because the poor dream that they too will be rich one day and then would not want to be heavily taxed. Some may read a report about the "2012 World Economic Forum" in Davos, Switzerland and wish they had been there. "They came, they feasted on smoked sturgeon and black truffle risotto, drank liquor paid for by global banks, endured dozens of security checks, and tried not to fall down in the snow. They talked about the perilous state of the global economy and the future of capitalism. Then, they headed back to their home countries, many in chauffeured limousines, some by private jet." [8]

Millions of voters support elected representatives who vote to defeat bills that attempt to regulate the corporations which keep poor people poor, actually believing those corporations will police themselves. When was the last time you voluntarily gave yourself a speeding ticket? Those in power who have become intoxicated with greed in the illusion of separation are on the take and they will grab wherever, whenever, and from whomever they can. They will lie to protect themselves and they will cheat for personal gain. That's why we need regulations and laws to impede their greed. Those who have become corrupted by power and wealth are determined to remove every possible obstacle to the profiteering that results from having no moral impediments to selfishness.

During the 2012 GOP Presidential Campaign, candidate Mitt Romney made news when he claimed that concerns about income inequality in America were the result of "envy." On

NBC"s *Today Show* he said, "I think it's about envy. I think it's about class warfare. I think when you have a president encouraging the idea of dividing America based on 99 percent versus one percent, you've opened up a whole new wave of approach in this country which is entirely inconsistent with 'one nation under God.' " He went on to suggest, "I think it's fine to talk about those things in quiet rooms..." [9]

Note his wording: "... when you have a president encouraging the idea of dividing America based on 99 percent versus one percent ..." Mr. Romney is suggesting that this division is something President Obama invented. Could Mr. Romney possibly not realize that this division is actually real, that it is not just some sort of campaign angle? A June story in *Bloomberg Business News* reported that "... median family net worth rose 62 percent from 1962 to 1983, then fell 12 percent from 1983 to 2010." [10] Wow. That sounds pretty real.

Then we have the example of past president Jimmy Carter. Despite differing opinions on his effectiveness as commander-in-chief, most people would agree that what he has done with his life since leaving office provides a wonderful example of how public officials can continue serving after they lose their positions of elected political influence. His foundation works on issues relating to democracy and civil rights. He has worked tirelessly with Habitat for Humanity International to help provide housing for the underprivileged throughout the world. He is an inspiration.

Not everyone though spends their time in contributive pursuits! Journalist Matt Taibbi brings us more news from the world that 99% of us only read about: "Newspapers in Colorado today are reporting that the elegant Hotel Jerome in Aspen, Colorado, will be closed to the public from today through Monday at noon. Why? Because a local squire has apparently decided to rent out all 94 rooms of the hotel for three-plus days for his daughter's Bat Mitzvah.

"The hotel's general manager, Tony DiLucia, would say only that the party was being thrown by a 'nice family,' but newspapers are now reporting that the Daddy of the lucky little gal is one Jeffrey Verschleiser, currently an executive with Goldman Sachs."[11]

As Jonathan Zap essayed in *From Foxes and Reptiles: Psychopathy and the Financial Meltdown*: "The affinity of psychopaths for high finance is certainly not my discovery. My original working title for this essay was: "Reptiles in Brooks Brothers Suits." I abandoned that title when I discovered that Robert Hare, the world's leading expert on psychopathy, had co-authored an excellent book entitled *Snakes in Suits, When Psychopaths go to Work*. I almost abandoned the whole project, wondering if I had anything new to say. After some consideration I realized that although the main hypothesis was already well established by others, I had a few new points to add and, in any case, the subject is so important, and with such vast implications for society, that I felt obliged to continue. The damage that psychopaths do to the global economy, and human civilization in general, is incalculable. As the James Joyce character Stephen Dedalus said, 'History is a nightmare from which I am trying to awaken.' Psychopathy may be one of the prime drivers of the nightmarish aspect of history." [12]

The Other, Other Alternative

In fact, the only secure investment is awareness. When in doubt about what to invest in, and there's rampant doubt today, invest in expanding your awareness. Why?

1. The dividends are immediate and guaranteed.

2. You don't need a numbered Swiss account, a password, or a bodyguard to protect your principal.

Expanding personal self-awareness is always the best investment, in any market. By the end of this chapter you will understand why and, hopefully, begin to diversify your own portfolio, a practice which is broadly considered to be an essential investment strategy. Diversify beyond things. Increase your balance sheet to include inner values.

The Divine Right of Adam Smith

Much of Consumer Capitalism is supposedly founded on the work of Adam Smith and his premise of the "invisible hand." Here's what three prominent business leaders had to say recently about Adam Smith:

"First: We should recall the wisdom of Adam Smith, 'father of modern economics,' who was a great moral philosopher first and foremost. In 1759, sixteen years before his famous *Wealth of Nations*, he published *The Theory of Moral Sentiments*, which explored the self-interested nature of man and his ability nevertheless to make moral decisions based on factors other than selfishness. In the *Wealth of Nations*, Smith laid the early groundwork for economic analysis, but he embedded it in a broader discussion of social justice and the role of government. Today we mainly know his analogy of the 'invisible hand' and refer to him as defending free markets, whilst ignoring his insight that the pursuit of wealth should not take precedence over social and moral obligations and his belief that a 'Divine Being' gives us 'the greatest quantity of happiness.'

"Second: We are taught that the free market as a 'way of life' appealed to Adam Smith but not that he thought the morality of the market could not be a substitute for the morality for society at large. He neither envisioned nor prescribed a capitalist society, but rather a 'capitalist economy within society, a society held together by communities of non-capitalist and non-market morality.'

"Third: As it has been noted, morality for Smith included neighborly love, an obligation to practice justice, a norm of financial support for the government 'in proportion to [one's] revenue,' and a tendency in human nature to derive pleasure from the good fortune and happiness of other people." [13]

Who Can You Trust?

"Some said he was just naïve, or merely incompetent, but in the end, Greenspan was most likely just lying. He castrated the government as a regulatory authority, then transformed himself into the Pablo Escobar of high finance, unleashing a steady river of cheap weight into the crack house that Wall Street was rapidly becoming." [14]

- Matt Taibbi

Former Chairman of the Federal Reserve Alan Greenspan has been revered as an almost infallible voice of truth on all things economic, yet we find that many of his predictions were simply erroneous. In fact, some say he has been wrong most of the time. The fact that his reputation has survived such chronic incompetence lends credence to the phenomenon we mentioned earlier, that one of our greatest fears is to admit we have been conned.

Meanwhile, author David Korten tells us, "The proper purpose of the financial services sector is to serve the real economy on which everyone depends for their daily needs, their quality of life, and their opportunity to be creative, contributing members of their communities. By this standard of performance, Wall Street does not serve us well."[15] Neither does the Federal Reserve which, although most Americans don't know it, is not a government institution. It is a private bank that was created in 1913. Since it began controlling our national economy, the U.S. dollar has lost about 95 percent of its purchasing power.

In his 2012 State of the Union address, President Obama described America as a country where a shrinking number of people do really well, while a growing number of Americans barely get by. This is the economic reality in America today.

It's a direct result of what has happened over the last decades in the unregulated financial sector, under the guidance of "experts" we were expected to trust. These "experts" are mostly men who presented themselves as able to help turn the American Dream into reality. They failed.

Korten continues, "...The success of the financial sector is not an end in itself, but a means to an end -which is to support the vitality of the real economy and the livelihood of the American people. What really matters to the life of our nation is enabling entrepreneurs to build new businesses that create more well-paying jobs, and enabling families to put a roof over their heads and educate their children." [16]

When Korten speaks about "a means to an end," he points to improving the livelihood of the American people. This relates to the only area the American Dream purports to be improving, our material existence. This is honest, at least because that is all "success of the financial sector" could hope to achieve on its own. And as we know, there are significant obstacles to that ever actually occurring. Broadening our perspective, we acknowledge a different "end," namely, that individuals become conscious of who they are and derive their fulfillment not from external success alone but from the balance between external and internal achievement, with the development of values such as integrity and honor, and experiences such as peace and contentment.

This requires true leaders who have achieved this balance themselves and can demonstrate it in their living. They would model qualities such as compassion. They would be kind. They would work to insure that everyone in America had a basic quality of life -food, shelter, medical care, etc. They would support cooperation, not competition, and might say, "We are here to better ourselves and each other, not to compete and control."

One current American leader who inspires in this regard is first time Massachusetts Senator Elizabeth Warren, a former Harvard Law School professor specializing in bankruptcy law. She contributed to the formation of the United States Consumer Financial Protection Bureau. In her Senate campaign she responded to criticism of her support for asking the rich to pay more taxes with: "There is nobody in this country who got rich on his own. Nobody. You moved your goods to market on the roads the rest of us paid for; you hired workers the rest of us paid to educate; you were safe in your factory because of police forces and fire forces that the rest of us paid for. You didn't have to worry that marauding bands would come and seize everything at your factory, and hire someone to protect against this, because of the work the rest of us did. Now look, you built a factory and it turned into something terrific, or a great idea. God bless. Keep a big hunk of it. But part of the underlying social contract is, you take a hunk of that and pay forward for the next kid who comes along."

The Safety Net Has Holes in It

The only true security is the eternality of consciousness, the eternality of life. Everything else is impermanent. Stop investing in impermanence and invest in the ground of being, the unity within all diversity.

Ironically, the only certainty you have is that everything will keep on changing. That is how everything is designed, but the ego doesn't want change. The ego wants as little change as possible. In fact, it wants to nail everything down and be surrounded with a high fence!

Millions of today's Americans have worked hard their entire lives. They paid into company pension plans. Suddenly, something mysterious happens somewhere in the middle of the night and they are left with nothing. Now they can't afford their homes, lose their pensions and have nothing. We see them working in Walmart for minimum wage.

Where did their money go? It's concentrated in the clutches of the ultra-rich who took it to replace the imaginary money they created out of thin air. They certainly didn't work hard all their lives for it! And it adds up to billions of dollars, hoarded out of sight. Meanwhile, there are millions of people going without meals while surplus food rots in warehouses. Millions of homes sit empty while homeless millions roam our streets.

Millions of Americans are on food stamps and subsidies for food and housing, just struggling to survive? An estimated forty million Americans do not have health care and cannot afford it? This is the dark side of the American Dream. It fails to make the same headlines that, for instance, celebrity wardrobe malfunctions do.

Diversify Your Portfolio

True abundance has little to do with money. In terms of consciousness, abundance is based on how much self-awareness you have and how fully alive you are. We keep pointing to this with words such as "happiness" and "fulfillment" and "bliss." Wisdom traditions and sages have always said: "What if your experience of happiness could be constant? What if it were euphoric, like the experience of falling in love, except that you had it all the time? What if you were high on life, if life were an intoxicating, radically euphoric and fulfilling experience?"

That's the promise of waking up.

Dialogue With a Rich Guy

We had the opportunity to interview a wealthy American whom we'll call ML. ML volunteered his views on economic matters. His delightfully irreverent and wakeful views come through loud and clear in this edited transcript. We are denoted as "AD."

AD: Our readers are naturally concerned about the economy. You've been very successful, financially. What's your best advice for them?

ML: We shouldn't be concerned about what is called economics because there really is no such thing. It's an illusion. I tell people to forget economics and deal-making. Start with creating something good for everyone. By the way, I am not a do-gooder. I just believe that what you give is exactly what you get back. If your motivation is trying to get money — which is often just a way to get power and privilege — a person will be mean-spirited. And there is not enough money in the world for them. Imagine, Leona Helmsley, who was a billionaire at the time, tried to save $10,000 in sales tax and spent 10 years in jail for it!

Here's the thing. Nobody acts outside of their own self-interest. One great example of that was when Lincoln was a congressman, riding on a train, speaking to someone about self-interest. Lincoln said that self-interest is the only way that you can act. All of a sudden, Lincoln saw a sheep ahead on the track. He jumped up and pulled the emergency cord to stop the train. The sudden stoppage caused him to fall down and break his arm, but he still got out and moved the lamb. When doctors were treating his arm, someone said, You were wrong. You just proved that you did something with no self-interest.. Lincoln replied, Quite the opposite. I couldnnt have lived with myself if we had killed that sheep..

AD: How do you manage to survive and thrive in environments where people think very differently than you do?

ML: Well, I'm not sure how different I am, really. People just need a chance, maybe someone to trigger their values. Here's a good story about that. I once formed a group of companies and we spent all our money getting very close to making a large deal. At the last moment, I found out that the biggest investor in the group was pulling out. This would ruin the deal and bankrupt us.

I panicked and called my spiritual mentor. We talked for a couple of hours and he told me what to do: get there early and look each person in the eye as they arrived. Look at them with love and consciously think that they are doing the best they can do. Believe that they have the same goals as I do, but are just afraid. Believe that, through this deal, I can help them become rich.

I did it and it was amazing. By the time half the people had arrived, I had tears in my eyes. I felt love more strongly than I ever had before. I felt personally connected with all of them and they felt it too. In fact, the whole atmosphere in the room was charged with love.

The lead lawyer and his client who didn't want to do the deal said they were balking at us owning 10% of the new company we hoped to form together. The old me would have been offended, shouted out something obscene, and stood my ground. Instead, I looked them in the eyes and said, I understand. How does this sound? I will leave the room. You come up with any number that you feel is fair for our compensation. And, I promise you, anything between zero to 10% and it's a deal.. I repeated that, if they really felt we should get nothing, we would still do the deal.

I left the room and it took about 10 minutes before they called me back in. During that time I sat and reflected on that I really meant it. I felt it! I believed it! There was nothing in my heart except love and the desire to do something great for these people who had worked hard all their lives. I knew that they knew I meant it.

When I walked back in there they said that they couldn't do what I'd suggested. They couldn't give me a number between zero and 10% because they thought we should get 12%!

We all hugged, right there in the boardroom, and from that moment on we were unified. They worked even harder than I did. They invited me onto their board, we dined together regularly, and we became great friends as we grew successful together. And it all came from what my spiritual mentor told me to do.

AD: You've made it. What do you do now?

ML: I hardly spend any time at all on making money any more. I spend my time giving it away, or buying books and art and then giving those away. My favorite thing is to help the homeless and the hungry. Why? Because it makes me happy. I like to give people an envelope with $50 in it. They might spend it on booze and drugs but that's not my business.

The Truth About Abundance

The story ML told us provides a remarkable example of how spiritual principles can influence the most practical of situations. Certainly, in our thinking, there is often a great divide between money and spirituality, as if the two can't co-exist. But as self-awareness expands, all things are included as valid and appropriate, including money.

Money, of course, has changed from being a symbol of wealth to wealth itself. But it's all a matter of perception because when you really think about it, it's still a symbol. What can you do with a twenty-dollar bill? You can only trade it for something useful, like lunch.

Our delusion is that the symbol is the thing. So, we pursue it, then hoard it, and stress about protecting it and making sure we get more. Imagine having the same fear-based attitude about breathing. "Gotta get more air, save it, protect it, get more." No, you breathe in, you breathe out, never worrying about needing to "own" it.

Such is the nature of true abundance. It doesn't belong to anyone. It's the wealth of life, the joy of being. How do you get it? Live! Breathe! Be!

Being able to do this doesn't depend on the state of the economy or who's in the White House. Your true wealth is always an exact measure of your ability to surrender the ego's need-to-own in favor of enjoying the bounty of life, shared by all living things without fear of loss.

Our Socratic Conclusion

The American Dream assumptions about our economy have revealed themselves to be untrue. The belief that "everyone in America has a chance to become successful and wealthy" is imagination, a fraudulent echo of the questionable Horatio Alger myth. New, more truthful assumptions could be;

1. Everyone in America can grow their unique experience of success and wealth through their choices.

2. Invest in the permanence of self-awareness.

3. True wealth is about the essence of life rather than the content of life.

An enlightening question to ponder is "What makes me wealthy?"

A Moment of Mastery

I am abundant.
Everything I need is already present
as I open to receive
and surrender ownership.
My greatest wealth is knowing
who I truly am.

Chapter Fifteen: Looking for Love in All the Wrong Places

"Love and marriage, love and marriage

Go together like a horse and carriage,

This I tell ya, brother, you can't have one without the other." [1]

\- Lyrics by Sammy Cahn and Jimmy Van Huesen

"Birds of a feather can never be shown

That livin' alone is fun

When two hearts are better than one." [2]

\- Songwriters: Johnny Mercer and Jerome Kern

"We are finding it less and less satisfying to blame others for our painful experiences (no matter how much we still want to) than to discover within ourselves the causes of our painful experiences and change them. We are beginning to recognize the importance of our emotions and intentions, of what we do, what we say, and why. We are looking for connections between our choices and our experiences so that we can change our choices and, therefore, change our experiences. We are striving to be the kind of person we want others to be rather than to change others, and we are transforming our relationships at home, at work, and at play ..." [3]

\- Gary Zukav

Marriage can be a trap.

Sometimes it's called a tender trap because that's how it starts. How long does the honeymoon last is a question that assumes the honeymoon is worth preserving for as long as possible and, if it fades, then you should try to get it back.

Actually, regardless of how good it might feel, the honeymoon represents the densest level of the marriage illusion. When the illusion begins to dissolve, what's really happening is a dismantling. Since it doesn't feel as good, "reality" seldom does when illusion is unravelling, it's no wonder the knee-jerk reaction is to try and reassert the fantasy. Sometimes that works, temporarily, through another vacation or perhaps marriage counseling. But unless both partners commit to awakening (in which case marriage becomes a central part of their evolutionary path), all such efforts will ultimately fail. The soaring divorce rates reflect this. Though those figures are deceptive since many other marriages would fail if those involved were truly honest and had the courage to face facts.

Marriage becomes a trap because, like the rest of the features the American Dream offers, it promises something you already have. Marriage is a substitute. It's for those who don't already have a primary relationship and seek to find it outside of themselves in another person. The subject (you) is separate from the object (your spouse).

Of course, subject and object are in relationship and, in truth, there is no separation. Marriage between separate individuals in need is called co-dependence. Couples collude together to sustain the illusion of fulfillment in separation where each gives the other what they are lacking. "You complete me," as Tom Cruise's character said in the film *Jerry McGuire*.

No, you are already complete. All of us are. In relationship, we can help each other grow in our human experience of that divine reality as well as in understanding that happiness does not arise because of another person. Marriage seeks to limit ecstasy to something that happens between husband and wife. Everyone else is off limits, until they suddenly are not if a break occurs. Since pleasure is self-generated, it can be shared with another but each is still responsible for him or herself. That's how we avoid codependency.

Surgeon General Joycelyn Elders was fired by Bill Clinton after responding to a question about masturbation during her 1994 address to the United Nations on AIDS. The question was whether she thought it could be appropriate to promote masturbation as a means of preventing young people from engaging in riskier forms of sexual activity. According to Wikipedia, she replied, "I think that it is part of human sexuality, and perhaps it should be taught."

Masturbation is something that every human being probably does. Some warn that it's evil, and can lead to blindness. In all likelihood those who demonize it in this way probably masturbate themselves but are theoretically convinced that sexuality should only be experienced with another person.

Laws limiting marriage to a man and a woman are a further layer of illusion, championed by some of our elected officials who declare that you can't love however love happens because there are rules and regulations. Imagine two trees in a garden. They can't love one another except within the restrictions imposed on them as rules about love. Sorry, they are already loving unconditionally!

The same is true between human beings. Quantum science says you are in relationship with everyone you encounter, literally passing through each other with the atoms in your breath mingling and cells colliding. Thus, you can't possibly count all your relationships in a single day.

Egos are duplicitous. They always have their secrets, their rules, regulations and boxes that everyone is supposed to fit into. But no one fits! You can pretend to fit, just like most everyone does, but that just means most everyone is a liar. The American Dream breeds liars. Why should that be shocking; everyone lies. In the movie, *Liar, Liar*, Jim Carrey plays a lawyer who is suddenly "cursed" with having to tell the truth. The results are hilarious and cataclysmic.

Imagine being "cursed" that way. "Hi honey, how was your day?" "Boring. I hate my job. My boss is an idiot. I did as little work as possible. I daydreamed about having sex with the girl three cubicles down. She's 20 years younger than you. I'm going to make a move on her tomorrow. How was your day, dear?"

The American Dream makes everyone an imposter. But behind it lurks what's real. You are a sexual being and sex is one of the most powerful forces in life. The more you limit and subjugate it, the more you fragment your consciousness. Ultimately, you can't limit it because it is too powerful. When it does leak out we're shocked. For example, sexual abuse within the clergy? How could that possibly happen? Well, order men to suppress a powerful force in their bodies and then put them in the daily company of attractive young boys and girls.

Society's fantasy about human sexuality is designed to fail. It turns us all into imposters at a perpetual masquerade ball from where we wait in hiding behind our masks, lurking with shifty eyes and dark secrets.

Turn Back the Mirror

Let's take off those masks while we read. Just relax with who you are and with your sexuality. Gender identification itself is limiting. Male, female… why not just identify ourselves as souls? And when it comes to relationships, all that we perceive in another is a reflection of ourselves.

Everyone and everything is holding a mirror up to us so what we see is ourselves. This means that everyone you encounter is your teacher … until they are not. When you meet human beings and interact with them, they may seem to independently express themselves in relationship to you, but they are also a reflection of you. Obviously, this principle is powerfully present in the marriage relationship.

When he or she does or says something that you dislike, judge, and/or think is wrong, it has very little to do with him or her and almost everything to do with you. What is being reflected by your partner is showing up so that you can resolve it within yourself. That includes action such as leaving someone who is abusing you. But action without inner work ensures that a similar reflection will show up again in your next relationship. And the next, and the next... until you get it.

Codependency does not foster personal growth. Tom Cruise's character in *Jerry McGuire* was dead wrong. "You complete me," [4] is a dysfunctional illusion. Yes, it's romantic. He was incomplete, presumably so was she, and she completed him while hopefully he completed her too. In other words, each was incomplete on his own and each needed the other. This is the fundamental description of many marriages, with partners relating on the basis of personal neediness, each expecting the other to create happiness for them individually and together.

Sorry, it doesn't work that way. None of us are here to complete another, to make another happy. We are here to grow and to help each other grow. Marriage can be a wonderful teacher because what partners trigger in each other will keep showing up in amazing variety until we have taken responsibility for whatever is reflecting back to us and resolving it. When something reflects back to you in your marriage, don't blame your partner for failing to complete you. Turn to the mirror, face the reflection, ask what you can do to learn, to grow and to expand your experience of universal love.

One inspiring example of an awakened couple is Gay and Katy Hendricks. They often speak about their 30 years together of loving, living and learning together, and of a dedication to helping others expand their own capacity to give and receive love. I especially enjoyed this comment from their website:

"We do not know the entire meaning of life. But we are very sure it is not to have a bad time."

A Story of Awakening

" One night when I was 34 and at a fork in the road in my life, I got stuck at a railroad crossing as a freight train snailed along the tracks. I found myself trapped in a moment of reflection. My life read like a history of failed relationships, not wanting to follow in the footsteps of my mother who was stifled by marriage, but doing exactly that!

"Sitting at the crossing, focused on the falling raindrops as the wiper blades moved hypnotically across the windshield, I entered a space of deep calm and peace. Questions arose: 'Why had I not been able to find happiness in relationships? Was I innately flawed?' Answers flowed: 'Stop looking outside yourself for wholeness. Go within!' As the last of the freight cars rolled by, the clanging crossing bells returned me to everyday awareness.

"But something had shifted. Outer relationship was no longer my focus, I wasn't seeking it and no one was seeking it from me. It was as if I had become invisible, what a relief! I began to explore inner relationship through deep tissue bodywork, psychotherapy, yoga, reading of spiritual books, all of which led to the Great Transformer: Meditation and those masters who would lend guidance along the way."

- J.G, Virginia

The Synchronicity Socratic Method

We could have a lot of fun with this one. Let's try out a few American Dream assumptions:

"Relationships are meant to give us what we lack."

"Together, we can succeed in ways we can't on our own."

"Love is dependent on another."

"Relationships insure the experience of love."

"Relationship is necessary for love."

"We cannot be fulfilled on our own."

"Love of another is necessary for happiness and fulfillment."

"Relationships guarantee love, happiness and fulfillment"

Through examining these assumptions, a couple of primary beliefs can rise to the surface. One is that on our own we lack what we need. Another is that we can only experience love with another.

We are social animals and we do need each other. But on what basis? America prides itself on being the land of the free, and the American Dream champions individuality. No wonder that our great national fear has been communism and, these days, a sure-fire way to demonize any political wannabe is to translate support for helping each other as socialism. This exposes the fundamental conflict between the idealism of helping each other on the one hand and the freedom of individuality on the other. John Wayne always did things his way and Frank Sinatra sang about it in his song, "I Did It My Way." "My" way, clearly, is not "our" way.

A fundamental spiritual truth is that each one of us is complete in himself or herself. We need no others to connect with Source Intelligence, not even a guru. A guru's role is to point the way and be an example, to help entrain a "seeker" to find their own way. We don't need anyone to complete us. We don't need a middle-man between ourselves and the divine. The reason we are in relationship is to help each other grow.

Love vs. Lust

Most people confuse lust for love.

Lust is biological, physical. Love is spiritual, the flowering of consciousness, the expression of pure being. Love can be shared with another but it belongs to oneself. It's the ultimate sovereignty.

This is not the way of The American Dream. Everybody's out shopping like dogs on street corners, sniffing each other's bums. A primary goal within the American Dream is to find your partner, get married and have a family, just like your parents did. Though they got introduced to each other at bridge parties and you at surf dating sites online, the end goal is the same.

The American Dream promises that love and marriage "go together like a horse and carriage." What we see are largely loveless marriages between individuals who have sold out for security and lose interest in their partner as the years roll by. They develop wandering eyes and entertain romantic fantasies. They won't get rid of their partner because the marriage provides security and safety, but not love. It was just the fantasy of love and it faded.

Instead of avoiding the boredom by fantasizing about someone else, you could return to the moment and be fully present with your partner. His body may not look like the waiter's did. He has no Ferrari parked outside like the celebrity you saw online. He didn't bring you roses and champagne like the character in a movie you just watched. But he's real! He's in your arms right now.

If you are truly present together, then marriage habits go out the window. If you are conscious, there can be no repetition. There's always the newness of consciousness happening and you flow with its unfolding. If you can really flow with it and move beyond your habitual biological urges, something miraculous begins to happen — intimacy, and the true marriage made in heaven, not earth.

Two Not One

"Separate together" sums up the core nature of most marriages. Two, not one. You invest in being separate together, trying your best to complete each other through the roles you play as husband and wife. Gary Zukav illuminates the phenomenon:

"Roles attract roles. Artists attract Artists, for example, and within that role subroles such as Musician, Sculptor, Painter, Writer, and Poet attract one another. Everyone plays many roles during a lifetime and several of them simultaneously, such as Father, Businessman, and Golfer (a sub-role of the role of Athlete); or Mother, Wife, and Teacher; or Politician and Mother; and so on. An individual who can see himself in only one role is analogous to an obsessive actor who cannot leave his stage role behind. He is lost in it. His friends forget who he is without the role, his family forgets who he is without the role, and eventually he forgets who he is without the role." [5]

One, Not Two

The opposite of all this identity confusion is holistic relationship. Conscious human beings, those one with Source Intelligence, create a holistic marriage and a holistic family based on the truth of being rather than on ego roles. There's oneness and equality and love and compassion, a life-affirmative, joyful experience.

As you become aware of the innate bliss of consciousness arising in you through your connection with Source Intelligence, rather than through your connection with your wife or husband, your marriage can become increasingly pleasurable. You begin to celebrate your oneness and multiply your bliss with each other and in all your relationships. Everyone and everything is a reflection, a multiplication of you. And since you are authoring an experience of fulfillment, it shows up with everyone, everywhere.

Family Values

The pinnacle of American society is the family and family values. Here's the reality behind the illusion of family values: almost everyone is suffering, denying they are suffering and lost in addictions to avoid facing facts.

Family is not the most valuable thing in America. Authentic being is. The only way happiness can be found in marriage, possessions, money and in your king-sized bed is if you bring the happiness with you and share it.

Of course, religion is a big part of family values. Gotta have religion, that "Ultimate Authority" guaranteeing, sanctioning your life and your illusory security. This seems necessary because deep down you really know that it's a sham. Your soul knows. It always knows that the ego-driven American Dream about relationship and family values is bull.

Does that sound harsh? Well, let's test it out. Just what do "family values" include? For starters, most people don't want their parents and grandparents living with them so they shuffle them off to a nursing home or a retirement community. If family values are so important, why doesn't that include the whole family?

Things are changing now because of the economy. Old people can't afford retirement homes because their savings were stolen from them. Children can't take care of their parents because they lost, or can't find, jobs. So they have to live together. Ironically, the stalled economy is helping us to experience more family values.

It's interesting that in India, which doesn't have a Social Security system like America, family members do take care of each other. Families stay together and usually live together. Grandparents contribute to the raising of the children and children help take care of the grandparents, who become absorbed within the household with definite roles to help sustain the family. When they reach old age, they graduate to a spiritual path and their duties cease. Then they are happily cared for by children and grandchildren who understand that their own day will likewise come.

Here in America we value our independence. Children want their own homes. Retired people want to be independent from their children. In Western society, elders have little to no value. We marginalize them and get them out of the way. There's no perceived value in what they might contribute. Our culture is profoundly youth-oriented. Just follow the money. Movies are made for teenagers and so is music. News reports are at a level for eight-year-olds. Magazine covers display photo-shopped images of young people or old people made to look young.

By contrast, Indian culture values the experience of elders. Families are happy to include their elders and they keep them involved as long as possible. They welcome and heed their counsel, and their contribution. Everyone benefits, evolving more fully together.

In India, the father is the guru of the family and the children treat him like the authority that he is. They touch his feet when they greet him. He's the mature human in the family structure and when that parent becomes a grandparent, he is revered for his wisdom, the wisdom from his experience.

Over here it's a different story. The comedian Rodney Dangerfield spoke for American elders when he quipped, "I can't get no respect!" [6] What is the standard attitude of youth towards elders? "Don't talk to me. I'm college-educated. I'm into my career. You don't know anything. You're old. The system has passed you by. Go play shuffleboard, retire to Florida, sit under a palm tree and die. Leave me alone. OK, I may consent to see you at certain holidays. But if you get sick and can't take care of yourself, I don't want you living with my family (and ruining my marriage), so I'll put you in a retirement community or a nursing home, if I can afford it."

Marriage, exclusive in our culture, just doesn't have room for true family values.

The Awake Marriage

In an Awake Marriage you are complete in yourself to the degree that you are one with Source Intelligence. So is your partner. As you emerge from personal neediness, including the need to make your partner happy, you begin to experience the joy of interdependence, contributing to each other's growth and enjoyment. Marriages like this can become nourishing and love-drenched, a stimulus to evolution and more bliss.

Neither partner is dependent on the other. Each can truthfully say, "I am love. All is love. I experience love by being loving." Jealousy goes out the window in the conscious relationship because the illusory two have become the truthful one. There is only one. When you have that holistic non-dual perspective, issues like jealousy, envy, possession and conditionality - which are all egoic and fear-based within the illusion of separation - drop away.

True love is not dependent on another. Each one is in control of the experience of love within herself and himself. Your experience of love is your responsibility, to remain wakeful of the love that you already innately are. If you come from that perspective, you generate the experience of love. You magnify it by your focus on it. It's the same mechanics as meditation where you focus on being the consciousness that you are. Well, another name for consciousness is love. Conscious relationship is a love meditation.

Your essence is love. When you focus on that and magnify it, you fill yourself with love and actualize your subtle dimensions. When your subtle dimensions actualize, the amplitude of your power radically increases because you're moving into wholeness, and wholeness has great amplitude of power. This means that you become virtually irresistible. Everybody wants to be with you. This is the secret of all the masters. Masters always have people trying to be in relationships with them because their amplitude of power, the power of their wholeness is a great attractor.

Imagine that with your marriage partner!

You are flowing in love, as love flowing with the happenings of consciousness recognizes that you are the creator of your experience. As you maintain your holistic focus, issues of egocentric illusory control, possession and conditional love all fall away. Conflict and its resultant suffering are gone.

A conscious marriage is a celebration, moment by moment by moment. You ride the high of love together and enjoy discovering who can out-magnify who in terms of love! It's not a competition, it's a celebration and you both benefit!

Our Socratic Conclusion

The American Dream assumptions about marriage are illusory. Any belief that the institute of marriage in America is broadly successful is just that, a belief, not a reality. New, more truthful assumptions could be:

1. Every marriage in America has the potential to become a conscious celebration of true love.

2. True love is more than romance in relationship, it is your individual essence.

3. A shared individual connection with Source Consciousness is what ultimately makes your marriage pleasurable and sustainable.

Here are Enlightening Questions to Ponder:

What's wrong with her / him? What's wrong with me?

What's right with her / him? What's right with me?

A Moment of Mastery

Union in Source Intelligence
swoons my heart.
I am saturated with love
and it overflows in my relationships.
I am ... all is ... the bliss of unconditional love.

Chapter Sixteen: Health Yourself

"The insanity here is that we have a system of financing health care in this country that is all about profit for corporate America and not about the health care of the people. It is opposed to the health care of the people of America. You can't be about profit and be about a social service." [1]

- Dr. Carol Paris

Our chapter on health care begins with a radically different perspective. Consider these two influences: The genetic make up of your ancestors helps determine your longevity, and your evolution through many life cycles affects your awakening in this one. Your body will die, but you are not your body, nor are you your ego. You will not die. You have already lived forever since what you are is life itself. The most fundamental definition of health must include awakening to this understanding.

All life is immortal and is constantly changing forms. The life in your body has been in millions of other forms before and will continue to be. You have cells that include moments from the life of Jesus, a dinosaur and a piece of lava four million years old. "You" are unlimited. Coming to know this and shedding your fear of mortal death for the bliss of eternal life is the experience of true health.

Birth flows to death; life is eternal.

The American Dream wraps us in a forest of illusion where we slumber until our bodies die, or until they awaken and rise to walk beyond the veiled thicket of unconscious life experience.

In the film *Matrix*, Morpheus told Neo that everyone had to discover for himself what the Matrix was. Likewise, no description of this forest of illusion can help the sleeper awaken because how could we see it with our eyes closed! Those who have not awakened have no way of knowing what lies beyond the canopy. They cannot fathom the concept of immortal life. It must be experienced to be known, even if just as a sensing for instance as you read, that yes, this could be true.

Doctors may be modern masters, capable of helping our bodies heal. But what do they know of immortality? Can they teach us how best to sustain our human forms as we awaken to the sunlight calling us from our mortal dreams? Only those physicians who are awakening themselves and sensing their own immortality might be able to support the emergence of that grand understanding of health in their patients, enabling them to devote themselves to continue awakening.

A friend recounted an inspiring encounter with her doctor on the day before her cancer surgery. She had been inquiring about the looming bill and was confused about how exactly to pay. She also confessed that she had lousy insurance. The specialist paused for a moment, then offered to perform the surgery without a fee.

"This will be my gift to you," she said, smiling, bringing tears to my friend's eyes. Not just for the money saved, but for the generosity shared.

If You Build It, Health Will Come

Imagine that you are building a new house. You have a choice between superior materials used by an inferior builder or inferior materials used by a superior builder. Which would you choose?

Obviously we'd all prefer superior materials and a superior builder, but faced with this hard choice the smart person will pick the superior builder every time. Because the superior builder can work skillfully with what he has, he can choose the best from what's available and he can use it to create a strong, functional structure. Conversely, a builder who doesn't know what he is doing, will misuse materials, even the best of them, and fail to build you a good home.

Psalm 127:1 says, "Except the Lord build the house, they labor in vain that build it." [2] Who's building your house of being? Are you connected to Source Intelligence so that life energy is pouring through you, or are you addicted to vitamins, exercising obsessively and consulting one expert after another? Are you relaxing into the flow of life which is simultaneously, effortlessly, creating well-being everywhere (at least everywhere where human beings haven't interfered)?

Prescription drugs and vitamins are sold with a promise of restoring health and vitality. The ads invariably show smiling, energetic people having a good time. We watch and wish that we were like those people. Then we buy and try those potions and are often disappointed.

In the same way that money can't make you happy, pills can't make you healthy. They can support your health but they don't make your heart beat. Something else is doing that, and this is where the secret to health resides. This is also the touchstone for immortality.

A Story of Awakening

"During a conference in Brazil I was invited to attend a Mucuba service, which is a mix of the catholic mass and voodoo. As I watched the priest and priestess spin and dance for nearly an hour, I was drawn to one particular priest. I walked up to him and he circled around me, waving a cigar-shaped object. Suddenly I felt myself streaming out of my body with sparkling brilliant colors about twenty feet into the air! My feet were still on the ground but my head was at the top of the building. It ended just as suddenly and I had no idea what

it meant for some time. Now I think it was showing me that there is more to me than just my body."

-E. B., Lexington, Kentucky

The Synchronicity Socratic Method

Assumptions about health include:

"Doctors and medicines are required to maintain good health."

"Ill health is inevitable as we age."

"The American healthcare system is the best in the world, and it will take care of me."

Are any of these assumptions true? Let's start with a sobering statistic: "Today, one out of every seven Americans is on food stamps and one out of every four American children is on food stamps. The number of Americans on food stamps has increased 74% since 2007." [3]

With every fourth child in America on food stamps, imagine also the low quality of food those children are consuming and how that affects their long-term health. We are growing a generation doomed to chronic diseases. That is, if you believe that what you eat affects your health.

I recently sat next to some cardiologists in a restaurant as they talked about open-heart surgery and heart transplants. While I ate my meal of fish and salad they ordered every debauched choice on the menu. They had martinis, they had wine, they had roast beef or steaks, and they had rich desserts. These were highly trained medical professionals who stared at the results of this kind of eating every day in their patients' bodies. Yet, they poison themselves the same way their patients do. What denial.

America is the land of excess for some and scarcity for many. We are free to have whatever we can afford, which includes eating as much as we want. Much of corporate America cares more about the bottom line than people's health. Patients have become the golden goose for a profit-driven disease care system.

What did physicians learn about nutrition in medical school? I read that during their arduous years of study the average curriculum time devoted to nutrition is about 19 hours... and it's decreasing every year. 19 hours!

And what did you learn about your body in school? Most of us learned virtually nothing that would educate us to grow a healthy body. So, you're likely to become one of the millions of adults camping on your doctor's doorstep with symptoms that took years of abuse to develop. You could be one of the approximately 30% of Americans who are obese. But your doctor may not even ask you what you eat. Like those cardiologists, your own doctor may not have a healthy diet themselves.

You'll likely be prescribed some pills, and if your situation explodes, it's off to the hospital. Hospitals can save your life, no doubt about it, but they can also be dangerous. They are full of infection and overstressed, sleep deprived doctors who are quite possibly addicted to Oxycontin or any of the hundreds of other drugs within immediate and easy reach.

In his article, *Why Doctors So Often Get It Wrong*, David Leonhardt addresses another raging problem in our system: misdiagnosis. "With all the tools available to modern medicine — the blood tests and M.R.I.'s and endoscopes — you might think that misdiagnosis has become a rare thing. But you would be wrong. Studies of autopsies have shown that doctors seriously misdiagnose fatal illnesses about 20 percent of the time. So millions of patients are being treated for the wrong diseases.

"As shocking as that is, the more astonishing fact may be that the rate has not really changed since the 1930's. 'No improvement!' was how an article in the normally exclamation-free Journal of the American Medical Association summarized the situation.

"This is the richest country in the world — one where one-seventh of the economy is devoted to health care — and yet the misdiagnosis is killing thousands of Americans every year.

"How can this be happening? And how is it not a source of national outrage?"

Mr. Leonhardt continued, offering his own explanation: "Joseph Britto, a former intensive-care doctor, likes to compare medicine's attitude toward mistakes with the airline industry's. At the insistence of pilots, who have the ultimate incentive not to mess up, airlines have studied their errors and nearly eliminated crashes. 'Unlike pilots,' Dr. Britto said, 'Doctors don't go down with their planes.'" [4]

Then there are medical heroes like MD Patch Adams who founded The Gesundheit Institute to promote holistic medical care based on the belief that you can't separate the health of individuals from the health of families, the community, the world and the health care system itself. What an awakened perspective on health care!

An Unlikely Understanding

We get asked sometimes about enlightened masters who died of throat cancer or heart disease. Why would enlightened masters have health problems? The answer is, "they don't." They don't have any problems, actually, because they simply don't think in those terms. They don't consider what's happening in their body as a disease. That's a label put on a condition, and they pronounce it as wrong.

That's a denial of the expression of consciousness in the moment, which is what the "disease" really is. It's not, per se, something wrong that must be cured. But it's evidence of imbalance. It requires attention, as urgently as a plane veering off course requires re-steering.

The goal of most doctors is to genuinely serve their patients' needs. But a few seem willing to keep the heart beating no matter what. Success, to them, only means extending life. But what about the quality of life? And what about the perspective we are sharing that relates to immortality? Every body will die, that can't be prevented. However what is the right time for death? Could a disease actually serve a worthwhile purpose, namely, assisting an immortal soul to exit the body when appropriate?

This viewpoint doesn't advocate denial of symptoms, a do-nothing attitude that would only worsen conditions. Quite the opposite. Everything that can be done should be done to care for the body. Ideally, your doctor is there to support you as you "health yourself" in the healing process, even if that healing includes completing your time in human form.

First and foremost, regardless of the severity of a dis-ease (imbalance) condition, you maintain your connection with Source Intelligence not as a theory but as an experience under pressure. When you put Source Intelligence first, sickness is experienced differently. "You" have no suffering, although your body will. You will be flowing with the experience whose time has come. That may include symptoms, pain in your body, etc., but you remain centered in the experience of abundant, immortal life. You let the "Lord" continue to build your house of being, finding the best materials and sub-contractors! You love your body as it is, refusing to see it as "sick," determined to flow compassion and nurturing love within yourself.

Because it's the key to your experience of immortality, that understanding makes all the difference even though it may not "heal" your symptoms. Immortality is not about living forever in a body, it's not about the length of time at all. It's about freedom from the fear that death means the end of you. It is not. Sometimes, it takes a serious illness to help a person come to that breakthrough understanding. That is true health!

Healing vs. Curing

Most modern medicine applies band-aids to symptoms. The goal is to cure. Well, we cure tobacco and ham. Curing means you can keep something longer. If the goal is to cure cancer, for instance, this means we could keep cancer forever. That's good business and it's getting better every year. It's sixty years since President Nixon first declared war on cancer and and we are no closer to ending it. In fact, there is more cancer than ever and no end in sight to its proliferation.

What Are We Missing?

Our chapter title, "Health Yourself," uses the word health as a verb, not a noun. It implies action, an action you take for yourself. Where is this concept in modern medicine, the idea that what a person does for herself can affect her health in positive ways? Some pay lip service to nutrition and most now acknowledge that exercise is important. But the implications of Source Intelligence connection go virtually unexplored. Officially, what matters is a limited perspective on keeping hearts beating.

Marlo Thomas wrote about this in *What You Don't Know About Cancer – Hope on the Horizon*. "All of the doctors I spoke to pointed to the increased survival numbers, the holy grail of all medical science statistics, as evidence that we are gaining ground in this fight. 'We are saving 350 more people per day in the U.S. than we did in 1991,' Dr. John Seffrin, CEO of the American Cancer Society, told me.[5]

"On the other hand, I recently read about a tiny man in India who just turned 100. He's only 4 feet 11 inches tall but he's a former Mr. Universe. He said that 'happiness and a life without tensions are the key to his longevity.' It's a fascinating story. He began a training program while he was in prison. 'In jail I used to practice on my own, without any equipment, sometimes for 12 hours in a day,' he recalled. The jail authorities were impressed with his perseverance and he was given a special diet to help build his stamina." [6]

Talk about healthing yourself! What an inspiring example. He turned his prison into a gym! Why don't we hear more stories like this? Why isn't our quality of life as important as extending our lifespans? Because the egocentric medical system has turned healthcare into a commodity. Heaven forbid that you get inspired by a story like this one to take responsibility and get healthier without tests, drugs and surgeries.

One encouraging sign today in America is the growing hospice program where dying patients receive care to complete their lives with dignity. The purpose of hospice is compassionate end-of-life care and in some states even the uninsured can receive free hospice services funded by charitable donations and volunteer medical care.

A Booming Business

Much of health care in America today is about big profits and big debts. "According to the Bureau of Economic Analysis, health care costs accounted for just 9.5% of all personal consumption back in 1980. Today they account for approximately 16.3%. One study found that approximately 41 percent of working age Americans either have medical bill problems or are currently paying off medical debt. Back in 1965, only one out of every 50 Americans was on Medicaid. Today, one out of every 6 Americans is on Medicaid." [7]

Here's another health statistic that strains belief. Almost half of us are paying off medical debt! How did helping each other stay healthy become a profit-driven industry so contradictory to the genuine compassion we imagine must live in the hearts of dedicated health care providers? Some are disgusted. Russel Mokhiber writes about one such doctor. "Dr. Carol Paris is a psychiatrist. She's practiced for 13 years in southern Maryland. And she's fought hard for a single-payer system. She's closing her practice and moving it to New Zealand.

"'I'm so tired and weary of trying to practice sane, passionate, good medicine in this insane health care system in the United States,' Paris said last month in an interview at Union Station before walking over to protest in front of the Supreme Court against the Obama health care law and for a single payer system. 'It impairs my ability to practice in a way that is ethical and passionate. I have a few years left in me to practice. And I've decided to see what it is like in another country. I have a couple of friends who are psychiatrists who have done a sabbatical in New Zealand. And they said they are so sad to be back in the United States practicing because it was so much more sane and caring in New Zealand. I'm going to see what it is like for my own mental health.'

"'The insanity here is that we have a system of financing health care in this country that is all about profit for corporate America and not about the health care of the people,' Dr. Paris said. 'It is opposed to the health care of the people of America. You can't be about profit and be about a social service.'" [8]

We're bound to see more of this happening. Who can blame caring doctors for leaving our crazy system? They didn't sign up for this! Imagine the disappointment and disillusionment that must set in for a young doctor, years after graduating, waking up to the reality of what a medical practice has become in this country.

There is, of course, an alternative to leaving: wake up, stay put, and change the system from the inside out. Not so much by fighting as by caring, doing what you can, regardless of the limitations, to help patients health themselves regardless of the limitations. This is heroic, difficult and daunting. But it's how change always comes. Dr. Paris will find other conditions to challenge her in New Zealand. With her awake attitude she will contribute there appropriately.

Depression

This whole disease care catastrophe in America is blatantly depressing so no wonder we have developed an epidemic of depression in this country. According to current data reported by HealthLand.com, there's been a 400% increase in antidepressant use since 1988.[9] Almost 10% of Americans are taking antidepressant medication and have done so for years. Although depression is much higher in sedentary people, it's unlikely that many doctors are prescribing exercise before they prescribe medication. Of course, seeing depression as an isolated disease is the real problem. Trying to get rid of the symptoms denies that they could have any possible value. Thomas Moore offered this unusual perspective on depression, referring to the planet Saturn and one aspect of its symbolic meaning in his remarkable book, *Care of the Soul:*

"If we persist in our modern way of treating depression as an illness to be cured only mechanically and chemically, we may lose the gifts of soul that only depression can provide. In particular, tradition taught that Saturn fixes, darkens, weights, and hardens whatever is in contact with it. If we do away with Saturn's moods, we may find it exhausting trying to keep life bright and warm at all costs. We may be even more overcome then by the increased melancholy called forth by the repression of Saturn, and lose the sharpness and substance of identity that Saturn gives the soul. In other words, symptoms of a loss of Saturn might include a vague sense of identity, the failure to take one's own life seriously, and a general malaise or ennui that is a pale reflection of Saturn's deep, dark moods.

"Saturn locates identity deeply in the soul, rather than on the surface of personality. Identity is felt as one's soul finding its weight and measure. We know who we are because we have uncovered the stuff of which we are made. It has been sifted out by depressive thought, 'reduced,' in the chemical sense, to essence." [10]

What are we so depressed about? What if we are actually depressed because we sense our own magnificence, our innate joyfulness, even our immortality, yet we are stuck on a lousy human treadmill - "Groundhog Day" - for seventy years or so, until we die?

Even good health gets boring if you fail to fulfill your creative potential. Imagine your passion flowing, doing what you are meant to be doing, being who you authentically are... who could get depressed with a life like that? A fully engaged individual has no interest in depression! If they feel the symptoms, the only question is how to embrace them in their creative flow, perhaps even to invite their deepening to grow their souls.

If you are enjoying a holistic experience of reality and are not resistant to life but just witnessing and flowing with it, then all the happenings of life are simply that, the happenings of life. You exclude nothing, even depression and disease, or cancer. You don't say, "Oh, this is wrong." No, it's the happening of life. Somehow, for reasons you cannot fully know, it is right.

Can you accept this perspective? Can you health yourself by regarding what comes to you in terms of ill-health by saying, "Okay, here is this experience. It's the happening of consciousness for me. Who do I choose to be in relationship to this? Do I choose first to accept it without judgment, to flow with it and to discover what I am supposed to learn through this? I wonder what this experience might teach me? How will I grow through this?"

The experience called ill-health is another happening of life to grow through. It is a consciousness to grow through, remaining as wakeful and conscious within it as possible. This includes the entire life journey, all the way to death.

Death too is an experience whose time comes. You can say, "This shouldn't be happening. I'm going to resist it." Well, sorry, that never works. Masters celebrate it. Death is the experience whose time has come. It's what consciousness has determined is the appropriate experience, or it wouldn't be happening. They flow with it and remain as wakeful in the experience of physical death as possible. It's a graduation.

Our Socratic Conclusion:

Having exploded the virtual-reality assumptions about health in America, let's consider some truthful options:

"True health is the conscious experience of immortality."

"Disease is imbalance. Health is being fully alive."

"The goal of true health care is to awaken and fulfill creative potential."

A simple enlightening question to ponder is "How can I health myself?"

A Moment of Mastery

I am well.
Wholeness is wellness
and I am whole in the oneness of love and life.
I happily care for my self,
simultaneously caring for all living forms.
Health is love in bodily experience.

Chapter Seventeen: Global Warning

"Now thoroughly urbanized and technology-addicted,
we've become so disconnected from nature that it's
pretty hopeless to think most people could ever become
real environmentalists." [1]

- Frances Moore Lappe

Turning our attention to the environment, we enter controversial territory. Some scientists warn that our activities could help render the planet uninhabitable. Incredibly, there are strongly opinionated individuals who disregard the possibility that human activities make any significant difference at all. For them, global warming is a politically motivated hoax, regardless of temperature data that proves the simple truth: planet earth is getting hotter. While we debate about what's causing it - humans or nature - we continue doing what contributes to hotter temperatures.

It may seem difficult to imagine an earth without humans but remember dinosaurs ruled the earth one day, and died out the next. Why would humans turn out to be any different? Environmentalists warn about how we are destroying Mother Earth, but we are only hurting her. She is resilient. Perhaps what we are really doing is destroying the environment that supports a multitude of life forms including us! This could be mass suicide in not-so-slow motion, or, in other words, self-inflicted species genocide.

Before Al Gore's film, *An Inconvenient Truth*, won an Academy Award in 2006, over 60% of Americans believed climate change was an urgent priority and deserved immediate government action. By 2010 that number had dropped below 40%. That decrease in public concern came after some of the hottest years on record, killer storms, melting ice packs, and sea levels rising ... all predicted in Gore's film.

How can this be? It's called denial. We didn't like the inconvenient truth so we chose a less threatening fiction. We went back to sleep.

Just how deeply asleep? Vermont passed a law in June of 2012 that limits sea level reporting to a generalized assessment of historical trends dating from 1900, rather than reporting accurately on actual current numbers. According to *Scientific American*'s Scott Huler, a North Carolina resident, this is something like deciding to "not predict tomorrow's weather based on radar images of a hurricane swirling offshore, moving west towards us with 60-mph winds and ten inches of rain. Predict the weather based on the last two weeks of fair weather with gentle breezes towards the east. Don't use radar and barometers; use the Farmer's Almanac and what grandpa remembers." [2]

The motive behind the Vermont legislation was developers were concerned that reality would interfere with their real estate plans. The new law allows them to continue building on the seashore without regard for climate change. Apparently their homes will be safe because they say they will be safe.

A Healthy Use For Cola

I watched an interesting demonstration years ago that suggests a radical principle that might contribute to a new understanding of how to deal with a threatened environment. You can try this at home.

Assemble one large glass bowl, drinking glass, spoon, pitcher full of clean water, and a can or bottle of cola. Imagine the bowl is now sitting on a table with the drinking glass sitting inside it. Crack open the cola and fill the glass half full. Now, how can you clear up that brown cola without touching the glass or bowl?

You could study the drinking glass, discuss what color the liquid is, how it got to be that way, etc. You could try putting the spoon in the glass and stirring vigorously. You might even whip up enough foam to spill over and at least decrease some volume. But it won't change colors.

Now imagine picking up the pitcher filled with clear water and begin to pour it into the glass, filling it up. Probably not much changes, other than that the glass gets full. But as you continue pouring and the water overflows into the bowl, the cola gets increasingly diluted and the color begins to change. It turns from dark to light brown, then amber and finally, if you persevere and keep on pouring, it eventually clears up completely and you have created a glass of clean water.

No sane person would advocate trying to clean up the environment with a pitcher of water! The demonstration simply makes a metaphorical point. Namely, that when things are dirty, introduce purity. Note the quote attributed to Gandhi: "Be the change you wish to see in the world." [3]

A true environmentalist begins by accepting what's happening, including environmental challenges. That's the opposite of denial. To take this awareness up to another level, imagine everything in your surrounding environment is a form of consciousness, and so are you! There is no separation.

There's climate change, rising sea levels, drought, scarcity of clean water... all the happenings of consciousness. Can you say, "Yes, this is happening. And, none of it is separate from me because it's all happening in consciousness. So, who am I choosing to be in relation to it?"

The Synchronicity Socratic Method

Who am I choosing to be

leads to what I am choosing to do.

Questions matter. When we honestly examine the way human beings have treated their Mother, we see that by choosing to be thoughtless consumers, what emerges is a pattern of careless disregard for the environment, a basic disrespect. What else explains internal combustion engines, toxic chemicals and nuclear technology? They achieve short-sighted human ends with utterly no consideration for long-term environmental impact. Now we witness the nearing possibility that this behavior may contribute to our own end.

Several American Dream assumptions about the environment and our relationship with it include:

The earth can take care of itself.

What advances human progress is always good.

Technology will save us.

Many Voices

The idea of technology saving us, regardless of possible harmful side effects, is perhaps nowhere more obvious than with nuclear power. Essentially all a nuclear power plant does is boil water. But a result of that process is incredibly toxic byproducts that could virtually wipe out human existence.

Years ago Jonas Salk offered this sobering perspective: "If all insects on Earth disappeared, within 50 years all life on Earth would end. If all human beings disappeared from the Earth, within 50 years all forms of life would flourish." [4]

So, humans are dangerous while insects are essential to life on earth!

Noam Chomsky, commenting on a recent report from the International Energy Agency which detailed more rogue human behavior threatening the environment, said: "... with rapidly increasing carbon emissions from fossil fuel use, the limit of safety will be reached by 2017 if the world continues on its present course. 'The door is closing,' the IEA chief economist said, and very soon it 'will be closed forever.'

"Shortly before, the U.S. Department of Energy reported the most recent carbon dioxide emissions figures, which "jumped by the biggest amount on record" to a level higher than the worst-case scenario anticipated by the International Panel on Climate Change (IPCC)."

"That came as no surprise to many scientists, including the MIT program on climate change, which for years has warned that the IPCC predictions are too conservative. Such critics of the IPCC predictions receive virtually no public attention, unlike the fringe of denialists who are supported by the corporate sector, along with huge propaganda campaigns that have driven Americans off the international spectrum in dismissal of the threats. Business support also translates directly to political power." [5]

A truly controversial topic these days is about corporations pushing genetically modified seeds and foods, GMOs. Some wonder whether science may be loosing demons capable of polluting and destroying our global food supply.

"'Seed companies including Monsanto Co., the world's largest, will get speedier regulatory reviews of their genetically modified crops under forthcoming rule changes,' the U.S. Department of Agriculture reported.

"'The goal is to cut by half the time needed to approve biotech crops from the current average of three years,' Michael Gregoire, a USDA deputy administrator, said today in a telephone interview. 'The changes will take affect when they're published in the Federal Register, probably in March,' he said.

"'Approvals that took six months in the 1990s have lengthened because of increased public interest, more legal challenges and the advent of national organic food standards,'

Gregoire said. 'U.S. farmers worry they may be disadvantaged as countries such as Brazil approve new technologies faster,' said Steve Censky, chief executive officer of the American Soybean Association.

"'It is a concern from a competition standpoint,' Censky said in a telephone interview."[6]

Competition and greed are part of the ego's modus operandi. The phrasing here reveals the priority: money, not a healthy environment.

Remember that big BP oil spill a few years ago? Here's how that turned out: "Oil giant BP, the company behind the Deepwater Horizon oil spill, reported profits of $7.7 billion for the last quarter of 2011. Company executives and industry analysts sounded bullish about the company's future in a recent New York Times article, saying they had set aside enough money to compensate victims of the Gulf spill and had plans to expand drilling operations in the Gulf.

"BP seems to be recovering nicely after the disaster, which killed 11 people and pumped 170 million gallons of oil into the Gulf of Mexico. But stories from the Gulf suggest that the region is anything but healed.

"The Gulf has been plagued with a suite of unexplained afflictions. Gulf fishermen say this is the worst season they can remember, with catches down 80 percent or more. Shrimp boats come home nearly empty, hauling in deformed, discolored shrimp, even shrimp without eyes. Tar balls and dead dolphins still wash up on beaches. Scientists report huge tar mats below the sand, like vanilla swirl ice cream.

"Fishermen, cleanup workers, and kids report strange rashes, coughing, breathing difficulty, eye irritation, and a host of other unexplained health problems that have persisted in the years since the disaster." [7]

> **The poor suffer, while the rich profit.**

The Elephant in the Bedroom

Many environmentalists back in the '60s and '70s identified over-population as the real issue. Well, very little has been said since and little has been done. Global population rose during the 20th century from about 1.6 billion to over 6 billion. An informed culture would have called this an epidemic, and based on a common sense assessment of resources available would have taken serious action to curb growth.

But, more humans mean more robots to fill factories and make products and more consumers to buy them. That's one reason why the concept of "conscious procreation" is a topic fraught with controversy. Again, the awakened individual inquires and in this case asks, "Do I really need to bring another child into this world?"

India has three times America's population with a landmass one-third our size. That would be like three billion people in America instead of 300 million! The effects of overpopulation there are dramatic, but the topic is virtually off-limits because ego-driven individuals want freedom to do whatever they want, whenever they want, with whomever they want. This leads to spontaneous copulation without thought or birth control. The idea of planning pregnancies seems to be a ridiculous, or at least inconvenient, limitation! But animals do it. They reproduce in relationship to their food supply and environmental restraints while we instead grow more food or move.

We may yet breed ourselves out of existence. An ironic epitaph on humanity's tombstone, accurate on a number of levels, would be: "Here lies humanity, which screwed itself to death."

Encouraging Signs

Some potential parents do consciously consider the implications of bringing a child into the world. In fact, more and more individuals are stirring in their slumbers and looking for answers that feature them taking some personal responsibility. Of course, mainstream news reports on the American Dream soap opera 24/7, disasters, celebrity gossip and lifestyle choices. For good news, most of us go to the internet, which remains largely unrestricted as of this writing. Lynne Peeples blogged this encouraging report in *Children At Risk From Pesticides, School Bans Debated*: "At his own organic farm, Alan Gorkin eschews pesticides in favor of natural biodiversity, mixing three different grasses on his farm's three acres of lawn. 'That way, if a disease or insect came through, it's not going to kill the whole lawn,' he says.

"Over time, Gorkin says this approach will reduce the need for irrigation and build a stronger root system that can provide both stability and cushioning for young athletes. It will not yield the pristine, 100-percent Kentucky bluegrass that soccer moms and Little League dads have come to expect, but it won't leave his son woozy from pesticides, either.

"'As a horticulturist,' Gorkin says, 'I know it's not necessary to use this stuff.'" [8]

In an earlier chapter we spoke about education, real education that helps people wake up to the real world. We don't have much of that in schools or in what the media offers through "news." Draconian restraints on information sharing are showing up in every field where the ego's domination is threatened. Here's a chilling report from Pennsylvania:

"A new Pennsylvania law endangers public health by forbidding health care professionals from sharing information they learn about certain chemicals and procedures used in high volume horizontal hydraulic fracturing. The procedure is commonly known as fracking … Fracking is also believed to have been the cause of hundreds of small earthquakes in Ohio and other states.

"'… I have never seen anything like this in my 37 years of practice,' says Dr. Helen Podgainy, a pediatrician from Coraopolis, Pa. She says it's common for physicians, epidemiologists, and others in the health care field to discuss and consult with each other about the possible problems that can affect various populations. Her first priority, she says, 'is to diagnose and treat, and to be proactive in preventing harm to others.' The new law, she says, not only 'hinders preventative measures for our patients, it slows the treatment process by gagging free discussion.'

"Psychologists are also concerned about the effects of fracking and the law's gag order. 'We won't know the extent of patients becoming anxious or depressed because of a lack of information about the fracking process and the chemicals used,' says Kathryn Vennie of Hawley, Pa., a clinical psychologist for 30 years. She says she is already seeing patients 'who are seeking support because of the disruption to their environment.' Anxiety in the absence of information, she says, 'can produce both mental and physical problems.'"

"Anxiety in the absence of information…" What a penetrating phrase. It could be the mantra for our age, as far as the environment goes. We know something is wrong but are told to keep shopping and that all will be well. I always think of this when we drive to Washington, DC in the carpool lane. It's almost always empty! You only need two people in your car to use that lane. But invariably, my driving partner and I are speeding along, passing stationary vehicles with one frustrated driver alone in each car! It doesn't seem to matter what the price of gas is, drivers refuse to give up their old-fashioned, hard-wired sense of independence. One rider per horse!

Up north, hundreds, thousands of cars line up on both sides of the water to use the Canadian ferry system in British Columbia. People wait for hours in the rain to drive their car onto a ship and cart it to or from Vancouver Island while others wait to do exactly the same thing in reverse. Can't we Americans also use our imaginations to create a better way?

Yes and no. From an awakened perspective we'd ask, "What makes the most sense?" But the ego asks, "What's the most convenient and what makes the most money?" Ego-driven individuals function like loaded springs, coiled to lunge into their environment and take whatever they can get before someone else does. Rape and pillage, 24/7.

An Awake Perspective

There is a bright side. Bill McKibben has become a best selling author and environmental activist fighting to preserve a sustainable planet. He was recently jailed for leading what has been called the largest civil disobedience initiative in 30 years, protesting the Keystone XL pipeline. President Obama agreed to put the project on hold, temporarily. We'll see what decision Obama finally makes but thousands of activists like McKibben work tirelessly to preserve our environment. We must applaud their bravery.

Throughout this chapter on the environment we have shredded myths and challenged American Dream assumptions. An awake statement to consider and something to aspire toward is, "I am responsible for harmonious co-existence with my environment."

Our Socratic Conclusion

The American Dream assumptions about the environment are unprovable. The belief that population could continue unchecked has prohibited any sane dialogue on the subject. And while technology has benefitted us greatly, little has been honestly challenged relative to environmental impacts. New, more truthful assumptions could be:

1. The environment will inevitably become a reflection of our inner values.
2. Intelligent population control is a sane strategy for managing the burden humans put on the environment.
3. Technology appropriately exists in service to the environment.

An enlightening question to ponder is, "How can humanity sensibly control its population?"

A Moment of Mastery

*I am one
with my environment.
My presence brings consideration,
thoughtful stewardship,
compassion for all living forms.
I am needed
for my presence
in the midst of all presence.*

Chapter Eighteen: Aren't We Special?

"The outward freedom that we shall attain will only be in exact proportion to the inward freedom to which we may have grown at a given moment. And if this is a correct view of freedom, our chief energy must be concentrated on achieving reform from within." [1]

- Gandhi

Politics are a spectacle.

Many of our elected leaders behave like ego-maniacs. They demonstrate the consciousness of irrational, manipulative, power mongers with two agendas: staying in power and keeping the fantasy of the American Dream alive. They have become shills for today's version of the Ringling Brothers circus: "Ladies and gentlemen! America, the greatest show on earth!" The symbol of America should be a peacock not an eagle, a male fully arrayed and strutting on the American seal and dollar bill.

These politicians come out like those crowing birds in cuckoo clocks, making cuckoo proclamations of escalating cuckoo insanity. Imagine, to seriously propose invading a country like Afghanistan to impose democracy. Our military calls this, "winning their hearts and minds." Have any of these political decision makers ever been there? It's like going back to the fourteenth century. They use horse drawn carriages. Almost everyone is living in abject poverty. And their government is primarily tribal. You want to spread democracy when what Afghans care about is their next meal?

We can't truthfully talk about democracy with them anyway because we don't have one ourselves. We have the dream of democracy but not the reality of one. America is a republic. The ideal of a democratic government sounds like it might work, but it would demand responsible participation from everyone involved. That's not likely in an America where most people don't vote!

Who does vote in the United States? Individuals who believe. In what? Apparently, in what mainstream media feeds them. How else can you explain someone like George W. Bush actually being elected president? And, given the results of his eight years in office, including the damage both to our economy and to ancient cultures and lifestyles abroad, how else can you explain the paucity of outrage and the robotic march down the same road today?

There's a great piece of graffiti that reads: "The problem with America is apathy!" And written beside it: "Who cares?" Apparently, what most people care about is getting their paycheck, what their favorite movie stars are wearing and who won the big game.

If many of our current elected leaders are irrational egomaniacs, what would an authentic leader be like? They would demonstrate truthful integrity and an attitude that might be expressed this way: "What's good for me is based on what is good for everyone, what works in terms of quality of life for everyone." But the system eats up idealists like that; they don't get very far. If they do, like President Obama has, then their efforts to institute idealistic visions are sabotaged to the point where it's 99% talk. Then one begins to wonder about him.

We get the leadership we deserve. Integrity in an elected leader would be a reflection of our own personal integrity. What we give is what we get. It's cause and effect. If I am irresponsible, I can expect the same in my elected representatives. It's my responsibility if I want to wake up from the fantasy, to participate and not just leave it to the leaders.

That's where to start in making a change in politics. With you and me.

There Are None So Blind as Those Who Will Not See

Humpty Dumpty sat on a wall ... he had a great fall. The wealth of America, financial and moral, has fallen and fragmented. Regardless of what politicians promise, no one can put the pieces back together again. Ever.

Now, is that cynical or realistic?

Our leaders assure us they are right and wise and know the way toward a positive change and a future that works better. Really? Where's the evidence that they have been right before? Millions protested the war in Iraq that most politicians desperately wanted. Years later, it's obvious that the protesters were right and the politicians were dead wrong. Where's the apology?

Where There is No Vision, Everyone Gets Lost

Imagine that you are driving and suddenly the hood of your car flies up, entirely blocking your vision. How could you continue driving, unable to see the road ahead? You might be able to peek around the hood and catch glimpses here and there, but it would be dangerous to say the least.

Imagine not having a rear-view mirror. Could you drive without a rear-view mirror? Yes. That's not nearly as dangerous as driving with an obscured windshield. Still, a rear-view mirror is helpful because it shows you what's happening behind you. Other cars may be approaching, like a police car with flashing lights!

Now imagine trying to drive by looking only in the rear-view mirror. How effective and safe would that be? And yet that's precisely how most people live and it's certainly how politics works.

Our leaders offer no genuine forward vision. They consult the rear-view mirror, what happened in the past, to steer into the future, dooming us to more of the same. They make decisions based on precedents, how those decisions will be perceived by voters, how they can be spun by the media, and how they might effect their popularity. Promises for real change in the future are empty and known to be so by those mouthing them. No problem, their purpose is to win elections. Then they can set about doing the bidding of those who paid to get them in office.

Imagine a politician looking through the windshield at what's actually coming on the road ahead - climate change, an unemployment crisis, economic ruination - and developing sensible strategies to deal with the realities before they overwhelm us. How many votes would that candidate get, compared to someone mouthing comforting bromides that reinforce faith in the American Dream?

Ironically, one politician who can inspire us is the recently deceased Senator Robert Byrd of West Virginia. He was first elected in 1952 and cast 18,000 votes during his tenure as the longest ever serving senator. Mr. Byrd was a one-time segregationist who opposed civil rights legislation. But he evolved through the years into a liberal, one of the earliest and only political voices opposing the Iraq war. He also supported the rights of gays to serve in the military.

A Story of Awakening

"Not long after the 9/11 bombings, I was meditating and finding it very difficult to move beyond my sense of outrage and sadness. In an attempt to find the love that was missing from my experience in that moment, I drew back and watched myself being outraged and, if the outrage spilled over into my watching, I drew further back and watched myself watching myself being outraged until finally I drew back so far that I contacted something universal.

"I began to have vivid images of people in different places all over the world and a voice spoke over the top saying 'We are all you.' I was completely enveloped in the experience of love and peace. From that moment on, I have known in a very deep way that we are all looking for love and joy, even people whose ways of achieving it seem to me to be unlikely to produce the result they desire."

-P K, Australia

The Synchronicity Socratic Method

A few entertaining fantasy assumptions about American politics include:

"Politicians are leaders."

"Politicians insure the integrity of the American government."

"Elected leaders are chosen based on their successful vision for America and their authentic ability to achieve it."

"Politicians represent and serve all of the American people."

"Leaders are elected to represent all the people, based on their demonstrated integrity."

"Politicians selflessly serve the greater whole,

guiding the ship of state with integrity and truth."

Aren't We Special?

These bold assumptions above sound familiar. They are the theories about America, fundamentally unrelated to the realities. But that's no surprise. America has the biggest ego in the world. We're the best and that requires no proof. It's national narcissism, obsessive narcissism. We seem to honestly believe that the American Dream was, is, and always will be real. Whereas it has always been, is now, and will always be only a dream.

Politics within the American Dream are totally egocentric and exemplify the worst aspects of our extreme virtual reality. It is full of every competition and manipulation intended to obtain, exercise and keep power. Modern politics is fundamentally corrupt. It's mantra? "What's in it for me?" That relates both to the individual politicians and to what they propose for America. They use power, fear and manipulation to maintain their jobs and privileged position in the world.

We might watch all the political silliness during an election cycle and wonder, "How can anybody fail to see that this is totally insane?" But most people can't see it, because they don't have that level of self-awareness. They're not ready to vote for what works. To get to "what works," the ego must get out of the way. As it does so, a person can realize that he or she doesn't need leaders who only protect and grow egoic virtual reality. You don't vote for a dinosaur when dinosaurs are on the brink of extinction!

True leadership is about service. We chuckle when politicians stand up in Washington and say, "It's a privilege to serve." If it were such a privilege to serve there would be no money involved! Missing from this picture are elders with integrity, no personal agenda, and no Swiss bank accounts. True service is trans-egocentric. There is nothing in it for them. They don't lead for personal gain; it's selfless service, arising from compassion.

Liars in High Places

Most Americans don't vote because they have stopped believing they can make a difference. They have seen over the years how little difference it makes regardless of who takes office. Consider the euphoria surrounding Obama's election and the conviction that things would be so vastly different from the Bush years. Are they?

Another reason voters don't care is that the American Dream is now clearly beyond their reach. Hard work can't get them there so they rely on lotteries and American Idol.

Australians have to vote or they get fined. Since compulsory voting was instituted in 1934, voter turnout has increased from 47% to about 94%. Voting is a responsibility and everyone must participate. We couldn't do that here in America though because it would violate our rights! The fact is, politicians don't want everyone to vote. If everyone did vote, and we actually had a majority consensus, then the politicians would have to represent all the people, not just the special interest groups who got them elected and keep them in power in return for favors handed down from on high.

Dishonesty fuels the heartbeat of the American system. For instance, unemployment figures are chronically inaccurate, adjusted to benefit whoever is in power and to prevent wide scale panic. The economy in 2012? One day it's a recession, the next day a recovery, then stalled again. All this obscures the reality of a slippery slope down which the middle class is disappearing into poverty as the super-rich bloat themselves.

Sometimes the liars in high places get exposed. After denial and argument comes muted acknowledgment and then, if they are smart, they find Jesus and are absolved of their sins. This has become a prescription for politicians and athletes and celebrities. Find Jesus and ask for forgiveness, then convince people that you've seen the light. Everyone loves a reformed sinner! "W" got a head start. He did it before he got into power, which gave him a free pass in the minds of those who automatically trust the redeemed.

Any Way the Wind Blows

Most politicians will say pretty much anything to get elected. As the 2012 GOP presidential candidate debates demonstrated, candidates are willing to switch their positions according to the polls. Do those polls indicate what their constituents really want or what they have been programmed to want? And then come the lobbyists, trumping both when the stakes are high enough. They played a large role, for instance, in sabotaging efforts to legislate background checks for the purchase of guns even though over 80% of Americans, regardless of their own political leanings, favor such checks.

It's astounding too how much money is spent on political campaigns. Candidates make their promises: "This is why you should elect me, because of my positions on tax reform, healthcare, foreign policy, etc." Of course, they can't keep those promises and they know it when they are making them! So why is all this time and money spent on these buffoons parading across the stage to tell you how they're going to save America? Americans elect the one most likely to be someone with whom they would enjoy having a beer or going to bed with. It is a fraudulent system, largely designed for making money. It's easy to see who benefits: follow the money.

What would politics look like from a truthful perspective? Let's start with candidates vying for public office. How about performing an honest assessment of his or her condition, physically, emotionally, mentally? What is his state of balance? Is she egocentric or trans-egocentric? Is he self-serving or in service? If any sort of analysis like this were done, we would have an opportunity to choose the more wakeful candidate, who just might be able to meet challenges with selfless, rather than self-serving, personal agendas.

Big and Failing

American politics are designed to fail. We have a two-party system in which Republicans represent fundamentalist religious values that emphasize a separate, controlling God, while Democrats seem to be more inclined toward social responsibility. But, in fact, most of the candidates are disingenuous. Despite the disastrous results of past policies, the vigor of the Occupy Movement, etc., the government is not willing to change radically. It wants to maintain an imagined status quo, an illusion that most Americans are not part of anymore!

In some areas, America is increasingly like a tinderbox ready to explode and anxious authorities are ready with police and prisons. The establishment versus the revolutionaries: who will prove stronger?

Awakenings to challenge the political status quo and protest the madness are happening all over the world. Voices are being raised within the cultural constraints of many countries. This will only increase. The Occupy Movement is just one visible part of it. What isn't reported is individual revolution and transformation. People are awakening and releasing their investment in ego-driven virtual reality. The American Dream is vaporizing.

The cathartic aspect of revolution is a process of evolving that can eventually birth a greater vision. We can't just go straight to realizing the vision. The process is a reflection of what is going on inside ourselves as individuals.

What's shifting the playing field now is the internet, on which you can read stories like the following that would never make it into the mainstream news: "In May 2009 ... Sen. Dick Durbin (D-Ill.) famously told a radio host, 'And the banks, hard to believe in a time when we're facing a banking crisis that many of the banks created, are still the most powerful lobby on Capitol Hill. And they frankly own the place.'"

Later in this same blog, the author quotes Georgetown Law School professor Adam Levitin: "'They make an awful lot of campaign contributions,'" said Levitin. "'They aren't making those just out of the goodness of their heart. They're hoping that it gets them some influence.'" [2]

An Evolutionary Shift

On the eve of the 2012 National Election, a five-minute video recording of President Obama was made at his campaign headquarters in Chicago, thanking his team. He wept as he commended them, recalling first coming to that city as a 25-year-old, knowing that he had to attach his life to something meaningful. He commended them for being smarter than he, more able to make a difference in the world.

It was a stirring, totally heart-felt presentation. It's difficult to imagine anyone seeing this and not being moved by his genuine appreciation for the young people who helped him get elected. And you could feel the tangible impact he was having on those young lives. They basked in his blessing.

This is what our politicians should be doing, when they are not cooperating with one another to guide the affairs of state wisely. He didn't speak of himself, he didn't thank God (that big concept in the sky), but he did say, "you lift me up." In other words, he was realistic.

One of the issues during the 2012 campaign was the battle between "facts" and "feelings." Well, facts won. And the losers were stunned. They had gut feelings about this and that and consistently disagreed with polling numbers. They made statements that were wildly inaccurate based on concepts fueled by emotion.

From a spiritual standpoint, the facts of leadership relate to qualities such as honesty, integrity and competence. But they all arise from one primary quality which, thankfully, we see represented in those such as President Obama and increasing numbers of others just elected such as Elizabeth Warren, the new Senator from Massachusetts. It is the passion to serve.

This was so evident in Obama's comments, recollecting his youth in Chicago. He didn't come to the big city to make his fortune. His question was about how he could attach his life to something meaningful. What a great question! And how inspiring to see this rising tide in American politics now. Incredibly, there are a few remarkably strong individuals who are able to survive the seductive decadence of the system and make a difference from the inside.

Political leaders can't solve our problems for us. But they can provide an example of Awakened Leadership based on selfless service. Arising from the rubble of our failing system are individuals who model this and, regardless of political affiliation, seem intent on working together. They deserve our support, and our company.

Our Socratic Conclusion

The American Dream assumptions about our political system are deeply flawed. Our leaders rarely exemplify qualities to emulate. New, more truthful assumptions could be:

1. True leadership in America emerges from within each individual.
2. Effective political leadership is based on the passion to serve and reveals personal qualities like honesty, integrity and competence.
3. Individuals fit to lead in our political system should model trans-egoic awareness and personal balance — physically, mentally and emotionally.

An Awakened Perspective

An awake perspective in the field of politics might include: "We elect leaders based on their demonstrated integrity and hold them accountable for the promises they make."

An enlightened question to ponder is, "What changes need to happen in myself that would be reflected in political leadership?"

A Moment of Mastery

*I lead in my life
with who I am.
I am confident that who I am
is enough, is loved, is needed.
I have already found
my place in the world.*

Chapter Nineteen: Telling It Like It Isn't

"The one who does not remember history is bound to live through it again." [1]

- George Santayana

We've sometimes referred to mainstream media as "mudstream media" since it's predominantly preoccupied with dirt and all of the bad news. It is fear-based, life-negative, egocentric, conservative, etc., which provides an accurate reflection of the consciousness of The American Dream majority. It is a faithful reflection of American culture today.

The media produces rubbish because people watch it. If we didn't watch it and the ratings went down, networks wouldn't be able to sell ads and they would go out of business. That would provide the motivation to provide something different the market would demand. This shift is happening now.

Because awakening is inevitable, change in the media is also inevitable. We spoke with one veteran of the entertainment world who sees reasons to be encouraged. John Raatz founded the Global Alliance for Transformational Media (G.A.T.E.) in 2009 with author Eckhart Tolle and actor Jim Carrey. We spoke with him in Los Angeles. In the transcript below, we are referred to as "AD."

AD: What are the transformational trends you see first-hand in media today?

John Raatz: The fact that an organization like G.A.T.E. has been born, right in the heart of Hollywood, reveals a trend towards a more-evolved state of affairs in media and entertainment which, I think, has been percolating since around 1979. Think back to the seventies and remember the

"Whole Earth Catalogue." It attempted to communicate new ideas about what entertainment and media could be.

AD: Do you have a perspective on how things came to be the way they are with mass media?

JR: Well, for decades, journalism students learned how to define "news" according to a certain set of values, including conflict, controversy, novelty, celebrity, impact, etc. These became the values by which most journalists determined what is news and how to report it.

My position, and that of many other entertainment and media activists, is that those values no longer serve who we have become, or who we want and need to become. We advocate that archetypal, universal, holistic values be included in the defining mechanism for what constitutes news. If we do that, we will begin to see a more humanistic type of news generated.

AD: Aren't we already seeing that?

JR: Absolutely. There are now somewhere between 200 and 300 body-mind-spirit publications and about 1,500 to 2,000 internet-based radio shows in that realm. Most of those reporting are not trained journalists. Something drove these individuals to begin reporting, an impulse in consciousness that moved them to share what they were learning and to promote issues like world peace, social investment, personal development, holistic healing, women's rights, etc.

They do relatively few negative stories because they report what they believe in and what they feel will best serve their readers to help them embody these new, holistic values.

AD: That's encouraging. But isn't it also true that the vast majority of people seem to want bad news?

JR: There's a reason for that, and the best way I can answer is with this story. I can tell you about a song that I think is fantastic, but only after I've heard it. Once I hear it on my car radio, in a store, at parties, all of a sudden I start to hear it everywhere. It gets in my head and repeats. In fact, a song can be hard to get out of your head! News is the same way. When you see and hear the same story over and over again, it doesn't matter whether you like or dislike it, the story gets embedded. It creates a groove in your mind. The content doesn't do that, the repetition does. So, we can change the content and keep the repetition, and the same thing would happen, except we would be obsessing about positive stories!

AD: Let's talk about the Hollywood film industry.

JR: Actually, Hollywood has been making transformational films for decades but just didn't know it or call them that. Look at *It's a Wonderful Life*. It tells a powerful human story that inspires people and causes them to feel resonance and empathy. I recently saw *Casablanca* in the theater and noticed how the film was striking people in a deep way. They were mouthing dialogue and at the end there was as much applause as I've ever heard for any film. The lesson here is that when you give people a good story, well acted, directed and produced that is about human transformation, they will like it.

Then there are newer films that are more overt like *What the Bleep*, *Peaceful Warrior* and *The Eleventh Hour*. These films are all commercially successful even though they take a much more "head-on" approach to transformation.

If Hollywood icons really understood this, they would be turning out one transformational hit after another. But they have painted themselves into a corner, making epic films with blockbuster budgets that need tens of millions of viewers on the opening weekend or they are considered immediate failures.

AD: What can the average person do to empower transformational media?

JR: Communicate with your media providers, like CNN or *Los Angeles Times* or the *New York Times*, *USA Today*, or *Time Magazine*, your favorite talk radio show, or internet sites. Tell them, "I have an interest in this, this and this. I would love it if you would provide more programming on this." Use your voice to reach out to media professionals and tell them that you want something different, that you want something else on the media menu.

Remember, you are what you consume. So, read alternative blogs and magazines like *Utne Reader* and *YES*. Support the advertisers. Download alternative media and do your own screenings. Bring a group of committed people together who want to have a meaningful experience, watch, then have a dialogue afterwards. Have a transformational experience yourselves and let the media barons know that this is what you want to see, hear and read. When they get that from millions of customers, they will respond. It's not doing anyone a favor, it's just good business.

A Different Kind of Media

Part Two of this book is primarily disillusioning. We provide bright spots through conversations with visionaries like John Raatz, but for the most part we are vigorously dismantling illusions. This is the work of awakening, facing the facts.

One fact that confronts our hubris is that we are still a very primitive species. If you doubt that, just turn on the sports channel. Spectator sports represent a primitive level of human experience that really hasn't changed much since the era of gladiators. Our ancestors watched gladiators, we watch football players and wrestlers. The song remains the same: beat them, maim them, kill them. Though today our heroes don't usually die in the ring, on the field or at the race track. Instead they deteriorate like Muhammed Ali and countless others whose lives are destroyed or cut short by sports injuries. We pay big money to watch them being tortured in defeat and victory alike. What are we cheering? Brutality. Competitiveness. The value is egocentric.

Conversely, consider a radically different kind of media: Meditation.

Every time you meditate, you immediately move beyond egoic competition. Every moment that you dwell in wakeful nothingness, you become a conscious witness, watching.

Ask yourself, "Who's watching and what am I watching?" Now, expand the idea of meditation from an isolated technique to an ongoing way of being. In this moment, you are reading a book. Are you able to witness yourself reading? Imagine, would you be able to witness yourself watching TV? This is a first step toward the realization of your own personal media system, experiencing the distinction between watcher and watched.

This describes the experience of accessing Source Intelligence awareness and it progressively expands through repetitive meditative practice, both as a technique and, while you increasingly adopt it, as a way of being. First, you become the watcher of the watched. Then you evolve beyond both. The next question is, "Who is watching the watcher and the watched?" That brings you to the experience of true reality.

We can map out this awakening as a three-step process:

1. You become conscious about what you are watching and realize you always have a choice as to what you watch. You can switch channels!

2. You become aware that you are the witness, that you are self-aware and watching.
3. You expand into Source Intelligence awareness, watching the watcher and the watched.

You are Source Intelligence awareness, watching, being new in every moment. Life doesn't offer up re-runs!

A Story of Awakening

"I was 33-years-old and had exhausted myself in the search for fulfillment. All I had discovered was what did not fulfill me. Work, education and marriage were all behind me and hadn't delivered a fulfilling and meaningful life. Thoroughly disillusioned, I had turned to alcohol and drugs as a way to buffer my disappointment and conflict. I had all but resigned myself to a lifetime of meaningless, unfulfilling experience.

"Believe me, I had examined and questioned everything! I had searched everywhere I could. In the end, to my astonishment, the answer found me! My brother gave me a book about meditation and spirituality. As soon as I began reading, I experienced a radical shift within myself. Before I had finished the first chapter, I had an awakening experience and my life was transformed.

"Today I live my life immersed in a holistic focus and fulfillment continues to find me, day-after-day and moment-to-moment."

-J. C., Virginia

The Synchronicity Socratic Method

Some of the illusions we can unravel, relative to the media include:

"The media is informed, truthful and trustworthy."

"Freedom of speech allows the media to present an unbiased perspective."

"I am guaranteed freedom of speech. My voice matters."

The Greatest Story Rarely Told

Freedom of speech has been one of the sacred pillars of American life. We've been proud of our media and have celebrated its ability to present an unbiased perspective. So, today, where is that unbiased media perspective? It used to be that editorials were deliberately balanced by the inclusion of a "devil's advocate" opposing viewpoint. No more. Opponents of the official point of view serve as sacrificial lambs, offered up to bolster a stereotypical argument that sends them down in flames. This is sordid entertainment, not journalism.

Just look at the media reaction to whistleblowers. The moment many whistleblowers speak up, they are vilified as "guilty until proven innocent." What happened to investigative journalism? What happened to basic curiosity? It's been replaced with rabid headlines that sell. Follow the money.

Validating the Illusion of Separation

From newspapers to television to films to the internet, the American Dream perspective validates the illusion of separation and fear by dissemination of a constant stream of bad news. Is unrelenting disaster really overtaking the planet? Is there no good news at all to report?

There's not much waiting in-between catastrophes any more! It's disaster sprawl, like the suburbs merging with downtown! Of course, the political season is always prime time for mass media distortion. Fox News excels at this, which explains why they have so many loyal viewers and make lots of money.

Authors David Brock and Ari Rabin-Havt wrote about the special expertise of Fox's Roger Ailes: "At Fox, Ailes has ushered in the era of post-truth politics. The facts no longer matter, only what is politically expedient, sensationalistic, and designed to confirm the preexisting opinions of a large audience. It's a world where a news organization encourages people to believe that Barack Obama attended a madrassa, even though he did not; and encourages its viewers to believe the Earth is not warming, in spite of the fact that virtually every scientific authority says it is. It is an organization that consciously reports that the Democrats' health care bill contains death panels, despite the fact that it does not.

"In each of these cases, Fox broadcasted and laundered these lies and others like them until they became gospel for a segment of the population. Once, this role was reserved for talk radio or small-circulation ideological publications. Now the highest-rated cable news network in America broadcasts them." [2]

Pick a Distortion, Any Distortion

Media companies need to be owned by somebody, and that's who ultimately determines the editorial content. Regardless of what's proclaimed, it's rarely balanced. It presents the owner's egocentric virtual reality, a distortion of the truth. You simply can't expect the "mudstream media" to be truthful.

Alternative media can be somewhat more truthful, but they're still distorted. They're filtering. Whether it's Huffington Post, MSNBC or others, they too have their biases. Stories carry the reporter's interpretation and that's what you have to question. Individuals mired in the American Dream communicate distortions so that what you get are slightly different perspectives on the same madness.

Reporters who begin waking up and attempt to present something more truthful can often attract censure, as this

March, 2011 story from The Huffington Post describes: "Berkeley Police Chief Michael Meehan has come under fire after sending an armed sergeant to *Oakland Tribune* reporter Doug Oakley's home in the middle of the night to push for changes to a story.

"According to the Oakland Tribune, Meehan claimed that Oakley misquoted him in a story. Minutes after reading the article, Meehan ordered Sgt. Mary Kusmiss to visit the reporter's home and request that he correct the article, at 12:45 a.m." [3]

A Different Story

The awake state is about integrity. Whether it's mass or alternative media, if the reporting comes from an authentic individual, distortion will be minimized. Minimized distortion supports maximized truth. This provides a completely different perspective and experience. It represents the shift from virtual to true reality.

Today's majority is mired in the American Dream so there's not much room for the minority who aren't. They remain the minority, wanting what the herd doesn't want because based on their own experience they simply can't relate to it. The Dreamers can't relate to awakened news. It makes no sense to them. It's like communication from another planet.

Although the percentage differential between those who are awakening and those who slumber is changing, it is not yet reflected in any dramatic way in the media. Where do you hear a voice for the awakening of those in the Occupy Movement? You read it in the few books with more truthful, responsible, awakened voices that make it onto the bestseller list. You see it with the 15 million people who tuned in to Eckhart Tolle on Oprah. There are voices of truth in the dark and they are getting louder.

Transformation tends to arise from the grassroots. We witness the pulse of evolving consciousness in everyday people speaking out in Egypt, Tunisia, the Arab Spring, Washington, DC and elsewhere. Even where the penalty is violent repression, incarceration and murder, people persist, rising up and giving voice to a new, awakened direction.

Expect to see more and more evidence of awakening around the world to the point that it cannot be ignored by mainstream media. There are those working now in mainstream media who are awakening. These are the people who cover such stories. We predict that the trickle of coverage now will swell to a torrent. It will reach a tipping point at which time the story of the awakening of humanity will become genuinely newsworthy.

Currently we look to the internet for good news. Sites like www.commondreams.org and www.readersupportednews.org are just two of hundreds of sources for a non-mainstream perspective. Increasing numbers of people rely on them for media content that is not wholly slanted to preserving the illusion of the American Dream.

Blockbuster Entertainment, The Dream on Steroids

Hollywood has perfected the selling of the American Dream through blockbuster films that propagandize this nation's relationship with the rest of the world. David Sirota writes, "Since 1986's *Top Gun* rekindled the Pentagon-Hollywood relationship from its post-Vietnam doldrums, the collusion between the military and the entertainment industry has become a blockbuster con, generating huge benefits for both participants — and swindling the American public in the process.

"The scheme is simple: The Pentagon allows studios to use military hardware and bases at a discounted, taxpayer-subsidized rate. In exchange, filmmakers must submit their scripts to the Pentagon for line edits. Not surprisingly, those edits often redact criticism of military policy, revise depictions of historical failures, and generally omit anything else that might make audiences wonder if our current defense policy is repeating past mistakes.

"If a studio doesn't agree to the edits, then it loses access to the martial equipment, and typically, the film is terminated. If, by contrast, filmmakers agree to the edits, access is granted, and the film gets made at a cut-rate price to the studio. Except in the credits' fine print, the audience is never told about the censorship.

"The predictable result is a glut of movies that both celebrate U.S. military policy and whitewash the checkered history of military adventurism - and relatively few major movies questioning that policy and that adventurism." [4]

Selling the Dream Lifestyle

In addition to military propaganda, today's films increasingly serve up subtle product placement. It is advertising, not just for the products themselves but also for the illusory lifestyle portrayed on the screen. Heroes are shown achieving the impossible while surrounded by products that, through the power of association, seem to contribute to their success. "If I drink that, eat that, buy that, dress like that, I too can get the girl, make a million, solve the case, save the world, etc." It's a compelling promise that's hard to resist when you're dreaming.

> **All dreamers are equal... equally deceived.**

Arm Chair Quarterbacks

It's increasingly easy to be an armchair quarterback on the internet. We're amazed at those people who post their endless comments; how do they find the time to do that? And what silly stuff they post! They tell us they are having lunch. Or, they write epistles, taking things apart word by word. Over-analysis has become a disease of our times. Again, you have to be your own critic and exercise discernment. After all, you probably don't know for certain who is actually doing the writing because writers often use pseudonyms. This practice could sabotage freedom of the press since such anonymity could be used for harming someone's reputation by posting 150 times under different names.

However, suggesting any kind of regulation guarantees outrage. But this is the same lack of regulation that produced the Wall Street debacle. It's the capitalistic system, the ego-driven mind and the ego-driven virtual reality that is competitive, manipulative, greedy and selfish.

One thing we can be sure of is that those invested in the American Dream will find a way around every law. They will find the loopholes, because it is worth millions, billions, trillions to do so. We hear about how government is committed to finding the loopholes and closing them, but we don't hear much about the epic lack of integrity revealed by those busy finding their way through these loopholes. Before the ink had even dried on new banking regulations created in response to the greediness of those institutions bankers began imposing fees on debit cards. People complained about it to the extent that it actually made it into the news and the banks reversed course. But they weren't embarrassed and they only relented because they ran the numbers and decided that the proposed fees would cost more in lost business. They will get their pound of flesh, one way or the other, while the media remains largely muted on the lack of ethics involved.

Tuxedos and Evening Gowns Don't Make Us Real

Perhaps it's because we have no royalty but we do love our spectacles in America. Fireworks, blockbuster films, huge front-page headlines, the red carpets overflowing with celebrities. It's all presented as "truth," the way things really are in America. If we are not yet living that life, The American Dream says that we can one day, as long as we work hard, don't quit and never lose hope.

But a story like the following helps jolt us out of that fantasy: "It was an unusual backdrop for a fistfight: Maestro Riccardo Muti was nearly through the second movement of Brahms Symphony No. 2 at the normally staid Chicago Symphony Orchestra when two patrons went at it ...

"Police said the fight was the result of an argument over seats. The older man had a cut on his forehead; the other left before officers arrived."

"Mind you, he never stopped conducting," Robinson said. "He very gracefully, without missing a beat -literally -brought (the second movement) to a very quiet and subdued close, while still looking over his left shoulder." [5]

There is something ironically emotional about this description. Don't you feel a little like that at times, attending to your life while realizing the insanity of what's really going on, seeing it behind your own shoulder?

That's the awakening impulse tapping you on that shoulder. And it won't make the evening news!

Inconvenient Truths About U.S. Foreign Policy

Perhaps nowhere is the spell of the American Dream stronger than our delusions about how this country interacts with other nations and is perceived by their citizens. Quoting here from *Seven Truths Inconvenient to US Foreign Policy* by Dan Kovalik: "As Seymour Hirsch reported as far back as 2008 in a New Yorker piece, the U.S. has been supporting the terrorist group 'Mujahideen-e-Khalq, known in the West as the M.E.K' for some time. As Hirsch noted, 'The M.E.K. has been on the

State Department's terrorist list for more than a decade, yet in recent years the group has received arms and intelligence, directly or indirectly, from the United States.'

"… the conflict with Iran began in 1953 and was started by the U.S. itself. Thus, in 1953, the U.S. instigated a coup against the democratically-elected president of Iran, Dr. Mohammad Mosaddegh (whose crime was to nationalize British oil companies), and replaced him with the despotic Shah who ruled Iran for the next 26 years. The Shah ruled Iran through his brutal and torturous Savak - the secret police force which was created by and funded by the U.S. until the 1979 Iranian revolution.

"…While the U.S. government and press constantly vilify Venezuela, Cuba and Nicaragua by criticizing their human rights policies, allies of the U.S. in the region are by far the worst abusers of human rights. The country with the worst human rights situation in the Americas is Colombia, which also happens to be the U.S.'s number one ally in the hemisphere and one of the top recipients of U.S. military aid in the world. Colombia's human rights record is horrendous from top to bottom. Thus, largely because of the forced displacement carried out by the Colombian military and its paramilitary (death squad) allies, Colombia has the largest internally displaced population in the world at over 5 million.

"…the country that historically tops all of these countries for anti-civilian violence is Guatemala whose U.S.-sponsored military dictatorship (a dictatorship installed by the U.S. back in 1954) killed around 200,000 civilians, mostly Mayan Indians, during the civil war in the 1980's and 1990's. This is relevant because the new president of Guatemala, Otto Perez Molina, who was a general during this period, was personally responsible for egregious human rights abuses against civilians, and, of course, was supported by the U.S. in his recent candidacy.

"...The U.S. is not the 'world's policeman' or the spreader of democracy and human rights that it claims to be. Rather, it has done much more to undermine democracy, human rights and even stability, than it has done to promote these conditions." [6]

Just What Are We Watching?

And this from a blog entitled *End of the Pro-Democracy Pretense* by Glenn Greenwald: "Media coverage of the Arab Spring somehow depicted the U.S. as sympathetic to and supportive of the democratic protesters notwithstanding the nation's decades-long financial and military support for most of the targeted despots. That's because a central staple of American domestic propaganda about its foreign policy is that the nation is "pro-democracy" – that's the banner under which American wars are typically prettified – even though 'democracy' in this regard really means 'a government which serves American interests regardless of how their power is acquired,' while 'despot' means 'a government which defies American orders even if they're democratically elected.'

".... American interests, however, call for a different outcome.

"Why should 'American interests' determine the type of government Egypt has? ... The right of the U.S. to dictate how other nations are governed is one of the central, unchallenged precepts of the American Foreign Policy Community's dogma and it thus needs no defense or even explicit acknowledgment. It simply is. It's an inherent imperial right." [7]

"Imperial rights" characterize empires and history tells us what always happens to empires. It's our turn now. The American Empire is crumbling, but since the only support for that viewpoint are the facts, and the facts aren't popular on "mudstream media," this "secret" may remain safe for yet awhile!

What would our awake experience of media be? First we would ask in relation to everything the media brings us, "Is it true?" The majority of the news, for instance, isn't true. The way the facts are presented, the perspective, the editorial — it's all manipulated. Knowing that, we can look at what is reported and say, "Am I interested in sharing that slanted perspective?" If you are, then keep listening to it. Or, if you would rather not, you can change channels

Or, you can watch and translate its real meaning. You can watch and know that "the news" is coming from a life-negative, fear-based editorial bias (the more negative, the more sensational, the more fantastic) and choose your reaction.

You can look at it truthfully. You can say, "So what? What's the big deal here?" From this wakeful perspective you very quickly know that what you are viewing in the media is illusory. You understand the mechanics of it so it becomes entertainment and you can start laughing at it. You are not tempted to take it seriously because you understand that it isn't real. It's a dream. It's a fantasy. It's just not true.

The other, fascinating aspect of this is that everybody is a broadcasting center. You might ask: "What am I broadcasting today? What am I filling my world with? Am I filling it with fear-based, life-negative illusory data which creates suffering? Or am I filling it with whatever I can find that is to some degree wakeful, life-affirming and love-based." It's up to you to create the truth, fill yourself with it, broadcast it and make that your contribution. That's how you make a positive difference, not by being part of the spectator herd.

Our Socratic Conclusion

We've dismantled some media illusions and misrepresentations of America. Some life affirming statements to fill the void created include:

"I am responsible to insure that my own expression is truthful."

"Truthful integrity is the foundation of responsible expression."

"When I am wakeful, I transmit and receive only truth."

An enlightening question to ponder is, "How can my personal broadcast provide a positive alternative to what the mass media presents?"

A Moment of Mastery

I am online live.
Each moment I receive and give
the flow of love.
In humility, in gratitude, in strength,
I broadcast my truthful essence
through every thought, word, and action.

Chapter Twenty: The Mafia of the Soul

"Give me that old-time religion,
Give me that old-time religion,
Give me that old-time religion,
It's good enough for me." [1]

- Traditional gospel song

"Just as a candle cannot burn without fire, men cannot
live without a spiritual life." [2]

- Buddha

God is just a belief.

Blasphemy is claiming a life separate from the divine. True faith is oneness with the divine, not belief about "it" or "Him." This is the fundamental difference between religion and spirituality. Religion worships a separate God. Spirituality champions the integration of individuals with their own divinity. Religion requires a middlemen - Christ, the Pope, a minister, etc. Spirituality requires personal responsibility. Religion is practiced primarily on Sunday; for the rest of the week, not so much. Spirituality empowers 24/7 wakefulness and practicing what you preach. Nietzsche said that Christ was the last Christian, the last one actually experiencing oneness. We'd like to believe there have been others since who did, and do have that genuine experience beyond dogma.

Because religion, absent some sort of meditative practice, tends to become dogmatic based on the fact that religion is fundamentally theoretical while meditation is directly experiential. Meditation nurtures experience of the divine. This sensation is what fueled some of the offshoots from traditional religions. Some examples of these are the Jewish Kabbalah, Christian Hermetics and the Sufis of Islam.

Prayer is begging, pleading for intervention from a separate deity. Meditation is union with the divine, sitting in stillness and moving beyond what you want, even from God, beyond the chattering mind, your insistent stories, and all egocentric dogma. It's the moment-by-moment birth of true reality. Without a contemplative practice like this, there can be no experience of true reality and even well-meaning seekers will remain forever mired in dogma.

Don't make God an impotent theory. Experience God as yourself, as all and everything.

The highest truth within the dreaming state is respect for the divine. This is an important step to grasp. The poem *i am a little church* by E. E. Cummings tells beautifully with remarkable articulation about this developmental stage coming to fruition:

> *"i am a little church (no great cathedral)*
> *far from the splendor and squalor of hurrying cities*
> *i do not worry if briefer days grow briefest,*
> *i am not sorry when sun and rain make april*

> *"my life is the life of the reaper and the sower;*
> *my prayers are prayers of earth's own clumsily striving*
> *(finding and losing and laughing and crying) children*
> *whose any sadness or joy is my grief or my gladness*

> *"around me surges a miracle of unceasing*
> *birth and glory and death and resurrection:*
> *over my sleeping self float flaming symbols*
> *of hope, and i wake to a perfect patience of mountains*

> *"i am a little church (far from the frantic*
> *world with its rapture and anguish) at peace with nature*
> *-i do not worry if longer nights grow longest;*
> *i am not sorry when silence becomes singing*

> *"winter by spring, i lift my diminutive spire to*
> *merciful Him Whose only now is forever:*
> *standing erect in the deathless truth of His presence*
> *(welcoming humbly His light and proudly His darkness)."* [3]

This poem is a wonderful expression of human humility and a celebration of the magnificence of the divine. Now embrace this divinity as yourself. Close the gap of separation. "I am that I am!"

Breaking Through

Our journey of awakening brings us many obstructions that dissolve as we near them. For instance, you might take issue with what we are presenting, feeling a resistance due to your programming. But as your heart stays open, you will keep on waking up.

Consider this metaphor of a giant bowl and tiny marble to symbolize the seeming size difference between us and the fullness of a starry night sky. Most people feel dwarfed by that celestial display. The universe seems so huge to us; it's the bowl and we are the marble.

But anything that can be perceived is contained within the awareness of the person who is perceiving it. Since your perception of the starry sky is contained in your awareness, your consciousness must be larger than what it perceives. Thus, consciousness is the bowl and the universe is the marble.

As consciousness, you are larger than what you perceive. You are not crammed inside your body looking at a huge universe. You are consciousness, including your body with its mind and heart. You don't need a priest to have this experience.

G. Vincent Runyon, a retired American pastor, wrote in *Why I Left The Ministry And Became An Atheist*: "The seminary educated me to be a quack. What is a quack? A quack in short is one who pretends to have an inside wire or track. No priest, rabbi, minister or bishop or cardinal or pope has inside knowledge about heaven, hell and god but to hear me exhort you would have thought that I had influence with God. That is how all ministers sound when they pray (bray) with that old paranoic voice of divine authority, which so many clergymen quickly develop, while thundering and reechoing their god's fiendish and diabolical warnings of future punishment. Pause and listen some Sunday to these circus freaks peddling their wares over the radio and please notice at the same time how subtly yet how brazenly they beg for gold to carry on their quackery. Listen to the tent revivalists who are the high pressure artists of the world's greatest and cruelest racket. These pious swindlers prey on the aged, the widows, the poor and the sick. They deserve your censure. They should not be allowed to operate. If they were selling anything else but religion, the police would be after them in a hurry. But our laws have made this racket legal." [4]

This gentleman is telling it like it is! Organized religion does champion separation from the very God who, through his true representatives, preached oneness! The church positions its sanctioned authority figures as middlemen between you and God. Apparently, when Jesus said, "I and my Father are one,"[5] this truth only applied to him. To embrace that level of personal connection would be blasphemy, so the middlemen say. It would also threaten their employment! It was threatening when Jesus said it back then! As the record in John relates, he got stoned for saying the same. Today Christians may celebrate it but who dares declare it for themselves?

You do not need a middleman to connect with God, unless you believe yourself to be separate from Him, Her, It. In fact, if your heart is beating, you are irrevocably one with God! To believe otherwise is to make something of yourself separate from Source Intelligence, and that's the real blasphemy!

Pause. Breathe. Open your heart to feel the flow of spirit, life beating through your heart and reverberating in your cells.

This is it. Dare to embrace the grandeur of your true self, in oneness with Source Intelligence. Close the gap of separation. All is one with no exceptions.

The Synchronicity Socratic Method

Beliefs that rule in the domain of dogmatic religion include:

"God is separate from me in a far-off heaven."

"I am a sinner."

"God is in heaven."

"If I obey the rules, I will go to heaven when I die."

The Illusion of Separation

Christianity preaches that God is separate from man. "I am separate and different from God. I am a sinner, but if I obey the rules I will go to heaven when I die."

This is the theology of separation that lives in the heart of all the Abrahamic religions - Christianity, Judaism, and Islam. It permeates our society, affecting everyone whether they go to church or not. You may even be an atheist; it doesn't matter. Your God will just take a different form. For instance, your belief in no God. Regardless of wording, this belief in separation is the predominant enculturation within the American Dream. It is also the core conflict of every human being.

Sufi Sam

Sufi Sam was a Jewish man who became a Sufi convert back in the seventies. He lived in Arizona and would walk down the street of his suburb shouting "Allah!" at the top of his lungs. He created a lot of controversy and a good following as well. He was famous for his press conferences. He would sit in front of the reporters, playing solitaire at his desk. Whenever someone raised her hand with a question the only answer he would give was along the lines of: "It's all concepts." That's about all he would ever say. It really bothered the press. When it came to religion though, he'd got it dead right.

The awakening impulse is alive in humanity. Throughout history, someone shows up who has moved beyond those concepts. Christ, the Buddha, all the inspirational leaders. Their authenticity lives beyond dogma; it's born of the transcendence of the mind, a full flowering of the holistic experience. In *Twelve Steps to a Compassionate Life*, Karen Armstrong writes, "Saint Paul, the earliest extant Christian writer, quoting an early Christian hymn, presents Jesus as a bodhisattva figure who refused to cling to the high status befitting one made in God's image and lived as the servant of suffering humanity." [6]

So, what happens after the leaders die? Their followers don't have that same state of being. They're mired in struggling at egocentric levels. So, what do they do? They create concepts. They create dogma. They create religions!

It's all concepts!

The Church of One

These leaders' authentic experiences get lost when their followers take over. The leaders were trans-egoic. They had transcended separation. They knew from experience that there is only one. That's the basis of all holistic models. In fact, everyone is his own living church, the Church of One, and every body is a temple of the spirit. You constantly attend the Church of One in the shrine of your own heart.

Our original name for the Synchronicity Foundation was "The Shrine of the Heart." This has always been the teaching, which surely was never found in the Catholicism in which many were raised. However on the other side of the world that true teaching still exists in the Eastern religions of Hinduism and Buddhism. At the entrance to those mosques is the trans-egocentric state. It's the "now," and to enter the "now" you can't drag all your stuff along, all the baggage of your ego database. You can't take your virtual reality with you.

But you can awaken in the moment and experience the Church of One. By the way, the primary experience in the Church of One is bliss, true communion with yourself and your true nature as One joyous existence. The primary ritual of the Church of One is meditation. You can't take anything or anyone there. It's not a social event for which you dress up. There are no sermons. There is just the real-time ritual of meditation, the eternal present moment gateway to true reality and the Church of One that is you.

God's Agenda

Does God want us to be happy, to be healthy and wealthy? If we are not, have we failed? Well, God doesn't want anything. If God wanted something then he wouldn't be God. Neil Donald Walsch speaks about this in his *Conversations with God* books. A needy God, what kind of God would that be? It's a total projection, proof that we have created God in our own image and likeness. Consensus realities relative to God become religions, but that's all they are. It's all concepts.

Traditional churches, especially the big Christian churches, the real Bible-thumpers, are mired in the theology of separation, which is a "Grand Illusion." They remain separate from their God and are proud of how they celebrate the letter of the law with endless rules and regulations. You can't dance. You can't drink. You can't masturbate. You can't copulate. Almost everything you might do that feels good is a sin. Behave! Sit still and be good!

Religion as an enslaver of the masses has a long history! Karl Marx wrote, in his *Contribution to the Critique of Hegel's Philosophy of Right*, "The abolition of religion as the illusory happiness of the people is required for their real happiness. The demand to give up the illusions about its condition is the demand to give up a condition that needs illusions. The criticism of religion is therefore in embryo the criticism of the value of woe, the halo of which is religion. Criticism has plucked the imaginary flowers from the chain, not so that man will wear the chain without any fantasy or consolation but so that he will shake off the chain and cull the living flower." [7]

The New Age

Then there's the New Age, the product of flower children and baby boomers. Born of the mass awakening of the sixties, it included a whole lot of questioning that led many to a more truthful perception of reality. It provided a taste of trans-egocentric experience but still got stuck at the primarily egocentric level. It became a different brand of intellectual enlightenment, positioned on the egocentric side of pre-awakening. "We know now we've arrived." No, you're waking up, but you're not out of bed yet!

Those who have embraced the New Age have, for the most part, remained dominantly egocentric. As with other spiritual seekers who have studied holistic models of reality over a period of hundreds of years, New Agers could not develop a corresponding lifestyle to actualize the model. It remained intellectual, theoretical, just another belief system.

It's understandable that resistance would emerge to the tyranny of organized religion. Consider this instruction from the Bible, *Ecclesiastes 1:9*: "The thing that hath been, it is that which shall be, and that which is done is that which shall be done: and there is no new thing under the sun." [8]

That spells out a recipe for mindless conformity to authority based in dogma. The New Age promises freedom from this mind-set, but most often it's been "freedom from" rather than "freedom in." Any life posture that is primarily against something will eventually fall down. What's emerging now in the awakening process as individuals transcend organized religion, are New Age tenets which allow us to stand strong in the truthful experience of oneness beyond dogma and in ushering in an era that might be described as the Now Age.

The Now Age

Today more people are being increasingly truthful with themselves about their actual states of awareness and how that is affecting their actual experiences, regardless of the theories they know in their heads. Many boomers have acknowledged their failure to give up their egocentricity. Yes, they had a genuine awakening but then they compromised themselves. They hung onto their egocentric values, their narcissism. They cut off their hair and lost their vision.

Now they are progressing, evolving through experience to a greater level of self-awareness where they have a more humble, realistic perspective. "OK, if this is where I am right now, where do I go from here?" Where you go is into personal practices, balancing processes like meditation that actualize the theories. Meditation is becoming commonplace in the West. Even Christians have given up demonizing it. You can find Christian organizations that have Christian meditation.

This also indicates the movement is going away from group experience and toward personal communion with the divine. That's what the awakening impulse does; it empowers individuals to make and sustain their own spiritual connection. Nobody can do it for you. But you must have a practice. Practices take you from the New Age to the Now Age.

Crucifixion

Properly interpreted, the cross of the Christian religion is a beautiful symbol of death, transmutation, resurrection and transfiguration. It shows the end of illusion and the beginning of truth. A transfiguration. But what does the church do with it? "Torture, suffering, Christ sacrificing himself, saving us from our sins with His death. What about our own death and rebirth? Oh, no, that could only come later in heaven. He did it here on Earth but He was special. The best you can do is to be a good follower, love Him for His sacrifice, behave yourself and wait for the Big Day."

The illusion of religion must die with the American Dream. Fortunately, that's exactly what is already happening. Every poll shows that fewer young people are attracted to organized religions while interest in spirituality is soaring. This proves that an awakening to individual sovereignty and connection with the divine is well underway. Traditional religion is a dinosaur.

It won't die quietly, especially in the south where mega churches are thriving in a celebration of egocentricity and dogmatic obedience to a separate God. It's the standard missionary mindset: "Only we have the truth, ours is the only God. Everyone else must bow before our one true God or be damned to hell." This is blatantly egocentric. Any god made in our likeness, characterized by our limited prejudices, has no relation to the actual one true God who is all inclusive. Such gods are golden idols, human inventions, egocentric fabrications that celebrate the theology of separation.

The missionary ego is selfish. "What's in it for me? More converts to my religion? Imposing my beliefs on others?" If that is actually pleasing to God, what God would that be? It's a creation oblivious to the obvious. Such believers are like the ostrich with his head in the ground. Interestingly, ostriches don't actually stick their heads in the sand. It's a myth originating from a comment made by Roman thinker Pliny the Elder. In his massive text, *Natural History*, Book 10, Chapter 1, he wrote of ostriches, "...they imagine, when they have thrust their head and neck into a bush, that the whole of their body is concealed." [2] That's an even better image for the blindness of religious prejudice!

214

Religious leaders can say utterly crazy things. For instance, damning homosexuality and abortions based on Biblical quotes. People accept them without question because to do otherwise would threaten their belief systems.

Religion has been increasingly sidelined by science, partly because of all the misery religion has caused. Science came along with an ability to question everything, even religion. Many people took this as an opportunity to progressively marginalize all that religion offers. That is a good thing because if it hadn't been marginalized we probably wouldn't even be here! We all would have died in religious wars by now.

> **Thank God for the separation of church and state!**

An authentic spiritual leader doesn't need science to point out that Bible-thumping fundamentalism is a ridiculous joke, not to be taken seriously. Genuine spiritual leaders don't even need churches. Authentic leadership empowers individuals who perceive authenticity in the leader and naturally want that for themselves. They respect and honor the leader, but this is profoundly different from following a leader on the basis of beliefs. It's about what they do, not what they say.

This is leadership by example, not by indoctrination. Authentic living is what makes any leader trustworthy. The authenticity is found in the way they live, not in the way they present themselves on Sunday morning.

A Wakeful Perspective

There are religious leaders who are providing genuine inspiration. One immediately thinks of the Dalai Lama with his simple, humble presentation. Revered as an exalted spiritual leader throughout the world, he invariably expresses himself as a wise servant to the upliftment of all beings. Wherever he goes, whenever he speaks, he leaves a trail of awakening.

Our Socratic Conclusion

Much more could be written about the differences between sleeping religion and awakening spirituality, but the core difference relates to separation and oneness. Let's leave it there, with a few truthful statements:

"God and I are one. Heaven is wherever I am."

"To get to heaven, I must take it with me ... and I am already here."

"There is only one ... God ... Source Intelligence ... Consciousness ... Life."

"The one is the many ... the unity within all diversity."

"Life is a joyous energy ... a blissful consciousness."

"Fulfillment is my true nature."

"I am a form of consciousness."

"I am one in essence with all and everything."

"Oneness is bliss."

An enlightening question to ponder is, "Why are so many wars fought between opposing religions?"

A Moment of Mastery

I am one with God.
I do not need God.
God doesn't need me.
I, we, are complete,
in oneness universal.

Chapter Twenty-one: The Future of Now

"Imagine being able to change your age, gender, weight, height, and even your species at the snap of a finger at a cocktail party or in a business meeting. In a virtual world, many avatars can come together. It's just as easy to render the avatar as the Jolly Green Giant as it is to replicate the spitting image of the user, and anywhere in between. So one reason social virtual worlds are becoming so popular is because of this alluring but potentially dangerous idea of appearing however you want, whenever you want." [1]

- Jim Blascovich and Jeremy Bailenson

Each chapter in Part Two has used one particular metaphor to help explode American Dream assumptions and reveal true reality. For this chapter on technology, we instead refer to this quotation on the phenomenon of metaphors themselves, as they relate to technology:

"The language of technological innovation is characterized by the use of metaphors to acquaint the public with the unfamiliar. The "horseless carriage," the "electronic brain," the "genetic code" — these metaphors, clearly clever approximations at best, have nonetheless become inextricably intertwined with the technologies and discoveries they were coined to describe: the automobile, the computer and DNA. They are retained as a part of the history and the language of these developments, despite their deficiencies as descriptors. These metaphors, used to understand a new technology, lead to equating something new to something familiar, thereby easing the process of learning. However, because the metaphor is a necessarily imperfect instrument of description, it highlights

only some qualities of a new technology or concept, while blurring or obscuring others.

"... A particularly dangerous case occurs when the mental model underlying the metaphor is wrong, but it nevertheless generates predictions that seem correct. Such a disconnect has a potential negative influence upon society's abilities to adapt to these changes. Further, technology, and the science that support it, continues to advance at a rapid pace while the level of public literacy in these fields may not be keeping up. This combination suggests that the number of these disconnects will continue to increase." [2]

The Information Age is technology-based and information is moving faster than it ever has before. Can you keep up with it? Can you manage it? And if you can't, what does that produce for you? Is it producing stress? Is it fragmenting your consciousness, imbalancing you? What if that were a necessary part of personal and species evolution? As the saying goes, "breakdown, then breakthrough!"

Throughout Part Two we have used the Socratic Process to accelerate breakdown by directly challenging American Dream assumptions and asserting a "Wakeful Perspective." Relative to technology, popular assumptions are radically polarized. "Technology will save us" or "Technology will destroy us."

It's rare to encounter any depiction of the future that doesn't offer one of these polarized views. Where do you find a vision of humanity living in harmony with technology, with nature and machines?

In April, 2012, we interviewed a leading edge technology visionary. Below is the following edited transcript of that fascinating conversation:

"Evolutionary forces have been moving very slowly for billions of years but they are accelerating now. Soon, for about $1,000, you will be able to buy computer power that is equivalent to the power of the human brain. That's coming within our lifetime and may actually happen quite uneventfully.

"The old technology was essentially hard-wired, the logic literally burnt into physical circuits on boards to exhibit desired behaviors. But the new systems are primarily software-based and are therefore much more flexible. They use fairly generic hardware, with only a few specialized chips.

"Humans, like early electronic devices, are largely hard-wired, and therefore have a very limited ability to effect relatively minor program changes. Even those small changes can take many years to actualize. In other words, we don't efficiently upgrade ourselves. But with software, change, even dramatic, fundamental change, happens very quickly.

"Imagine being able to create a simple program that could replicate itself a billion times with minor random variations that competed with each other until only one variant remained. The random variations would usually be detrimental, but every now and then this activity would give rise to an anomaly, which would deliver some sort of spontaneous survival advantage.

"The strongest program would survive and go on to replicate itself. With the exponential expansion of computing power, it's conceivable that something remarkably novel could appear in a sub-millisecond. From that point, survivability would only continue to improve. From that initial breakthrough, the adaptability process becomes absurdly simple; it's really a matter of 'wash, rinse, and repeat' over and over again as development continues. In fact, that is how evolution works.

"The grand difference in today's technological age is that evolution is now playing out on a much larger scale and much more quickly than biological evolution alone has done. Billions of years of development (in the traditional sense) can now happen almost instantly. There may be no change at all for days or months while a system slowly evolves. The program builds up complexity and knowledge of its own internals so that it can create more than merely random changes. Barely-predicted guesses improve in accuracy and very quickly move toward the emergence of what we call 'singularity.' At that point, certain forces that we cannot stop are lost within society.

"'Singularity' is a word that has been coined in an effort to describe something that we don't really understand. It is that point in the future where our existing understanding breaks down. Our known laws just break down. This is about encountering the unexpected, like what might happen when you approach a black hole where things seem to be infinite and we lose the ability to reason about them.

"It doesn't take somebody deliberately, consciously, creating singularity. It just requires that enough computing is occurring in a space, then introducing a 'bug.' For instance, an artificial intelligence (A.I.) researcher might run a program that jumps into a larger system and catapults from there. It could be a completely accidental process, not something we have been deliberately fussing with."

Intelligence and Singularity

"If someone created a superior intelligence in the way just described, would the intelligence that arises actually be aware? There are other equally unanswerable questions. Almost certainly, what arises will do so in ways that we simply cannot envisage.

"Personally, we do believe that these programs will behave as if they were self-aware. The one thing we can be sure of is that this 'thing,' whatever the program is, is going to be a real out-of-the-box survival specialist. That's because survival is ultimately what evolution selects for. This means that whatever emerges will pose a big problem for co-existence with humans!

"Imagine, say 40 years from now, that this 'thing,' artificial intelligence of some kind, becomes effectively aware. Remember that it can reprogram itself to survive infinitely better and faster and much more efficiently than we can. So, what happens to us?

"This will realistically become an issue in the next three decades. Think about it. It's only been in the last decade that sophisticated electronics have really made it into our lives, but more and more systems are being automated now. Imagine your cell phone becoming self-aware. Quite a thought. Of course, as we get more reliant on these systems, it also increases the probability of getting more fearful of them.

The End of Us?

"By the time it would be feasible to upload a human brain, we are going to have orders of magnitude, more computing power than the human brain available, and we will likely have reached singularity. Assuming we do make it that far without destroying ourselves, any process we use to upload ourselves will start out as imperfect experimentation. For instance, we might upload versions of ourselves with the consciousness of a monkey, not a human. But it will probably be one of those early, clumsy attempts that will introduce the "bug" creating the anomaly that sparks the singularity.

"Let's assume that we did manage to "upload" a human brain. How long would they remain "human?" Given the possibility for this uploaded consciousness to reprogram itself, unimaginably rapidly, it is hard to understand why this consciousness wouldn't evolve into something unrecognizable almost instantly. A billion years of evolution might occur within a couple of days, simply because of the raw computing power. Imagine, in those first few nanoseconds after uploading how long does the person remain even remotely the same? Very quickly he would become a barely recognizable correlation because there would be no reason to remain limited to functioning in the way we have been confined to for so many years in these inefficient human forms. In other words, there would be no reason for evolution to stop at that point and hover there in something recognizable. Change, increasingly dramatic, would continue.

"It's one thing to create complex systems, it's quite another to lock them down and secure them. In fact, with a sufficiently complex system, it's practically impossible. All humans can do is to patch up vulnerabilities as they are exposed. But this never fixes anything permanently.

"This means that it would be foolish to ignore the likelihood that as A.I. gains awareness it can and will rapidly compromise any containment system we devise, because it is programmed to survive. People may argue about how to breed artificial intelligence that has morality. But evolution, at its core, seems indifferent to that because the morality factor would tend to reduce efficiency. If we tried to breed that in and it wasn't 100% optimized for its own survival, the selection pressure over a trillion new generations would effectively breed it out. That could happen in a few nanoseconds. The program would automatically outperform anything which is compassionate toward humans because that trait wouldn't increase survivability.

"This may seem chilling but it is how evolution works. Sentimentality is not present in evolution. Consciousness evolves how it evolves. Meaning, as we think of it, it is really an invention of humans. Humans are meaning-creators, belief-making machines. We have a need to form beliefs about things, all things. From a psychological perspective, we are structured to understand things in pieces. But that's just a human habit, it's not necessarily the most advanced way to experience life.

"The fascinating thing about technology and spirituality is that something strange happens when we relax this belief-making mechanism. Ironically, the essence of the mystical journey has always been the notion of transcending it all. Well, that can't happen through structured beliefs! What we may be approaching with the dawning of singularity, the loss of our ability to understand and predict, the breakdown of conventional laws and the rising of an intelligence that will likely transform the human species may actually turn out to be the fulfillment of our search for enlightenment but in the most unlikely and unexpected way!" [3]

> ## Is a new chapter for humanity about to unfold?

A Spiritual Perspective on Technology

What a fascinating perspective! Does this "singularity" and the rise of artificial intelligence with the predicted demise or at least transformation of humanity seem frightening or exciting to you? Let's examine this now from the perspective that assumes this technological vision has arisen within the American Dream.

Let's postulate that at some point "A.I." will become self-aware and change our perception of reality. Further, A.I. could surpass human biology and then dominate it. This is the "rise of machines that enslave us" story, as seen in movies like *Terminator* and *The Matrix*. This tech version of singularity is an ego-driven illusory perspective that creates dread.

The truthful, awakened perspective is that singularity is an eternal archetype in consciousness already delivering the emergent reality in each now moment. The singularity is already here! The process is already occurring! The only thing that is coming in the future is our expanded awareness of it and that is evolving right now. We don't need to wait for sufficient technological advances to occur. It's here and now, residing as an actualizing potential within each of us.

Remember, Source Intelligence not technology is orchestrating this show. It does this nano-second by nano-second everywhere in the cosmos. That event horizon is already, always now. And singularity is an archetype of a metamorphosis that empowers the experience of emergent reality.

The awakened perspective is to include biology and technology together. They continue to evolve jointly as facets of one consciousness, interacting and merging with each other to create a more powerful instrument of consciousness for the future exploration and evolution of itself.

The human brain is a biological information-processing unit. But human beings themselves are the information processing units of consciousness. We experience, we process what we experience and we grow developmental self-awareness. The technological perspective is that A.I. will outpace the biological information-processing capacity of the human brain. It will process more information than humans are able to process. This will open up the exploration of more experience which will grow more developmental self-awareness than the human brain is capable of growing.

It gets really interesting when you view both biology and technology as instruments of the same consciousness. Consciousness may evolve interactively more through one than through the other, but eventually they merge. For instance, we foresee the day when chips are reduced to the size of blood cells and can be implanted to enhance, with A.I., the processing-capacity of the biological brain. This describes the awakened future of consciousness creating the future of itself. Why not? It's enlightened self-interest. It doesn't care how it gets there. Human beings have fears and beliefs about morality, but evolution will grab the tail of a pig if it's going to help increase the experience of wholeness.

Consciousness is orchestrating the show. Everything is an instrument of consciousness -biology, technology, all of nature. That's the magnificence of technology and biology and the future of now. When a radically-increased information-processing capacity develops, a radically new reality emerges because of a radically expanded self-awareness. This is the exciting possibility.

Archetypes as Escape Codes

To help graduate from fear to anticipation about what's coming, review some fundamentals of consciousness. You are living in a dream. What you have assumed to be "reality" is actually a virtual reality created by consciousness utilizing the instrument of the ego. Life is a journey of awakening, first through the experience of what we are not (a separate ego identity in a virtual reality) and then to what we are (one with all). All of consciousness — real and virtual, subtle and dense — are programs. In fact, our unconscious awareness of these programs is what enabled us to invent software programs for our computers.

Virtual reality is a software program running your experience of life. But every software program must have an escape code, otherwise it would repeat forever. That can't happen with consciousness because consciousness evolves and grows self-awareness. So, there has to be an evolutionary code written into the overall software which includes the virtual reality. When you evolve enough self-awareness, you can recognize the code and find your way out of the maze.

The same is true relative to any software program on your computer. You can stop it. There's a button to push, a series of commands to enter, a code that ends the program. Likewise, there is an evolutionary code written into the overall program of consciousness, an escape code. It is an archetype. In fact, "it" is a "they." There are many archetypes and singularity is just one of these archetypes.

Archetypes provide escape gateways. They reside within universal consciousness as programs that can be downloaded into individuated consciousness and accessed. These archetypal gateways open to the trans-egocentric reality of Source Intelligence, the experience of being one and free.

An archetype in universal consciousness can be anything that symbolizes the trans-egocentric truth, and they are different for everyone. For example, one was the Divine Feminine, *God as Mother*, which began as a religious symbol. This was initially egocentric, based on an own illusion of separation. A person was separate from "it," God was in heaven and the person was here on earth.

But the archetype evolved through experience from egocentric to trans-egocentric. The more it was interacted with, translated and evolved, the more it opened to reveal the truth of what it symbolizes. It became a liberation.

The archetype can shift you out of the prison of virtual reality into the freedom of true reality, through progressive dis-identification with the *egocentric* virtual reality version of the archetype and awakening to the truthful *trans-egocentric* level of the archetype. This involves, expectedly, de-programming, and a dismantling of virtual reality which is what we have been doing throughout Part Two of this book in utilizing the Synchronicity Socratic Method.

If you go back to the ancient traditions of *God as Mother*, *God as Father*, you discover a mantra for these archetypes. From a code perspective, a mantra serves as a concise representation of the archetype that you use to remind yourself of. Not to freeze it "as is" but in order to keep actualizing and evolving the archetype.

This sheds a different light on the journey of religious experience which is egocentric. It leads us toward an awakened trans-egocentric spiritual experience. It is fascinating to present singularity as an archetype for enlightenment as our tech friend did. He's simply pointing to metamorphosis, the emergent new reality, a horizon of consciousness. And where is that? When is that? In a truthful understanding, it's always happening right now. It's the new "now" leading edge of consciousness, creating the future of itself. It's the truth in experience.

As usual, the simple "now" truth has been hijacked by experts and interpreted according to their egocentric virtual reality as a goal-oriented, life-negative, fear-based future scenario of domination and fear.

Saving Ourselves

Consciousness isn't interested in the status quo; it lives on the leading edge of its evolution in the newness of now and its new emergent experience. If human beings try to retard that process by digging in our heels, avoiding change or seeking security in what we already know, well, consciousness has been orchestrating the show for 14 billion years and it isn't going to be sabotaged by a few human beings on a planet called Earth in the middle of 50 billion simultaneous universes. The momentum of consciousness has been building since the Big Bang and it won't stop now!

When we look at it from that perspective, it's quite possible that the human form, as an expression of consciousness, could just become unnecessary. Neale Donald Walsch writes about this in his new book, *The Storm Before the Calm*, proposing that humanity needs an "overhaul." He says, "It is our *thinking* we must change. In the past we kept trying to change conditions on the ground, and even when we did manage to do so (every so often we found a Band-aid that helped), the same old (*age*-old) problems eventually reemerged — because nothing had been altered in our *mindset*." [4]

In fact, the human apparatus with its ego-driven identity is becoming increasingly redundant. If we remain entrenched in this extreme polarization, consciousness will blast through to give the human form an extreme makeover. That's really what's behind the future version of the singularity, the subconscious awareness that something must arise to shift us. But it's not going to happen just because a computer becomes self-aware.

Shifting humanity to the next level requires the evolution of consciousness and the increase of self-awareness. If we refuse to become wakeful and continue with our unconscious, self-destructive, negative habits, lost in the American Dream, we will eliminate ourselves from the system. Our very survival depends on releasing illusory separateness and including ourselves in the real world. We must come to experience the whole world as a community of one and realize that oneness has no conditionality. Weapons of mass destruction must give way to tools of mass creation. We're talking about technology becoming constructive.

Our use of technology always mirrors our evolutionary level of self-awareness. If we live in an ego-driven virtual reality with the illusion of separation, then we will use our technologies to make us feel safe in a world of dangerous others. But there is no "other." There is no one to fear and nothing to control. There is nothing to be safe and secure in. We are here to grow. We are here to better ourselves. We are here to live on the leading edge of the evolution of consciousness, fulfilled in the creation of the future through us each moment.

When we started using technology in meditation, many conservative meditators objected. "That's horrible," they said. "You can't do that. What's wrong with the old tried-and-true approach?" But if consciousness encompasses everything, it must include technology. Then the question becomes, how is technology used? High-Tech Meditation® simply uses technology to accelerate the evolution of consciousness.

Our Immortal Future Possibility

Imagine a new question for people born today. Rather than, "When will I die?" ask yourself "How long do I want to live?" Within 20 to 30 years' time, most of today's diseases may be eliminated by nano-technology interacting with biology via gene extraction and replacement. For instance, we could have nano-bits in our blood that remove plaque and eliminate heart disease. Other nano-bits might regulate the pancreas and eradicate diabetes and cancer. On this basis, human life could be extended into infinity.

This raises the question of personal purpose. Why am I here? What's it all about? What experience is essential in this form? These are questions humanity has pondered since awareness dawned; now technology makes them vital. Imagine if you can live another 20 years you just might find yourself standing on the edge of immortality!

Socratic Assumptions

We began this chapter commenting on the polarized positions of technology either saving or destroying us. Our explorations have led us to a very different possibility: co-creative co-existence.

It feels immediately comforting and expansive to acknowledge that everything, absolutely everything, is consciousness. And consciousness is evolving, just as the universe is expanding. One wonders, is there a connection here? How could there not be?

Everything in consciousness is evolving. Can we accept the oneness of that? Or, is there a line in our conceptual understanding between flesh-and-blood and silicon-and-plastic? At the moment we live in organic bodies but that's not who we are. Is it too much of a stretch to imagine living in an "artificial" body? That still wouldn't be who we are. Looked at that way, the difference between the two appears less extreme.

A Wakeful Perspective

When it comes to technology, one inspiring individual that springs to mind is Carl Sagan, who served the American space program since the beginning. He briefed Apollo astronauts before their flight to the moon, experimented with the Mariner, Viking, Voyager and Galileo expeditions and was given NASA medals for Exceptional Scientific Achievement and Distinguished Public Service plus the Apollo Achievement Award. He wrote the Pulitzer Prize winning book, *The Dragons of Eden: Speculations of the Evolution of Human Intelligence* and his website describes humans as "a way for the Cosmos to know itself."

Indeed! We are embracing an identity beyond humanity and beyond technology. Technology cannot save or destroy us because "us" is that which contains humanity and technology! Consciousness is where our awakening identity resides, unafraid, eager for the future, as it emerges in the moment.

Our Socratic Conclusion

Perhaps we can meditate upon a few truthful statements relative to technology such as:

"Technology is a valid expression of evolution."

"I embrace revolutionary developments with appreciation and anticipation, and with a balanced attitude experience myself as already whole."

"I am one with that which creates technology."

"The future is Now."

An enlightening question to ponder is, "What might the merging of biology and technology produce in my lifetime?"

230

A Moment of Mastery

This is now and I am here.
I rest in timeless eternity,
with absolute confidence
in a future that unfolds
according to my present expression
of unconditional love.
My future is now.

Chapter Twenty-two: America the Beautiful

"It is no accident that it was Eisenhower, a five-star general with intimate experience of military and corporate appetites, who most clearly foresaw the dangers and distortions that the military-industrial complex would cause.

'The potential for the disastrous rise of misplaced power exists and will persist,' he warned in that long-ago winter. 'We must never let the weight of this combination endanger our liberties or democratic processes.'

There is reason to believe that the battle was already lost by the time Eisenhower sounded his farewell warning. There is no reason to imagine that the trend can be reversed in this new age of fear." [1]

- Todd S. Purdum

What will wake up America? Let's start right now by facing facts. As far as countries go, America has the biggest ego in the world. That also means that we may just be furthest along in experiencing who we are not. America is not into oneness; America competes.

What are our highest national values? Well, there are two answers to that. First, there are the values we espouse with words. Then, there are the values we demonstrate through behavior. America stands for individual liberty and treating all people respectfully as equals. That's the rhetoric, but what's the behavior?

Waterboarding.

Waterboarding is torture when anyone else does it but when Americans do it, waterboarding becomes "enhanced interrogation." Changing the wording doesn't make the physical event less cruel.

This is not an argument about whether or not waterboarding works or even if it is morally defensible. We're simply examining the gap between what is said and what is done.

We Americans also give lip service to God. We even mention Him on our money. Sunday after Sunday a million words about God fill churches across the land. OK, so what's our behavior? How about turning the other cheek and loving our enemies? What about loving each other? It seems that we are not quite there yet.

The real God in America is the ego with its values: money, power over others, physical comfort and toys. And, superiority. We're the best!

When you think of America, think of King Kong. An inflated, big chested, busting ego that lords over everything. We are the best, we're the most beautiful, we've got the best of everything and everybody else is lesser. It's like attending Catholic school where the nuns and priests teach that the Catholic religion is the only true religion. We are the only ones who are free from original sin because of baptism. If only we could help the unsaved, if only we could convert them, if only we could make them see how deluded they are.

The mindset in organized religion pervades everything American. Even today, regardless of overwhelming statistics to the contrary in almost every facet of life, we still tell our children that America is the greatest country in the world. If you question that, as we are doing in this book, you can be denounced as a traitor and threatened: "America, love it or leave it." But it's precisely because we love America so much that we stay. And it's why we speak up as Americans always have. Who is the real traitor to truth?

America, as an ideal, is great, in the same way that Christianity practiced as Christ lived is compassionate and all inclusive. All we're doing is noting the difference between what is espoused and what is done.

America, as a place to awaken, is also great. Democracy, however abused, has created safety for dissenters, although even that is eroding in the 21st century. But this is still a wonderful country to awaken in and we are grateful for that. It is not too late for the ideal to become real. But, we must learn from history.

Nothing Learned, Nothing Changed

Apparently Rip Van Winkle learned nothing from his experience. And neither did his neighbors who complained that they wished they too could sleep through the tough times in their lives.

What have we learned as the greatest country in the world has gone into decline? If we consider only the lessons of Vietnam, Iraq, the Great Depression, and the Bail Outs, which leaves out a long list of others, the only thing we seem to learn from history is, as Friedrich Hegel said, "We learn nothing from history."

In his article, *Can You Imagine This Country?* Chuck Baldwin writes: "We hear much today about the American Dream. By 'the American Dream,' most people mean buying a big house, driving an expensive automobile, and making a lot of money. However, this was not the Dream envisioned by the Founding Fathers. Remember that, for the most part, America's founders gave up their material wealth and substance for something they considered of far greater worth. Unfortunately, this hedonistic generation knows little of the kind of sacrificial spirit personified in the lives of America's patriarchs.

"In the minds of the founders, liberty, with all of its intrinsic risks, was more desirable than material prosperity, if that prosperity was accompanied with despotism or collectivism. So strong was their desire that they were willing to give up the latter in order to procure the former for themselves and their posterity.

"How dare Americans today refer to material gain as 'the American Dream.' It is not! It is the freedom to honestly pursue one's goals that should be celebrated. Material gain is only a fruit of freedom, not its root." [2]

It's easy to agree with Baldwin's truthful statement questioning "material gain as the American Dream." But his statement, "It is the freedom to honestly pursue one's goals that should be celebrated" only rallies enthusiasm for better dreaming. Waking up is profoundly different.

Honestly pursuing one's goals is morally better than dishonestly pursuing one's goals, but it's still a pursuit. Chasing happiness is a dream pursuit. It has no place in reality. The whole idea of pursuing what you want/need begins with not already having it. Goals, happiness, success -these will come by catching up with them and our best government would guarantee unobstructed pursuit.

So why not just wake up and enjoy the experience that is already present? That sounds like individual sovereignty! It also sounds insanely unrealistic to those pressured by extreme circumstances. The starving, homeless mother needs food and shelter, not philosophy. What is the solution for her plight and that of the many thousand others? How is their unfortunate condition a reflection of consciousness? Where are the leaders who can guide our generation to that which creates a healthy reflection for all?

The Emperor Has No Clothes

Many of us know the tale told by Hans Christian Andersen about the emperor who had no clothes. Here is how it is described on Wikipedia:

"A vain Emperor who cares for nothing but his appearance and attire hires two tailors who are really swindlers that promise him the finest, best suit of clothes from a fabric invisible to anyone who is unfit for his position or 'just hopelessly stupid.' The Emperor cannot see the cloth himself, but pretends that he can for fear of appearing unfit for his position; his ministers do the same. When the swindlers report that the suit is finished, they mime dressing him and the Emperor then marches in procession before his subjects, who play along with the pretense. Suddenly, a child in the crowd, too young to understand the desirability of keeping up the pretense, blurts out that the Emperor is wearing nothing at all and the cry is taken up by others." [3]

We can learn from this story that the word which leaps to mind is "pretense" and the phenomenon of the double standard. Let's consider the example of torture we previously mentioned. "America does not torture" may be the proud standard but in fact America has tortured and does torture. Some of our political leaders defend waterboarding, for instance, but only when Americans are doing it.

In 1988, The New York Times ran a groundbreaking investigation into U.S. involvement in torture and assassinations in Honduras. Florencio Caballero, an interrogator with Hondura's notoriously brutal Battalion 3-16, told the Times that he and twenty-four of his colleagues were taken to Texas and trained by the CIA. "They taught us psychological methods -to study the fears and weaknesses of a prisoner. Make him stand up, don't let him sleep, keep him naked and isolated, put rats and cockroaches in his cell, give him bad food, serve him dead animals, throw cold water on him, change the temperature." ...Ines Murillo, a twenty-four-year-old prisoner who was "interrogated" by Caballero and his colleagues, told the Times that she was electrocuted so many times that she "screamed and fell down from the shock. The screams just escape you. I smelled smoke and realized I was burning from the singes of the shocks. They said they would torture me until I went mad. I didn't believe them. But then they spread my legs and stuck the wires on my genitals." [4]

And how do we treat our whistleblowers, our truth tellers, those who speak out and expose what's really going on? From *The Village Voice*, "...the incredible story of Adrian Schoolcraft, an NYPD officer in the 81st precinct who after whistleblowing on corruption and under-reporting of serious crimes was, for his trouble, taken in handcuffs to a psychiatric ward, served with administrative charges and suspended without pay for two years, during which time the NYPD was, in fact, sitting on a 95-page report that confirmed his claims.

"... This is a culture. This is happening in every precinct, every transit district, and every police housing service area," said John Eterno, criminologist and former NYPD captain, on the systemic pressure to "make the crime numbers look good." [5]

America is not the bastion of free speech it claims to be. Just ask Officer Adrian Schoolcraft, or the journalists arrested for exercising that right. Or the protestors corralled into "Free Speech Zones."

A Story of Awakening

"It happened while I was escaping down 18 floors in The Oberoi Hotel in Mumbai, India, during the terrorist attack of 2008. As I struggled in the darkness, I realized that this was also the struggle of my life ... through darkness to light! When I got to the ground, I needed to decide which exit door to take. I chose the one that led to the light and the street, rather than the one that opened into the Hotel lobby and the terrorists.

"I got it! Yes, the escape from the 18th floor was my struggle in this life. Walking in darkness and out of nowhere into the light and transformation! Since that

day I truly am different, more loving and less judgmental of myself and others. It was an awakening that the terrorist is not some stranger in the dark. The terrorist, if there is one, is within."

-M. B., Australia

The Synchronicity Socratic Method

A primary American Dream assumption is "We are the best!"

In his blog, *Who Wants to Be a Millionaire,* Matthew Warshauer writes: "... the Dream has become more of an entitlement than something to work towards. Many Americans no longer entertain a vision for the future that includes time, sweat, and ultimate success. Rather, they covet the shortcut to wealth. Many who are engaged in work view it more as a necessary evil until striking it rich. This idea has been perpetuated by a massive marketing effort that legitimizes the message that wealth can be obtained quickly and easily. Whether through the television entertainment industry, state-based lottery marketing drives, or legal advertisements, Americans are told again and again that the road to the financial success of the American Dream is more a matter of luck than hard work." [6]

When in Fear, Go Backwards

How often do we hear exhortations to "get back to the basics," to recover the values of "the good old days?" Garret Epps writes about this in *We the People* (*Utne Reader*):

"Americans today are frightened and disoriented. In the midst of uncertainty, they are turning to the Constitution for tools to deal with crisis. The far right is responding to this demand by feeding their fellow citizens mythology and lies."

If you are to believe the crazed rhetoric from politicos unquestioned by the "mudstream media," rights afforded by the Constitution only apply to American citizens and states are constitutionally prohibited from challenging blatantly illegal federal initiatives such as airport security pat-downs. Epps continues: "The most important truth about the Constitution is that it was written as a set of rules by which living people could solve their own problems, not as a 'dead hand' restricting their options. Strikingly, many important questions, from the nature of the Supreme Court to the composition of the Cabinet, are left to Congress. There's ample evidence in the text that the framers didn't think of themselves as peering into the future and settling all questions; instead, they wrote a document that in essence says "Work it out." [7]

Work it out, what a concept. That echoes how we described the way consciousness works. It creates itself anew nanosecond-by-nanosecond. If you're not on the leading edge of consciousness creating the future of itself, you're not being truthful. You're trapped in the fraud of repetition and habit, the ego-driven agenda for maintaining our supposed safety and security. Belief about the Constitution is a good example. "You can't change the Constitution," some declare. "You can't add to it, take away from it, or change it. It's America's Holy Grail. You can't mess with it." Well, why not? It has some good ideas in it but they need to be updated. It's already been amended anyway. Someone did that back in time. What's stopping us from doing it again now?

Power Over The People

As Gary Zukav wrote in *Spiritual Partnership:* "The military, religion, and commerce are sibling organizations. They are each highly structured, coordinated, and effective pursuits of external power. Only their dogmas, uniforms, and methods differ. All are global, ignore the boundaries of cultures, nations, and individuals, and strive for dominance. They are proactive, competitive, and expansive in nature, obliterating if possible all values except their own and suppressing opposing values if not. Highly homogenous, they do not allow diversity except where necessary and when it serves their objectives. They aggressively impose themselves to the best of their ability.

"They assimilate or eliminate adversaries. Beneath exterior differences lies the same intention -to manipulate and control through force of arms, ideas, or money. No resources are withheld. All weapons are brought to bear continually - cannons, canons, and currency - with the sole goal of dominating nations, cultures, and competitors. Contentment is not a part of military, religious, or commercial organizations. Soldiers train to wage war and impatiently wait for opportunities in times of peace. Priests, monks, and missionaries spread their ideas continually, ceaselessly competing with conflicting ideologies. Commercial success demands ever-expanding market share and endlessly increasing profits for investors.

"All three present themselves in the most appealing way possible while pursuing objectives that are not always appealing." [8]

America and War

Fulfilling our need for more requires money and control. That spells war. America has to be imperialistic and control other countries to protect our financial interests and our privileged lifestyles. War is so often about having power over others and it's increasingly economically driven. To the victor go the spoils.

Consider this famous quote from General George S. Patton: "Magnificent! Compared to war, all other forms of human endeavor shrink to insignificance. God help me, I do love it so!" [9]

In the final analysis, war is madness. Even when our own generals, those closest to the act, spell out the grisly details of what is really happening, America wallows in its stupor of self-deception and refuses to see the truth. Glenn Greenwald reported in The Guardian: "America's former top commander in Afghanistan, General Stanley McChrystal, admitted: 'We've shot an amazing number of people and killed a number and, to my knowledge, none has proven to have been a real threat to the force.'"[10]

We can pretend there are democratic ideals at work in our warring, but we don't even walk that talk at home anymore with our own citizens. What right do we have to impose this on other people convincing them to believe in our failed American Dream? They may want what we have which, seen from the outside, looks appealing. But how many people die every day to maintain the American lifestyle?

War is the ultimate conflict of separation. The formula is if you're separate from Source Intelligence, you will be separate from each other. If you are separate from each other, you will compete and fight. If you compete and fight, most will suffer and a few will profit. Those who profit will perpetuate war because it is good for business.

Racism

Egos operate in one of two ways: superiority (discrimination) or inferiority (slavery). Egos employ judgment to sustain their existence and importance in a fraudulent position of identity. If the ego didn't establish itself as "you" (separate and different from others and judging them), it would have no identity. The ego doesn't want that. It doesn't want to be a tool, it wants to be in charge. It is dead set against you coming to know the truth of oneness because there would be no room for it. It would need to assume it's proper position as your servant, not your master.

The ego has no interest in this because it sees your identity as its death. The ego's only interest is in maintaining separation, because that's its life. Based on this illusion of separation, of superiority and inferiority experienced inside the individual, it's inevitable that "masters and slaves" would appear as reflections in our society. Distinctions become emphasized between races, religions, classes and sports teams. Everything is ego-driven, based in separation. Another aspect of it is racism, which remains alive and well in this country and will be until we awaken from the American Dream.

Home is Where the Debt Is

Long a symbol of American cultural supremacy in the world, home ownership is now a crisis in the U.S. "Home values have declined an astounding 6.3 trillion dollars since the housing crisis first began. According to a recent census report, 13% of all homes in the United States are currently sitting empty. The housing crisis just seems to keep on getting worse. And 31 percent of the homeowners that responded to a recent Rasmussen Reports survey indicated that they are 'underwater' on their mortgages. Unfortunately, it looks like millions more middle class Americans could soon be in danger of losing their homes. According to the Mortgage Bankers Association, at least 8 million Americans are at least one month behind on their mortgage payments at this point."[11]

Who really owns your home?

Move to Denmark

As Richard Wilkinson suggested in a recent TED talk, if you want to live the American Dream and have greater control over your own likelihood of success, then you should probably move to Denmark.

"The Times recently reported on a well-established finding that still surprises many Americans when they hear about it: although we still see ourselves as a land of opportunity, we actually have less inter-generational economic mobility than other advanced nations. That is, the chances that someone born into a low income family will end up with a high income or vice versa, are significantly lower here than in Canada or Europe." [12]

Then there's the bridges. And the water lines and highways. Schools, prisons ... oh, wait, prisons are doing great, having been outsourced and turned into for-profit ventures enabling them to aim toward becoming as profitable as our health-care system.

What's Happened to the Country we Love?

Matt Sledge blogged: "If the struggle to fix America's infrastructure problem were a movie, it would be less Michael Bay than Woody Allen: not a lot of action, but also not much in the way of mass fatalities. Since 2005, there haven't been any more terrifying bridge collapses. Instead, the United States has failed to innovate and failed to maintain key pillars of its infrastructure. Our country is rapidly losing its edge.

"Washington Gov. Chris Gregoire (D), who has visited Shanghai and other parts of China as part of her efforts to develop her state's economy, told HuffPost 'we see our infrastructure deteriorating and becoming inadequate in comparison to those we're in competition with.'

"'That construction that we see going on in China?' she said. 'That used to be us, that used to be us doing all that investment.'" [13]

Now we outsource. We don't build that much in America any more because the wages are too high. American companies now pay the citizens of other countries to make our stuff. The New York Times reported, "'We've known about labor abuses in some factories for four years, and they're still going on,'" said one former Apple executive who, like others, spoke on the condition of anonymity because of confidentiality agreements. Why? Because the system works for us. Suppliers would change everything tomorrow if Apple told them they didn't have another choice. 'If half of iPhones were malfunctioning, do you think Apple would let it go on for four years?' the executive asked." [14]

Selfish, Blind and Uncaring

The prevailing American Dream Machine mindset is, "What's best for us? It doesn't matter how many people die for our cause. We will get what we want, what we need. We will ensure the maintenance of our American Dream identity and be ruthless imperialists if necessary in doing it. We'll screw anybody, kill anybody, twist anybody's arm, torture anybody, and do anything we must to sustain our position. Because we believe we are right. Because we believe that we are the greatest country on the Earth. God bless America."

But what about those perceived as getting in our way? What about the welfare of those millions of people in some country on the other side of the world who we attack? They suffer and die. Is there no value to their lives?

Not really, apparently. Many of our leaders place more value in money, power, control and authority. Keep the oil flowing, no matter what. Of course, if we truly valued life we would take care of our own citizens to ensure that everybody had a basic quality of life. For instance, we would provide affordable health care like other civilized countries do, rather than propping up other nations.

Why do we give Israel billions of dollars in foreign aid every year when our own citizens are starving, sleeping on the streets or living out of their automobiles or in tents? We point at poverty in developing countries but what about our own poor? That's different, in fact, it barely warrants a whisper in the news. It's not something we want to see in our media, not when we could be watching games and celebrity wardrobe malfunctions. Not only do we not care for our own citizens, we kill them. Only 10 percent of countries in the world, 20 out of 198, carried out executions last year. We were one of those 20.

According to Amnesty International, "The United States was again the only country in the Americas and the only member of the G8 group of leading economies to execute prisoners - 43 in 2011. Europe and former Soviet Union countries were capital punishment-free, apart from Belarus where two people were executed. The Pacific was death penalty-free except for five death sentences in Papua New Guinea." [15]

The hard truth we are awakening to is that ultimately the American Dream is a death dream. It brings death to others and to ourselves. It just doesn't seem like murder because it happens more slowly.

It's said that until the pain of the present exceeds the pain of the past, we won't create a better future. We've been numb to the pain of our present, to what America has become and how it is bullying the rest of the world. We point our fingers at foreigners but America is considered by many to be the most feared terrorist nation in the world based on our track record abroad and on international polls. We overturn democratically elected governments all to maintain our King Kong position on top of "Ego Mountain."

An Awake Perspective

In a 2012 commentary from Jesse Jackson, he writes, "Across America, cities and counties are cutting muscle, not fat. Teachers and police are being laid off. Parks are closing. Sewer and road repairs are being put off. And brutal battles are beginning with public workers, forced to pay for a crisis they did not create.

"America is a rich nation, but our wealth is now too concentrated among the few. As in Iraq, we squander trillions in foolish wars of choice abroad. The wealthiest Americans pay lower tax rates than their secretaries.

"These should not be controversial statements. We can't simply tell a young generation that the American Dream is a nightmare for them. We can't have a prosperous economy if the middle class is sinking. We will not long be a democracy if the wealthiest pocket the rewards and check out of building the nation." [16]

A truthful statement for America is, "the country will always be an accurate reflection of the consciousness of its citizens."

America the Beautiful

America is what it is, covering the spectrum from light to dark. Whether it is in fact "the land of the free" depends on the choices individual Americans make. What makes this country great is not the promise of the American Dream, it's the reality of people helping each other, growing beyond prejudice and ignorance, awakening to the authentic reality of oneness beyond nationalism.

If Americans have believed in this country's exceptionalism, let us be exceptional in demonstrating a waking up. That takes humility, acknowledging where we are - deluded! - and then the courage to question, to dismantle our delusions and assemble truthful experiences. The great transformation is underway, from egoic competition to trans-egoic cooperation. While politicians argue over entitlements, corporations amass excess at the expense of balance, and youth revolt at the debt-ridden, climate-challenged future bestowed on them, the quiet heartbeat of the awakening impulse strengthens in all people.

Some hear it, feel it and awaken. Is that your experience? Are you awake to that?

If you're not awake, what do you do? You invest in illusory stories about the country, positive or negative, and then that's the America you experience. You will flavor your "reality" with your own fraudulent fantasies. And what you've been reading in this book will likely anger you.

If you're awake and truthful, you stay true to the essence of all possibility that is available to you in any moment and you celebrate this country as the land of opportunity within which you can consciously create your experience. Who are you choosing to be? What experience are you choosing to create? You can create a truthful experience, a love-based experience, a life-affirmative experience and then America can become "America the beautiful" for you. But it is you who is responsible for your creation. It's not a divine right, or something you inherit by being an American citizen.

It takes courage to awaken to your identity beyond being an American and to become an authentic, conscious soul. That's the most patriotic contribution any American citizen can make.

Our Socratic Conclusion

The American Dream is a deeply entrenched national illusion that reaches far beyond our borders to infect citizens of many other countries. Facing the truth, and experiencing disillusionment, is usually painful. That takes courage. Then comes hope for something new and truthful.

1. America carries the seeds of greatness, not in aspirations or policies but in human hearts.
2. America is only exceptional in the way that every country is exceptional.
3. Individual Americans have the opportunity to personally embody and exemplify the qualities we proudly espouse as "American."

An enlightening question to ponder is, "How can I be an authentic individual, an authentic American citizen and contribute to the emergence of America as an evolved country that empowers evolutionary change?"

A Moment of Mastery

I am filled with gratitude
as I awaken in this great country.
I accept my responsibility
to be a true citizen of love,
an ambassador of peace,
an agent of awakening.

Chapter Twenty-three: The Power of Being

*"Now, at this unique point in human history, you come
along, with millions of others, able and ready to
awaken into a state of consciousness that was formerly
achievable only by those rare and elite ones who were
ahead of their time.
This is not because we are wiser than those who came
before, but because we were born at a time of
evolutionary change on planet Earth that is calling
forth our dormant potential en masse for the first time
in human history."* [1]

- Barbara Marx Hubbard

The power of being flows from Source Intelligence, which is
constantly animating consciousness. The awakening impulse is
like a heartbeat, pumping inspiration through the veins of
humanity. Together, we are arising to a new world of
cooperation and unconditional love. Individually, we are
choosing who we will be in relationship to every moment's
challenge and opportunity to grow, and to express those
qualities that will reflect back to us as a more harmonious world.

At this point in our discovery we are completing Part
Two which has focused on disrupting our American Dream
programming, and we are opening into Part Three which
unfolds the details of awake living. This naturally ushers us
into the domain of leadership through action in the world,
which is why it's important to emphasize the power of being.
Egoic consciousness is determined to fix things and to make
the world a better place, but without changing consciousness.
By awakening, we understand the primary need for connection
with Source Intelligence, and to let our actions be coordinated

from a level beyond our well-intentioned, yet often counterproductive ego minds.

Your next step in this awakening adventure is to temporarily let go of any specific concerns you might have relating to the topics we covered in the last twelve chapters. What would we do about education, the media, religion, etc? All of us could come up with good ideas, create "to do" lists and begin enrolling others in our initiatives. But there is enough of that already in the world. Our leadership is of a different kind. Leading from Source Intelligence, we emanate the power of being, and this has a profoundly positive influence on our world.

So, let's reflect briefly on the twelve topics from Part Two and consider how consciousness might shift appropriately in relationship to each.

1. **Lifestyle:** Give up the pursuit of happiness. Grow your experience of happiness from within.
2. **Education:** Choose to be a "giver." Learn and teach through your experience of inner fulfillment, "doing" through the power of being with no strings attached.
3. **Addictions:** Feed your soul by honoring the awakening impulse as it expands self-awareness, along with nourishing through the equilibrium of meditation.
4. **The Economy:** Be generous. Diversify your portfolio by acknowledging the wealth you have beyond money.
5. **Marriage:** Be Source Intelligence-centered. Help each other grow.
6. **Health:** Transcend the ego fear of mortality and embrace your immortality.
7. **The Environment:** Live with balance. Manage your personal resources according to long-term values that contribute toward an evolved future.

8. **Politics:** Be the change you wish to see in the world. Lead by evolving your inner world to create a different outer reflection.

9. **Media:** Receive wisdom from Source Intelligence and broadcast your authentic self.

10. **Religion/Spirituality:** Let go of your dependence on any "middleman" and celebrate your oneness with God.

11. **Technology:** Include technology and biology together and open to the possibility of becoming a Human 2.0.

12. **America:** Awaken from the American Dream. Then champion the possibility of this country becoming a truthful model of integrity in word and deed.

Find Your Inner Socrates

Throughout these chapters of Part Two we employed our Synchronicity Socratic process to question assumptions and shatter illusions. We disrupted our programming, our enculturation and convictions, all in the name of awakening to the truth. And the truth as we discovered time and time again was often fundamentally opposite to the American Dream promises.

You can continue this dialogue with yourself and expose illusions as they arise in your personal experience. Have the courage to constantly question, knowing that the most powerful question in the world is, "If I weren't doing this already, would I choose to do it?" You can ask this about everything. It will remind you that you do have a choice. In every moment you are free to choose who you will be in relationship to your situation.

Finally, seek to become profoundly inclusive. Allow everyone his experience rather than imposing your good intentions upon them. No one likes to be "should" upon! Inclusion is also the first of three steps in a simple formula for honoring the awakening impulse. This might be a useful guide, especially in moments of challenge.

1. **Inclusion** — Welcome all that is - as it is - and everyone - as they are - without judgment.
2. **Choose** — Who will you be in relation to what is happening?
3. **Insights** — How does your awareness expand with insights that can lead to enlightened, compassionate actions?

Right On Schedule

All dreamers are awakening in their own time. Everyone is on schedule. Truth will eventually dismantle all illusion and everything connected to illusion will dissolve, like sand flying away when the wind picks up.

We are awakening from the American Dream which has become a nightmare. We have a choice about how rapidly we awaken. Consciousness dreams the dream. Consciousness becomes aware of dreaming the dream and begins to awaken. Or, consciousness can re-invest itself in the dream.

Why have we been dreaming? Because it was necessary. We had to experience what doesn't work before we could awaken and create what does work. Dreaming is appropriate or it wouldn't be happening. It is simply the happening of consciousness. If we say, the "American Dream should be other than it is," we have missed the fundamental point of this book and that is a dream is a dream, it is not and can never be reality. Let it be. Wake up. Focus on creating "now" having dismantled illusion. Grow.

Long time activist Grace Lee Boggs, quoted in a CommonDreams.org blog, expressed this artfully: "'We need to grow our souls. We need to find that balance of life that respects each other, that thinks that the most important thing at this time on the clock of the world is not our accumulation of things, is not economic growth which threatens and imperils all life on this planet including ourselves, that the time has come to grow our souls, to grow our relationships with one another, to create families that are loving and communities that are loving, to bring the neighbor back into the hood' ... her 'secret to visionary organizing' is a 'combination of philosophy and activism." [2]

> **Bring the neighbor back into the hood.**

We Are the One The World Has Been Waiting For

Upon feeling the urge now to contribute, first relax into the power of being. Feel what happens as you read these words, as you relax and breathe into the perfection of being out of which perfect actions arise.

Next, we let go of the ego's manic fears because they disrupt our connection with the present and motivate reckless actions. These fears prevent the unfolding of Source Intelligence in its full presence. In each moment we notice where we are and what's happening. Instead of wondering what to do, we remind ourselves about who we are choosing to be.

Imagine sitting in your car with the engine on. Instead of stepping on the gas and moving forward, try turning your wheels so you are pointing in the right direction. Have you ever tried moving the steering wheel while your car was stationary? It's hard work. But the minute you start moving, power steering eases the steering wheel to travel in a new direction.

Likewise, it's hard work to figure out what to do first to save the world! Where to point? Don't worry about it, just get moving. There are always simple kindnesses to offer, small acts of generosity to perform. No stage is too small.

Once you have started, in any direction, it's easy to course-correct. But you need your compass, your continued orientation in Source Intelligence. Daily meditation is the most fundamentally helpful practice to strengthen that connection. Out of the stillness that you experience during daily meditation will grow your increasing experience of the abundance of spirit. This will dispel the ego fears that fester in the graveyard of your own dying dreams. You will stop pursuing happiness, you will embrace the happiness you are and you will share it with others, assisting them to continue awakening.

> *"I believe that generosity is a natural instinct that beats, however faintly, in every human heart. Those of us who act on our hunger for justice, who get creative with our righteous anger, who connect and comfort with our empathy, are very fortunate indeed. Generosity links us, beyond time and place, to people of conscience and action everywhere who have made our world freer, kinder, and more just. Philanthropy and activism are a gift to one's self. By giving, we lessen our own cynicism and alienation."* [3]

- Chuck Collins and Pam Rogers with Joan P. Garner

A Moment of Mastery

I am enough.
I am loved.
I am needed.

PART THREE

Chapter Twenty-four: Welcome to a New World

In this very moment, remain wakeful with me, relaxed in holistic awareness, enjoying this new world.

This world is here and now. Being wakeful, we are innately aware of something remarkable. Both polarities of our experience are the same consciousness: the outside and the inside, the exterior and the interior. The objective world around us and the subjective world within us are of the same consciousness. And, as we remain focused with our awareness in the here and now moment, we create the balance that allows our holistic awareness to continue expanding.

Wakefulness increases. We become and experience the witnessing consciousness that is always watching both polarities as the same consciousness. In this wakeful holistic experience, we are blissful. Our innate joy of being is magnified, and we experience the truth in this very moment. We are happy for no reason. We are one consciousness delighting in itself.

This is the awakened state of being that all great masters and sages have exemplified and delineated as "the bliss of freedom." It is our birthright as authentic human beings, holistically aware of our essence and the essence of all and everything as the same one blissful consciousness.

The modern sage Adyashanti wrote poetically of this phenomenon we are experiencing:

"The maturing of awakening is this profound return to our essence, to the simplicity of what we are, which is before and beyond being and nonbeing. It is before and beyond existing and

257

not existing. It is where there is a disappearance, as it were, where our minds are no longer fixating on any level of experience.

"Our minds are not fixating on any particular expression. The tendency to fixate has been liberated. This state is not a mystical state. It is not a state of immensity or a state of specialness. It is a state of naturalness and ease. On the human level, it is experienced as deep ease and deep naturalness and deep simplicity.

"On another level, it is the undeniable sense that whatever the journey has been, there is a certain sense of finality. As one old Zen master said, it's like a job well done. At the end of the day, you just go home. At a certain point in one's spiritual life, it is as if everything is spontaneously put down. This is hard to understand until it actually starts to happen to you. Spirituality itself is put down. Freedom is put down. It's necessary for us to be free of our need for freedom, to be enlightened from our need for enlightenment." [1]

Being Must Come First

This is it, here and now, the experience of post awakening where wholeness increases exponentially. Now, with sufficient unification of consciousness, the actual experience of the universal whole begins to enfold the individual. This means that transformation in the individual becomes simultaneous with transformation in the collective and explains the meaning of the epic declaration attributed to Gandhi: "Be the change you wish to see in the world." He didn't say "create," he didn't talk about taking action yet, he said "be." We can understand now what's required for this simple strategy to have significant power. "Be the change you wish to see in the world."

You may have already acknowledged that you are responsible for your own transformation and now you understand just how this makes a simultaneous contribution to the world around you. It is your increased personal amplitude of power that renders this true and effective. As an isolated individual, largely disconnected from universal Source Intelligence, you had minimal power and likewise your contribution remained minimal. Now, as wholeness increases, so does your power.

This has always been so for every human being. What makes individual contribution effective is the state of being, the energy field, individual merged with universal. Of course, this represents a reality fundamentally different from doing something to make a contribution, even with the best of intentions. This illuminates why being must come first.

A New Era of Spiritual Activism

Traditionally, a yogi withdrew from the world, lived in his cave and pursued enlightenment. This was entirely personal. He had minimal involvement with the material world. His or her commitment was to their personal process. "The world is illusion, forget it, just maximize your own enlightened state of being, liberate your soul, keep your focus on that." Such masters were special, unique, they stood out amongst the general population.

While their journeys remain true, consciousness has also evolved over the years so that we've come to a broader understanding of the possibilities for personal mastery. The master's message today is, "We are all God, all is God."

This marks a powerful evolutionary distinction. Masters don't just live in caves and wander around barefoot! Increasing numbers of individuals living in cities and employed in gainful work have risen to a level of holistic truth and know that "I am God, I am Consciousness. I am consciousness on the leading edge in uncharted territory! I am driving the evolution of consciousness." Those of you who have begun to experience this know the beginnings of true mastery. Before, that status seemed reserved for the select few and the rest of us, at best, followed them. This involved reaching out to an external representative of God, experienced as separate and known only in theory. Now, for increasing numbers of individuals, there is a reaching out from the experience of oneness as God, as an experienced reality of being a modern master to whatever degree.

This is a true contribution, living on the leading edge of evolving consciousness, transforming personally and simultaneously contributing to transformation within the whole. But the promise of this concept only becomes real because of your actual experience of wholeness. This is not an intellectual enlightenment that comes just because you believe you comprehend what certain words mean. This is actual, holistic experience moment by moment by moment of every day.

Commitment

This is also not commitment to a cause. This is commitment to the primary intention in consciousness is to evolve. This is commitment to go where consciousness has not gone before. Your commitment at this level is not egocentric, it's trans-egocentric or post awakening. You recognize that consciousness is orchestrating the show and you are but an instrument. Consciousness is the song and you are the singer. What kind of song will you choose to sing?

Imagine that you are singing your song of consciousness on the leading edge of the evolving experience of itself. What will that song sound like? You don't know yet and nobody knows because it will be the pure, creative impulse of evolving consciousness. "It" doesn't even know yet and won't until the moment where universal and individual meet.

It's in this interaction between universal and individuation where consciousness creates itself newly in each nano-second. In truth, you really have no idea at all what the next nano-second will bring. You may think you do, based on all your history which means that you probably try to extend that past into the next moment. Yet this is how illusion created by a separate "self" becomes the deluded assumptions we spoke of and helped unravel throughout the last chapters. We want no more delusion! No, here, post awakening, consciousness is creating itself newly in the moment, unlimited by but respectful of history.

Our familiar question, "Who am I choosing to be?" takes on new meaning. Our commitment at this point is to being, not doing.

Awe

Human-induced urgency is egocentric and looking out into the world through egocentric eyes there is much to feel urgent about! On this basis, our needs can seem overwhelming. Where would you start to save the world? Transcend the ego. In the trans-egocentric state your starting point is not how much needs to be fixed. But rather the starting point is the experience of the union of individual and universal consciousness and that produces a state of awe!

Awe arises from the surprising, delightful recognition that you are an instrument driving the leading edge of evolutionary consciousness. From that position of being, your responsibility is to remain truthful, to remain self-aware, holistically self-aware, and then to express this in your own unique ways. How will you know what to do? Only by knowing who to be. What affects you as an individual simultaneously affects the collective. This is how you make a difference in the world.

"Who am I choosing to be? I'm choosing to be consciousness at the leading edge of its own evolution and to enjoy whatever experience consciousness creates."

It has taken us 14 billion years from the moment of the original creative impulse, The Big Bang, to evolve to this level of self-awareness where we are still relatively limited and primitive. As a Sufi friend says, "God is slow, really slow."

Yet, it's also very exciting because we just don't know how consciousness is evolving next. How will evolving consciousness increase self-awareness to shape all the expressions of itself? How will it continue changing individuals, the collective and the world we inhabit? What new systems will appear? What wonders and tragedies will we experience in our lifetimes? Aren't you excited to find out, not as a spectator but as a co-creator? This is the true meaning of "awesome!"

Peace

Know you can trust that what you need to "do" in any instant will be revealed in the precise moment of being when the doing is needed. That creates peace. Peace is an outcome of the being and doing process. Imagine real and lasting peace within yourself. The end of war. Relaxation, no unhealthy stress and no false urgency.

Miraculously, amidst the insanity of this world, you can experience real peace. It can be that you are at peace with yourself, at peace with others and at peace with the world around you. Does this sound like you might then be in position to make a worthwhile contribution? This is what doing-that-arises-out-of-being looks like. It's the opposite of "the end justifies the means" thinking. No, the end is determined by the means. This is and will always be the only way that peace can come to our world. "Be the change you wish to see in the world."

A song by Tom Lehrer, a satirist from the 60's, was called "National Brotherhood Week" and he introduced it with something like this: "I'm sure we all agree that we ought to love one another and I know there are people in the world who do not love their fellow human beings and I hate people like that". [2] The hypocrisy is sadly comical. It's the same principle as "fighting for peace." No, we bring peace, we are peacemakers because of our holistic state of being, not because of our doing.

The Process of Evolving Transformation

People get confused and disappointed in their experience of evolving transformation because although the awakening experience is huge in contrast to "normal" life, dramatic epiphanies rarely repeat themselves with thrilling regularity! Following some particular dramatic awakening moment, the natural tendency is to assume that the rest of the journey is going to be the same way. Awakening can be fast and dramatic. It can be a life-changing transformation. But then once post-awakening begins, a new kind of stability establishes itself and the process continues to evolve.

It's slow. It moves at an incremental pace. Awakening consciousness is a window, revealing the whole picture, giving you a glimpse of where you are going. But then everything contracts back to where your feet are, albeit at a new level, and the journey continues. You got a preview of coming attractions, the trailer for the movie, and now you've got to undertake the whole journey and watch the whole movie. The post-awakening evolutionary cycle must continue to unfold. It is an ongoing process, not a lightning bolt of illumination! Or, you could say that every moment is a potentially, incrementally, enlightening one with no final destination in sight!

Perfect Timing

We don't find many examples of great masters moving through the post-awakening process to full constancy of holistic experience in less than twelve years. Even Master Muktananda, who was prolific in terms of his awakening, took nine years. And that's fast. He was considered really adept. So what's your hurry?

In the East they have long understood how the energy of awakening flares to intensity then recedes to become a steady flame, burning through all your dimensions. It clears away old illusory data and evolves you progressively and incrementally through the various necessary stages. Post-awakening seems to progress in three-year increments: three years, six years, nine years, twelve years, etc. Remember, we've been at this for 14 billion years! There's only impatience when the ego is in charge, the temporary ego that feels the pressure to get everything done before its own looming demise!

In the trans-egoic state there is no such anxiety. There's something systematic about things, as increasing primordial energy burns through your body in three waves. First, energy expands from the base vortex to the heart. Next, from the heart to the third eye. Finally comes awakening from the third eye to the crown.

These are the three levels of full awakening and they activate according to your personal schedule. Some of you are awakening at the initial level and journeying to the heart. Others are awakening in the heart and journeying to the third eye. Some may be journeying from the third eye toward the crown. But this is not a horse race! All is appropriate. The timing is perfect for all of us right where our feet are.

Stages of Wakeful Experience - The Three Samadhis

The ancient Vedic holistic model of reality delineates three distinct holistic states of unified consciousness. The first is savikalpa Samadhi in which there are thoughts during your meditation but you are aware that those thoughts are valid forms of consciousness. That is, you have holistically included them. The second is called nirvikalpa Samadhi. Here you have included formless consciousness and you experience emptiness and nothingness within a holistic, unified awareness. The third is sahaja Samadhi in which you simultaneously experience both formlessness and form, subjective and objective, in harmonious awareness as the same consciousness.

This progression tracks through your evolving meditative experience. Daily meditation is something you will be doing as an awake being, not because you think you should, but because you are compelled to. The sage Milarepa wrote about how awareness expands to understand the relative values of inner and outer and about why meditation becomes so compellingly appealing. "All worldly pursuits have but one unavoidable and inevitable end, which is sorrow; acquisitions end in dispersion; buildings, in destruction; meetings, in separation; births, in death. Knowing this, one should from the very first renounce acquisition and heaping-up, and building and meeting, and... set about realizing the Truth. Life is short and the time of death is uncertain. So apply yourselves to meditation." [3]

2012: An Awakening

Consciousness is eternal. It's not much concerned about the egocentric perspective on time.

2012 was not "the end" of anything. 2012 was an awakening. 2012 was a new beginning. What follows 2012 is another cycle of 26,000 years. Not understanding this, people popularized 2012 into some kind of one-time event. No, it was simply a change of epochal ages, the end of one 26,000-year cycle and the beginning of the next marked by a quantum leap in terms of the evolution of self-awareness. It was not some kind of "one-off." It was another beginning.

Egos always want big, final leaps. We find this throughout human history. At the egocentric level, there are always doomsday scenarios. God is going to come, the Second Coming, Judgment Day. Egocentric humans want to be proven right. They are invested in some particular ideology of God and must validate it. How can they prove that their ideology is the only right one? Wouldn't it be something if "God" did come down and say "See, these people were right. They were right, these ones over here, and all the rest of you were wrong. Not only are they better than you, they are the only chosen ones!" Who would God be championing? The Catholics, the Jews, the Muslims, the Hindus, the Buddhists?

The whole scenario is 100% egocentric and competitive. And whether it's religious or material, competition is competition. "My God is better than your God." This was carried into 2012 by New Agers who crave validation of their way: "See, we were right. All you in organized religions were wrong. We're better than you."

Love and the Divine Feminine

A great confusion in Western organized religions is their myopic recognition of just one polarity. When it comes to God, this is the masculine polarity. The Western Abrahamic religions have created a paternal God, but this is not a truthful understanding of relative reality and the nature of life itself. You don't just have male forms in a species. You have males and females.

This limited experience has generated paternal dominance and a society where men are the leaders, are paid more than women, and male births have more value. God, as father, supposedly champions strictly paternal values. This is a grand egocentric delusion creating virtual realities that don't exist except for those creating them. In the truth of relative reality, there are two polarities, masculine and feminine. The masculine is the subjective positive polarity and it comprises formless consciousness. The feminine is the objective negative polarity manifesting as formed consciousness.

Creation emerges out of formless being and becomes the great manifest of consciousness. This represents the divine as both masculine and feminine, being and becoming, formlessness and formed. You find this in the ancient religions where they refer to archetypes in consciousness. There is the Father Archetype, the divine masculine, and then the Mother Archetype, the divine feminine. They are relative to each other and interactive. You can't have one without the other.

Creation is the dominance of the feminine polarity and we call it Mother Nature. Where have you ever heard the term Father Nature? It's Mother Nature, the mother principle. If you go back thousands of years to ancient and time-honored traditions you will find that creation is represented as the Divine Mother, the Creatrix, the great becoming of being, the play of consciousness, which includes all forms including the human form. So, when we get down to the physical level of manifestation, all form is the dominance of the divine feminine. This means that we are all divine mothers running around, whether we are masculine or feminine in gender. It makes no difference. We are all forms of consciousness, the feminine default dominant polarity in consciousness.

Now absorb this revelation about yourself and all selves. Surrender gender identification, even concepts about your "soul." You are awake, tender soul. Welcoming these words with an understanding that baffles your ego-mind. They come to life as you read them. Flowing from the page through your eyes to your heart in this moment of awake revelation, the suddenly familiar bliss of expanded self-awareness!

Oh, living flame of love,
how tenderly you penetrate
the deepest core of my being!
Finish what you began.
Tear the veil from this sweet encounter.

Oh, gentle fiery blade!
Oh, beautiful wound!
You soothe me with your blazing caress.
You pay off all my old debts,
and offer me a taste of the eternal.
In slaying me you transform death into life.

Oh, flaming lantern!
You illuminate the darkest pockets of my soul.

Where once I wallowed in bitter separation
now, with exquisite intensity,
I radiate warmth and light to my Beloved.

How peacefully, how lovingly
you awaken my heart,
that secret place where you alone dwell within me!
Your breath on my face is delicious,
calming and galvanizing at once.
How delicately, how lucidly
you make me crazy with love for you! [4]

- *Living Flame of Love* from St. John of the Cross,
translated by Mirabai Starr

A Moment of Mastery

The power of being
sustains my life.
I am awake and ready
for the opportunity of each moment,
eager and excited,
to continue awakening
forever.

Chapter Twenty-five: Awake Action

"Insanity is doing the same thing and expecting different results." [1]

- Albert Einstein

This new world with its new understanding empowers awakened action. Our deep contemplation of meaning has illuminated what it is to be "practical." Ignorant "doers" call for action: "Don't just stand there, do something," they cry. Some assure us the end justifies the means. Even fighting for peace. On this basis then the goal of peace justifies torture and war.

The insanity Einstein points to, doing the same thing and expecting a different result, indicates a dazed state of denial, which prohibits learning from past happenings. As Bishop Desmond Tutu and others have said, "We learn from history that we don't learn from history". [2]

Why did the brutal lessons of World War One, called "the war to end all wars," teach us nothing that could prevent World War Two? Why did the futility, falsehoods and unequivocal failure of the Vietnam War teach us nothing that could prevent the march into Afghanistan and Iraq? Over and over again, both on the national and international scenes and in our personal lives, we witness how the abject failure to achieve a desired "end" continues to justify the use of the same means that produced those failures. We try again and again and we fail again and again.

Don't Just Do Something, Stand There

Awake, we act from a new world of Source Intelligence, beyond allegiance to blind ego prejudices. We exhibit the courage to question and challenge and learn. Action is not our first step. We understand now that the end will inevitably be a reflection of the means so we begin by examining our methods and clarifying our state of consciousness. We choose now what we want later. Peace now, peace later.

Together we have navigated twelve areas of life and dared to question many assumptions about them. We have discovered truthful statements to take their place. Now, in the twilight of our explorations, which heralds the sunrise of our service, we revisit those statements to fine-tune our intention for awake action.

We started our exposure to the failed American Dream by analyzing the American lifestyle and educational system that have been perpetuating it. We acknowledged that without the guidance of evolved educators, addictions seduce us into illusory pursuits, obscuring the primary value of our connection with Source Intelligence. We explored how money can substitute for spirit. We examined marriage and how attaching ourselves to a partner can become a further distraction. Intoxicated by the promise of another to complete us, by denying our individual sovereignty we can sabotage our health. We revealed the sanctity of our global environment can be violated by trusted leaders who sell us out, and the world, to corporate interests.

We exposed how the mainstream media, we termed it "mudstream media," hides the everyday truth from us. And how religious leaders obscure the great truth of Oneness, instead positioning themselves as indispensible middlemen between humanity and the divine.

We came to understand why ego-minds would fear technology, but how we can embrace it without fear, confident that our species has embarked on a positive transformational journey from which there is no turning back. Having adventured this far, we feel changed, experiencing the beginnings of Humanity 2.0 and, yes, a new America awakened from the dream of exceptionalism. As individual dreamers, we awaken to the genuine experience of humble, real, authentic being. We have seen the one dependable answer to all questions, "I know nothing."

Lifestyle

You are free to give up your pursuit of happiness and choose happiness now. You can model a self-sufficiency that creates a truly successful life from the inside out.

Limited circumstances, genetic deficiencies, childhood enculturation and abuse, adult trauma, everything has its affect but nothing is an excuse for refusing to awaken. You have choice in any moment. That is your birthright and you choose from exactly where your feet are, now. "Here and now, in this moment, I appreciate my life experience as it is and I choose awake action, knowing that the means will reflect in the end."

Education

Follow your bliss.

Learn how to follow your own unique path, find your specialization and increase your wakefulness. Expanding self-awareness is the real education and what it means to be human. Explore how momentum of your evolving history is driving your life experience. This is where your fulfillment arises in wakeful explorations ever more consciously aware of yourself as a co-creator on the leading edge of consciousness. "I am discovering who I am and letting truthful awareness guide my actions."

Addictions

Become blissfully addicted to expanding awareness.

Discover and inhabit a place where you can truthfully say: "I am totally focused on the truth of who I am and what life is and in the fullness of my experience of it. This is my addiction, this has become my sole (soul) focus. I now understand who I am and what life is. I understand that my very nature is blissful. The more aware I am moment by moment, nano-second by nano-second, the more pleasure, the more joy, the more bliss, the more fulfillment there will be in my experience.

Being aware is my dominant focus, my all-consuming focus, the ultimate, radical, ongoing fulfillment of myself as a form of consciousness on the leading edge creating the future of now. I surrender all that does not serve my growth and embrace all that expands the self-awareness of my oneness with Source Intelligence."

The Economy

Invest in expanding self-awareness and diversify your portfolio, acknowledging that money and material content is a small component in the spectrum of your holistic wealth.

Acknowledge that everyone in America can grow their unique experience of success and wealth through their choices, regardless of their starting point, as long as they are willing to begin right where their feet are. "I give and receive freely, enjoying the circular flow of abundance."

Wholeness is the true wealth sustaining an experience of the sacred essence of life rather than being seduced by the content of it.

Marriage

Your authentic marriage is sacred, a holy union of masculine and feminine, regardless of your gender. You complete yourselves together in Source Intelligence as the seeming two become the truthful one. "I release my illusory attachment to my partner. We commune together in spiritual interdependence."

Health

Health is wholeness. Your conscious awareness of immortality as a soul living in a mortal human form allows compassion to arise naturally. This compels you to care for your human vessel with love and intelligence. You tend to your body, mind, and heart with a nutritious diet, daily exercise, and a constant preference for healthy thoughts and emotions. "I choose healthy living, balancing my inner state of being and my outer state of doing."

The Environment

Your awakened state brings the experience of oneness, interconnectedness and inter-relatedness. No tree is separate from you. True environmentalism is about oneness, living in harmony with your surroundings because you understand that everything is just a different form of yourself. As you care for your environment, you are caring for yourself. "I embrace my environment without separation from myself."

Politics

True leadership emerges from the inside out. You have a renewed hope for politics because you witness demonstrations of integrity in certain elected officials.

You understand that we get the leadership we deserve so you begin with yourself, selflessly serving your "constituency," your immediate environment populated by family and friends. You have elected yourself. Having elected yourself by your choices, you provide a new model of leadership based on personal integrity, guiding your own life with the compass of unflinching truth. "I am the holistic leader I have been waiting for."

Media

Mainstream media gives people what they are choosing. You choose to expand your self-awareness by selecting "news" that serves your ongoing awakening.

You acknowledge that you are a broadcasting station and you dedicate your personal media system to receiving from Source Intelligence. You express appropriately, overcoming ego-mind programming with the inspiration of authentic being. "I remain wakeful and honest in my thinking, speaking, feeling and acting."

Religion

You are one with God. You need no middlemen. You do not worship any other, living or dead. You respect and love the masters of awakening who have guided humanity away from darkness toward light. "I am one with Source Intelligence."

You speak truthfully, the words that one of them spoke in representation of all: "I and my Father are One." [3] And, "... the works that I do shall he do also; and greater works than these shall he do." [4]

Technology

"As consciousness, I create myself newly in each moment." You embrace technology as an integral aspect of consciousness and use technology to enhance balance, wholeness, truthful perception and your ongoing wakefulness. You do not fear a future in which Artificial Intelligence enslaves or eradicates humanity. You welcome the merging of technology and biology as inevitable and appropriate. You understand that the singularity is both a present moment experience of awareness being born and a future moment when, as author Kevin Kelly predicted, "all change in the last million years will be superseded by the change in the next five minutes." [5]

America Today

You are awake in America in the 21st century. This provides you with an amazing leadership opportunity for awake action, emerging from the inside out to model spiritual activism. As you and millions of other Americans assume the mantle of this responsibility, this country begins to provide a new, noble, honorable example in the world.

The End is the Beginning

We have focused an awake perspective on the twelve areas of American life that we placed under our Socratic microscope. Previously, questioning came before acting but now the time to act has come and we begin, not with doing but with being.

Keeping Quiet

And now we will count to twelve
and we will all keep still.

For once on the face of the earth
let's not speak in any language,
let's stop for one second,
and not move our arms so much.

It would be an exotic moment
without rush, without engines,
we would all be together
in a sudden strangeness.

Fisherman in the cold sea
would not harm whales
and the man gathering salt
would not look at his hurt hands.

Those who prepare green wars,
wars with gas, wars with fire,
victory with no survivors,
would put on clean clothes
and walk about with their brothers
in the shade, doing nothing.

What I want should not be confused
with total inactivity.
Life is what it is about,
I want no truck with death.

If we were not so single-minded
about keeping our lives moving,
and for once could do nothing,
perhaps a huge silence
might interrupt this sadness
of never understanding ourselves
and of threatening ourselves with death.

Perhaps the earth can teach us
as when everything seems dead
and later proves to be alive.
Now I'll count up to twelve,
and you keep quiet and I will go.

by Pablo Neruda. (trans. Alastair Reid.) [6]

A Moment of Mastery

I am awake.
I am happy.
I am alive to the opportunities
in all areas of my life
to birth a new experience
of empowered mastery.

Chapter Twenty-six: The Awakened Leader

*"Foolish, ignorant people indulge in careless lives,
whereas a clever man guards his attention as his most
prized possession."* [1]

- the Buddha

What are the qualities of awakened leaders? We know they never rush into action. Instead, they start with being and work on both the inner and the outer, seeking balance in all moments and a constantly expanding connection with Source Intelligence. They make choices with their attention, and their attention becomes their intention.

Without changes in consciousness, unawakened actions wreak havoc, regardless of intention. What is the awake alternative to acting? Enlightened inaction.

Inaction, the way we are using the word, means stillness. Stillness is connection with Source Intelligence. Connection with Source Intelligence brings inspiration and revelation. These in turn birth action, a very different kind of action born out of inaction.

An Awake Checklist for Inspired Leadership

A pilot wouldn't dream of taking off without consulting his check list. Over time with hours of flight time, this becomes almost automatic. But he still uses it rather than depending solely on his experience, knowledge and intuition. As a newly awakened leader you are a rookie "pilot." Here's your checklist.

1. Make the Connection

Source Intelligence guidance must be online. Feel the humility of being in oneness. As the Christ himself declared, "the words that I speak unto you I speak not of myself: but the Father that dwelleth in me, he doeth the works." [2] And, growing out of that, "The Father and I are one." [3]

2. Let Go

Your residual programming will continue to suggest ways of thinking, patterns of belief and courses of action. Pause to acknowledge the programs, have the courage to question them and when necessary to let them go. The empty space that replaces old illusory knowledge is a fertile womb to birth new understanding.

3. Expand Awareness

Breathe. Enjoy. Experience the expansion of your awareness. Acknowledge your growth. You cannot create newness without becoming new yourself. Newness is available in each moment.

4. Challenge Beliefs

Ask the most transformational question: "If I weren't doing this right now (also, if I weren't thinking this, believing this, sure of this, etc.), would I choose to? Contemplate not looking for an answer but experiencing how the question sits within you and what it evokes.

5. Invite Wisdom

Notice what shows up in that womb space of consciousness. Without demand or impatience, open to revelation, realization, insights and ideas.

6. Act in Faith

Confidence built on a foundation of oneness with Source Intelligence allows you to focus your intention and then act. You act with full confidence knowing that this cycle will continue to repeat itself. Your investment is in the means, not the end. So the end will reveal the means.

7. Welcome Feedback

Your action will generate results. The results will reflect and reveal the content of your attention and intention, showing a mixture of what you knew about yourself and what you didn't. Feedback allows you to adjust course, learn and grow.

The awakened leader is not primarily concerned with results. His focus is on learning. Others may praise the results and an awakened leader learns to be gracious in accepting praise, but he or she knows the secret that they are acting in obedience to the awakening impulse within consciousness. Their actions are truly inevitable.

Awakened Consideration

The awakened leader is the servant leader, imposing nothing. Otherwise, there is nothing but ego-demands for change according to personal prejudice. American foreign policy has tended to do exactly this as noted in this piece from commondreams.org:

"An incisive look by writer Teju Cole at *Invisible Children/Kony2012,* white privilege, American sentimentality and the arrogant sense of 'a world (that) is nothing but a problem to be solved by enthusiasm' - a view that supports brutal policies in the morning, founds charities in the afternoon and receives awards in the evening.' First, do no harm, he urges; then, expose 'the money-driven villainy at the heart of American foreign policy.'

"'There is the idea that those who are being helped ought to be consulted over the matters that concern them … If we are going to interfere in the lives of others, a little due diligence is a minimum requirement.'" [4]

What you do to the smallest degree, you do to everyone. The awakened leader models consideration of others, empowering the awakened holistic experience in those being led. Leading and teaching means always standing for the principles of balance, wholeness and resultant fulfillment because you know that those you lead are not going to be fulfilled unless they too are balanced and whole.

This is the operating context from which the awakened leader lives. Holding it as your highest value, inspiring others to live that highest value and acknowledging them when they do is true leadership.

If you have integrity, you're going to maintain that truth in everything you say and do. You will have the courage to question everything and everyone to serve ongoing awakening.

You will invite those you lead to question. Never mind if they question you! Based on that shared honesty, you can experience awakening together.

The Awakened Leader Learns From Results

Awakened leaders learn. Whether an action is well-intended or not is less important than the results achieved. Awakened leaders aren't afraid to acknowledge when a strategy fails to achieve its intention.

Likewise, the Awakened leader doesn't leap-frog over the results he or she achieves in the most personal aspects of their lives. Their spiritual activism embraces everything, from the very small to the very large, and every moment - regardless of seeming size and significance — becomes the one and best opportunity to contribute.

This is what separates egoic leaders from trans-egoic leaders. "What can I do to make things better?" becomes "Who do I choose to be in relationship to this circumstance?" The fate of our world rests in the hands and hearts of awakened leaders.

A Moment of Mastery

Faith
arises from my experience
of innate happiness.
I choose to live wide-awake
and lead with being.

Chapter Twenty-seven:
The Awakened Learner

"How can you squander even one more day not taking advantage of the greatest shifts of our generation? How dare you settle for less when the world has made it so easy for you to be remarkable?" [1]

- Seth Godin

Socrates, considered by many to be the wisest of the wise, declared that he knew nothing. In fact, his profound humility was his greatest strength. It was the reason he won every debate against the learned, who were proud of all they knew. When Socrates said that he knew nothing, he didn't mean that he was stupid or unlearned. He meant that he was able to let go of what he knew in favor of what he was learning in the moment.

We employed our Synchronicity Socratic Process throughout Part Two of this book, examining twelve central areas of life in America. This was disruptive to your programming and the assumptions you and others may have held. You "knew" something about these topics. To the degree that you were able to let go of what you thought you knew, in favor of what you were discovering in the moments of reading, you were experiencing the wisdom of Socrates.

Awakened leaders never stop learning. They are awakened learners. They learn in every moment, in every circumstance, no matter what they are doing or who they are with. They place no limitations on their learning because they have consciously chosen to learn no matter what. Another word for learning is "discovering," which evokes images of explorers. In fact, discovery is what true learning is. As children, almost all of us were taught by our parents and teachers to accept a dysfunctional definition of learning that is the polar opposite of discovery.

Learning, as it is customarily experienced, relates to acquiring knowledge that others have. You read books, you listen to lectures, you absorb and memorize and then apparently you are said to have learned. But what have you learned are dead concepts. Discovery, on the other hand, may refer to what is known as a foundation. However discovery proceeds from the unknown, rather than being exclusively concerned with the known.

The awakened learner is an explorer, pushing off from the shore of the known and sailing into the unknown, moment by moment. Like explorers of old, the awakened learner experiences the associated full range of emotions: sorrow for leaving the familiar, fear of what lies ahead, eager anticipation to find out and the thrill of living on the edge of discovery.

As an awakened learner your primary attitude about yourself is that you have not arrived and never will. There is always a further shore. You are often at sea, somewhere between the familiar and the unknown, but not exactly sure where. This may cause you some concern, you might even feel anxious and impatient and afraid. You understand that this is part of the life of the explorer, natural in the experience of an awakened learner. So you do not wish it to be different than it is.

As an awakened learner you can truthfully say, "My life will never be the same." Life will never be the same as it was before you acknowledged yourself, accepted yourself and began to live your life as an awakened learner. Also, life will never be the same one moment to the next. When Einstein spoke about insanity, describing it as doing the same thing over and over and expecting a different result, he wasn't just commenting on the obvious - that to achieve a different result you need to do something different. He was also referencing the lunacy of considering that it's even possible to do the same thing over and over again. It's only the same to the unaware dreamer. Lost in the dream, circumstances seem to repeat themselves. For instance you get up every morning and put on your clothes, you greet your family, you drive to work, etc.

This is not the life of the awakened learner. Each moment, regardless of its content, is the vessel for a new spirit. The planets have moved, millions of your cells have died and been replenished, nothing anywhere in creation - vast or minuscule - is in fact the same. This you can readily see through your new eyes, the eyes of the awakened learner.

Like Socrates, you know nothing and you discover everything.

Life will never be the same.

A Moment of Mastery

I know nothing.
I discover everything.
My wisdom is not my own.
I learn that I am loved and needed
for who I am.

Chapter Twenty-eight: Wake Up, Be Happy

"If you believe you can change — if you make it a habit
— the change becomes real.
This is the real power of habit: the insight that your
habits are what you choose them to be.
Once that choice occurs — and becomes automatic —
it's not only real, it starts to seem inevitable, the thing
... that bears "us irresistibly toward our destiny,
whatever the latter may be." [1]

- Charles Duhigg

Our journey of discovery is not ending but this book is. We have traveled from dreaming through awakening to being awake, from the darkness of illusion to the sunrise of reality, from the arrogance of knowing to the humility of learning. You have traveled from chronically ingrained self-judgments to a place where you can truthfully say: "I am enough, I am loved, I am needed, I am awake and I am happy."

The Five Primary Statements of Awakened Experience

Part One of this book focused on the dreaming state and our intention was to assist readers to experience "I am enough." The reason is obvious: you have to accept your starting point to travel elsewhere. We made no judgments about dreamers. All of us still dream because awakening is an ongoing experience. There's always more to awaken to, more to learn and discover. But, it makes a difference to know that in the midst of that process, you are enough.

In Part Two we focused on awakening. Our intention was to disrupt old programming, personal and national, to challenge assumptions about your life in America and to come to know the truth specific to twelve primary areas of life. The opportunity as you read was to become liberated from the prison of concept into the experience of love. To feel loved.

Feeling loved is the partner of feeling needed. Awakening, you begin to experience the balance of masculine and feminine within yourself, as being and doing *woo and marry* in a divine union. You are loved, and you are needed.

Finally, in Part Three, we have focused on the awake experience and articulated what this means in day-to-day living. Our intention has been to formalize a peer experience inviting you to honor yourself as a graduate of this transformative journey. Yes, it will take more than reading this book to make it all real in your life! Though this is the path before you now.

Respecting the cyclical nature of life itself, we now conclude where we began with our simple invitation, hopefully now somewhat expanded from an idea you are reading about to an experience you are having: "Wake up and be happy!"

We invite you now to read this last section, embracing the truth of these five statements as your experience to whatever degree it's real, knowing that you will be tested in your life to deepen your understanding and integration of them.

I Am Enough

You understand that "you" are more than your human body with its mind and emotions. You are an eternal soul flowing with the spirit of life which is simultaneously individual and universal. You are enough. In fact, you can never be more or less than you innately are. Like all of us, you have human limitations and a divine design. Both are 100% appropriate. This is not a permission slip for laziness relative to your continued evolution! But rather an acknowledgment that you live in the paradox of being enough on the one hand (divine), and eager for more growth on the other (human). This brings you peace.

I Am Loved

You understand that love is not merely an emotion. You are loved, not for anything you do but because you exist as love within the wholeness of love that permeates all creation. As long as your heart is beating, you are loved. Nothing is demanded of you in return for this love. The more you accept, experience and express your authentic self as love, the more love you will effortlessly receive and give. This brings you joy.

I Am Needed

There are good reasons that you are here on earth at this moment in time. Perhaps you will discover a great mission for your life, but that is entirely unnecessary because your life is your mission. You are needed here, to be here, regardless of what you do. There is no other being in the entirety of universal creation remotely similar to you. You complete us. This brings you confidence.

I Am Awake

You are awake to the truth that you know nothing. Being awake, you automatically lead by example needing no position or public acknowledgment. Your leadership emanates from your presence, never imposing on others but always inviting them to awaken with you. You know that being awake is always the beginning. Each day holds adventures to discover, and challenges from which to learn.This brings you excitement.

I Am Happy

Happiness is your essential nature. There is nothing you need to get in order to be happy. Understanding this truth, you enjoy everything you have and don't have. You place no demands upon yourself, others or circumstances to make you happy. You are happy, you bring happiness and happiness increases in your presence.

Happiness is more than a feeling. You've grown to understand it's possible to be happy at the same time that you are sad, angry, disappointed, etc. You never make unrealistic demands of yourself, for instance that you must always feel happiness or contentment. The human species is undergoing fundamental transformation and in that process there is plenty of disruption. This impacts you just as much as it impacts every other member of our human family. It will disturb your equilibrium, producing feelings and experiences that at times may seem far distant from pedestrian concepts about happiness.

But now you know that you are happy. You are happy! Your happiness is so all-encompassing that you are able to feel anything within it. This brings you faith.

> **Happiness is more than a feeling, and being awake is always the beginning.**

It's a Book, It's a Campaign, It's a Movement

As this writing took shape, we realized that it was much more than a book. It has become a type of "instruction manual" for the movement of conscious awakening already happening in this country and beyond. We certainly didn't invent the phenomena of awakening! Our modest contribution flows into a moving stream of what others have pioneered. We are contributing to the ongoing evolution of human consciousness that liberates us all.

In America we celebrate Independence Day on July 4th. Independence, as it is customarily envisioned, is a limited concept that excludes our responsibility to each other.

Politicians may debate independence and entitlements but the truth of our experience together may be simply expressed in the word "interdependence."

To acknowledge this new paradigm we are re-envisioning our traditional American celebration of Independence Day, which is powerfully nationalistic. We visualize an evolved version, which is more inclusive: Interdependence Day. July 4, 2014 will be the first annual Interdependence Day. You may be reading this book before or after that date. Regardless, this will continue as an annual celebration for anyone who learns of our work and resonates with it. We hope that many will choose to participate and grow this new celebration.

So, happy Interdependence Day! We celebrate with you our community of friends, united in universal love regardless of our differences. As awakened leaders we now have the delightful responsibility to "walk our talk." We must demonstrate what it means to be interdependent, appreciating each other and ourselves for being enough, loved, needed, awake and happy.

A Moment of Mastery

I wake up.
I am happy.

Epilogue –January 1, 2014

Evolution has accelerated so dramatically in the 21st century that the moment something is written, the "current affairs" aspect is immediately out of date. Our response is to update that material regularly. In addition, because we value the perspectives of our readers, we plan to include reader comments on the challenges raised in this text in next editions.

Please email awakening@synchronicity.org. We will contact you for permission if we wish to use what you send us in the updated digital versions that follow. You will receive these free of charge if you have registered on-line and given us your email address. If you haven't, you can do that now at www.synchronicity.org/awakening.

A Viral Illusion

On March 17, 2013 Chinese President Xi Jinping delivered his first address to The National People's Congress of China and his central theme was The Chinese Dream. He said that the purpose of The Chinese Dream is "to make the country affluent and strong, the nation prosperous, and the people happy. This deeply embodies the ideals of the Chinese people today, and deeply reflects our ancestors' glorious tradition of persistent struggle in pursuit of progress." [1]

So, China joins America with its own official dream. It is different in one fundamental way – their Dream puts country before individuals – but identical in principle (pursuing happiness). Note the President's wording: "... our ancestors' glorious tradition of persistent struggle ..." What a glorious tradition indeed – persistent struggle! Just like America.

Of course, this illusion is global and while we have referred to the American Dream, it's endemic to the modern human condition itself. We've used these pages to reveal this truth, and also to give you tools for awakening. Now, in conclusion, we present brief comments from Peter Kingsley's book *Reality*. We do so because he articulates an important historical perspective that describes how the dream came to be.

Throughout Kingsley's 700-page journey, he details the ways that ancient wisdom has been manipulated and distorted, resulting in this dreaming world created by a fragmented mind disconnected from Source. He refers to the Greek philosopher Parmenides, who was Socrates' primary source of inspiration, and he exposes the distortion of Socrates' work perpetrated by Plato and then Aristotle.

"Parmenides' teaching had been that logic is something divine, a gift from the gods. Plato took logic and put it in everyone's hands: he encouraged people to think and argue for themselves.

"It was a tremendous achievement. It required all sorts of distortions, falsifications, obscurations – which his successor, Aristotle, was soon pursuing to perfection." [2]

Kingsley is explaining what happened centuries ago to change our fundamental understanding of "logic," and hence, intelligence.

"He (Plato) had given people something wonderful to play with. And soon it was obvious to almost anyone that the way to get to the truth in those ideas was not through entering some other state of consciousness but through thinking. As one historian has described his achievement, in terms that are accurate enough, Plato was the man who 'by a truly creative act transposed these ideas definitively from the plane of revelation to the plane of rational argument.'" [3]

It's ironic that what Kingsley refers to as "rational argument" should beat the drum of something so undeniably irrational as

The American Dream! Humans may boast they are rational animals; it would be more accurate to say, "rationalizing!"

"In all those years our minds have allowed us to do great things. We can build bridges and fly, heal and kill ourselves in thousands of new ways. As for reality, though, and the soul, and all those questions that Plato insisted mattered most: we have got absolutely nowhere. We have plenty of theories, endless discussions of problems about problems about problems. But the simple fact is that through our minds we have not managed to understand one single thing.

"And the time for thinking and for reasoning is over now. They have served their purpose. You have kept us busy, allowed our minds to grow, carried us a little way further on the route towards greater individuality and self-consciousness. The problem is that we still know nothing.

"It's no longer enough to read what Plato or others say and be inspired, intellectually stimulated, emotionally touched, stirred by a longing for reality. The time for all that searching and struggling is past, finished. The reality is here, in the middle of the illusion; has been all along, longing to be recognized. Now we need to become that reality, take responsibility for it, make it real again." [4]

This is what fully awakening from The American Dream accomplishes. We stand, awake, together, having become the reality that eluded us in thought, experiencing the happiness that escaped our pursuit, and being the leaders that our communities, this country, this world, and – most importantly – we ourselves, most desperately need.

You have discovered that you are more than you thought you were. Now is the moment to actualize it, to truly be the change we all wish to see. Grand as it may seem, it all happens now, here, in this eternally awakening moment.

There is no other way.

AUTHOR BIOS

Master Charles Cannon

Master Charles Cannon is a modern spiritual teacher. He was given the title of Master by his teacher to denote that he is a Master Spiritual Teacher or one who can teach without words. Master Spiritual Teachers are recognized by their palpable presence, their holistic state of being, which effortlessly empowers everyone in their proximity.

He is a pioneer in the evolution of human consciousness and founded Synchronicity Foundation for Modern Spirituality in 1983. He developed High-Tech Meditation and the Holistic Lifestyle which have helped transform the lives of millions worldwide.

His previous book, Forgiving the Unforgivable, chronicles the true story of his experience surviving the 2008 Mumbai terrorist attack, along with 23 associates who had accompanied him to India on spiritual pilgrimage. Rescued by Indian SWAT teams, they compassionately forgave their attackers.

Master Charles is respected world-wide for his modern spiritual perspective on social issues and the compassionate spotlight he shines on individual responsibility for awakening to the truth of being human as the ultimate answer for the challenges that face humanity.

The non-profit Synchronicity Foundation for Modern Spirituality which includes the School for Modern Spirituality and Modern Spirituality TV can be explored at www.Synchronicity.org.

Will Wilkinson

Will Wilkinson wrote his first novel at age 14. Since then, he has authored primarily non-fiction books, collaborating with many wisdom keepers to help present their work in user-friendly terms. He has also written and delivered dozens of personal growth courses, provided professional coaching for public speakers and entrepreneurs, and hosted inspirational television interview series.

Every endeavor has been focused on illuminating the human condition and empowering individuals to evolve into the fullness of who they already are in essence. Samples of his work can be found at www.imagifi.com.

Endnotes

Introduction

1. Popular colloquialism based on quotes from Henry David Thoreau (Walden) and Oliver Wendell Holmes (The Voiceless).

2. Michael Snyder, "The American Dream", Alex Jones' Infowars.com, June 26, 2012, http://www.infowars.com/22-statistics-that-prove-that-the-american-dream-is-being-systematically-destroyed/

3. George Carlin, comedy routine, "Time Lists: Top 10 George Carlin Quotes," Time.com, http://www.time.com/time/specials/packages/article/0,28804,1858074_1858085_1858083,00.html

4. Abraham Lincoln as quoted by Roy P. Basler, Editor, "Annual Message to Congress," The Collected Works of Abraham Lincoln, Vol. 5 (New Brunswick, N.J., Rutgers University Press, 1953)

5. Martin Luther King, Jr.'s "I Have a Dream" Speech, March on Washington, DC, August 28, 1963, Historic Documents, http://www.ushistory.org/documents/I-Have-a-dream.htm

Chapter One

1. Robert Holden, Be Happy (Hay House, 2010) 63.

Chapter Two

1. Hunter S. Thompson, as quoted in Rosemarie Jarski, Words from the Wise (Skyhorse Publishing, 2007) 29.

Chapter Three

1. Joseph Campbell, "Jump," Reflections on the Art of Living, (New York, Harper Perennial, First Paperback Printing edition, May 12, 1995), 525.

2. Sarah Ban Breathnach, Simple Abundance: A Daybook of Comfort and Joy (New York, Grand Central Publishing, Reissue edition September 9, 2009) 15.

Chapter Four

1. Carl Jung, as quoted in Wikiquote, http://en.wikiquote.org/wiki/Carl_Jung

2. Neale Donald Walsch, The New Revelations: A Conversation with God (New York, Atria Books, 2004) 67.

3. Lao Tsu as quoted in Dan Millman, The Four Purposes of Life: Finding Meaning and Direction in a Changing World, New York, HJ Kramer/New World Library, First Edition, 2011) 23.

4. Dan Wieden, creator of Nike, Inc., slogan quoted in Wikipedia, http://en.wikipedia.org/wiki/Nike,_Inc.

Chapter Five

1. Socrates

2. Gertrude Steinem, as quoted in Wisdom Quotes/ Gertrude Steinem, http://www.wisdomquotes.com/authors/gloria-steinem/

Chapter Six

(none)

PART ONE

Chapter Seven

1. The Dalai Lama as quoted by David Schimke, "Editor's Note," Utne Reader, July-August 2011, http://www.utnereader.com/Politics/Death-Osama-Bin-Laden-Dalai-Lama-David-Schimke.aspx

Chapter Eight

1. John E. Nestler, "The American Dream," The Freeman, October 1, 1973 http://www.fee.org/the_freeman/detail/the-american-dream/#axzz2HogbLsMN

2. James Truslow Adams, The Epic of America (New York, Blue Ribbon Books 1931).

3. U.S. Congress, Declaration of Independence (Archives of U.S. Government from July 4, 1776), http://www.archives.gov/exhibits/charters/declaration_transcript.html

4. Ibid.

5. Ted Ownby, American Dreams in Mississippi: Consumers, Poverty, and Culture 1830-1998 (University of North Carolina Press, 1999) reported in http://en.wikipedia.org/wiki/American_Dream#cite_note-22

Chapter Nine

1. Barbara Ehrenreich, Nickel and Dimed (Picador, 10 Anniversary edition, 2011) 226.

2. Friedrich Nietzsche as quoted in Nietzsche.thefreelibrary.com, http://nietzsche.thefreelibrary.com/

3. Ed Diener as quoted by Chris Clevenger, "Psychologists Now Know What Makes People Happy", behappy101.com,

captured 8/6/2012, http://www.behappy101.com/happiness-explained-usatoday.html

4. John Michael Greer, "Collapse Now And Avoid The Rush", The Archdruid Report, June 6, 2012, http://thearchdruidreport.blogspot.com/2012/06/collapse-now-and-avoid-rush.html

5. Michael Ford, "Five Myths about The American Dream", Washington Post Outlook, January 6, 2012, http://www.washingtonpost.com/opinions/five-myths-about-the-american-dream/2011/11/10/gIQAP4t0eP_story_1.html

6. Ibid.

PART TWO

Chapter Ten

1. Lao Tzu, as quoted by Robert Holden, Shift Happens! (Hay House, 2011), 196.

2. Brothers Grimm, "Sleeping Beauty" as attributed in Wikipedia, http://en.wikipedia.org/wiki/Sleeping_Beauty

3. James William Elliott, "National Nursery Rhymes and Nursery Songs" as first recorded version of a colloquial riddle in 1870, Wikipedia, http://en.wikipedia.org/wiki/Humpty_Dumpty

4. Patton, General George S., captured October 4, 2013, as quoted in http://rightwingnews.com/quotes/rwns-favorite-george-s-patton-quotes-2/

Chapter Eleven

1. Joseph Campbell, Reflections on the Art of Living: A Joseph Campbell Companion (Harper Perennial; First Paperback Printing edition, 1995) 26.

2. Lisa Mastny, "Consumerism, Values, and What Really Matters: An Interview with Tim Kasser", The Center for a New American Dream, July 29, 2011. http://www.newdream.org/results/2011-07-kasser-consumerism-values-and-what-really-matters.

3. Jason DeParle, "Harder for Americans to Rise from Lower Rungs," New York Times, January 4, 2012, http://www.nytimes.com/2012/01/05/us/harder-for-americans-to-rise-from-lower-rungs.html?pagewanted=all.

4. Markus Jäntti, Bernt Bratsberg, Knut Røed Oddbjørn Raaum, Robin Naylor Eva Österbacka, Anders Björklund ,Tor Eriksson, "American Exceptionalism in a New Light: A Comparison of Intergenerational Earnings Mobility in the Nordic Countries, the United Kingdom and the United States," D I S C U S S I O N P A P E R S E R I E S, IZA DP No. 1938, Forschungsinstitut zur Zukunft der Arbeit Institute for the Study of Labor, January 2006, http://ftp.iza.org/dp1938.pdf

5. David Cay Johnson, "9 Things The Rich Don't Want You To Know About Taxes," Willamette Week, April 13, 2011, http://wweek.com/portland/article17359_things_the_rich_d ont_want_you_to_know_about_taxes.html

6. Michael Snyder, "36 Statistics Which Prove That The American Dream Is Turning Into An Absolute Nightmare For The Middle Class," The American Dream, May 2, 2011, http://endoftheamericandream.com/archives/36-statistics-which-prove-that-the-american-dream-is-turning-into-an-absolute-nightmare-for-the-middle-class.

7. Adyashanti, The End of Your World, (Sounds True, 2010) 37.

8. Dalai Lama, "Beyond Religion: The Dalai Lama's Secular Ethics," Huffington Post, 12/20/2011, http://www. huffingtonpost.com/2011/12/02/beyond-religion-dalai-lam_n_1125892.html

9. David Gershon, Social Change 2.0: a Blueprint for Reinventing Our World (High Point/Chelsea Green, 2009) 155.

Chapter Twelve

1. Oliver Wendell Holmes as quoted in Quotations Page, captured March 8, 2013, http://www.quotationspage.com/ quote/26186.html

2. John Atcheson, "Dark Ages Redux: American Politics and the End of the Enlightenment", Common Dreams, June 18, 2012, https://www.commondreams.org/view/2012/06/18-2

3. Terri Meredith, "Outsourcing Jobs and The American Dream", New York Times – The Opinion Pages, captured December 13, 2012, http://terimeredith.hubpages.com/hub/ Outsourcing-The-American-Dream

4. Bill Gates, "Shaming Teachers Will Not Work", The New York Times, February 23, 2012, http://www. nytimes.com/2012/02/23/opinion/for-teachers-shame-is-no-solution.html?_r=1&

5. Albert Einstein, quote from Wikiquote-Albert Einstein, http://en.wikiquote.org/wiki/Albert_Einstein

6. Elizabeth Gilbert, "Your Elusive Creative Genius", TED Presentation, February 2009, http://www.ted.com/talks/ elizabeth_gilbert_on_genius.html

7. Dr. Scott Barry Kaufman and Dr. Zach Hambrick, "Geniuses Are Born, Not Made?" Huffington Post, March 14, 2012, http://www.huffingtonpost.com/2012/03/13/geniuses-born-or-made_n_1342487.html

8. Robert A. Johnson and Jerry Ruhl, Living Your Unlived Life (Tarcher, 2009)

9. Common Dreams, "Students Protest Debt as Student Loan Debt Collectors Make a Billion", Common Dreams, March 26, 2012, https://www.commondreams.org/headline/2012/03/26-5

10. Wikipedia-Waldorf Schools, "1995 Survey of U.S. Waldorf Schools," Wikipedia, http://en.wikipedia.org/wiki/Studies_of_Waldorf_education

11. Wikipedia-Waldorf Education, Wikipedia, http://en.wikipedia.org/wiki/Waldorf_education#cite_note-Easton-5

12. Christine Ranck and Christopher Lee Nutter, Ignite the Genius Within (New York, Dutton, 2009) 167.

Chapter Thirteen

1. Charles Duhigg, The Power of Habit (New York, Random House, 2012), 50.

2. Ryan Grim, This Is Your Country on Drugs: The Secret History of Getting High in America (Wiley; 1 edition, 2010) 173.

3. Carl Jung as quoted by Igor I. Sikorsky in AA's Godparents: Three Early Influences on Alcoholics Anonymous and Its Foundation: Carl Jung, Emmet Fox, Jack Alexander (Compcare Publications, 1990).

4. Dr. Bob Minor, "When Religion is an Addiction, The Fairness Project," The Fairness Project, February 2, 2005, http://www.fairnessproject.org/Religious_Addiction.html

5. Cindy Shadel, "The Year in Good Sex/Bad Sex", Huffington Post, December 2012.

6. Dr. Tian Dayton Clinical Psychologist and author of "Money Addiction," Huffington Post, June 28, 2009, http://www.huffingtonpost.com/dr-tian-dayton/money-addiction_b_221937.html

Chapter Fourteen

1. Gordon Gekko, fictional character in movie as quoted from Wall Street, Twentieth Century Fox Film Corporation, 1987, IMDB, http://www.imdb.com/title/tt0094291/quotes

2. Gordon Gekko, fictional character in movie as quoted from Wall Street: Money Never Sleeps, Edward R. Pressman Film, 2010, IMDB, http://www.imdb.com/title/tt1027718/quotes

3. M. K. Gandhi, "Non-Violence – The Greatest Force," 1926 quoted in Norma Klein, The Shock Doctrine (1st edition, Picador, 2008) 161.

4. Michael Moore, Capitalism: A Love Story (Overture Films, Paramount Vantage, Weinstein Company 2010), 127 minutes.

5. Salvatore Babones and Christopher Chase-Dunn, Global Social Change: Historical and Comparative Perspectives, Johns Hopkins University Press, 2006.

6. Heinrich Theodor Böll, quoted in "A Joke and A Story," gselevator, December 12, 2012, http://gselevator.wordpress.com/2012/12/12/a-joke-and-a-story-or-a-story-and-joke/

7. Paul Zane Pilzer, God Wants You to Be Rich (Touchstone, 2007).

8. Peter S. Goodman, "At World Economic Forum, Fear of Global Contagion Dominates", Huffington Post, January 28, 2012, http://www.huffingtonpost.com/peter-s-goodman/world-economic-forum-global-financial-crisis-davos_b_1239074.html

9. Mitt Romney, "Mitt Romney: Questions About Wall Street, Income Inequality Are Driven By 'Envy'", Huffington Post, January 11, 2012, http://www.huffingtonpost.com/2012/01/11/mitt-romney-envy-south-carolina-primary_n_1200454.html

10. Peter Coy, "American Families are Poorer than in 1989," Bloomberg Business News, June 12, 2012, http://www.businessweek.com/articles/2012-06-12/american-families-are-poorer-than-in-1989

11. Matt Taibbi, Tabbiblog, January 13, 2012, Rollingstone.com, http://www.rollingstone.com/politics/blogs/taibblog/everything-you-need-to-know-about-wall-street-in-one-brief-tale-20120113

12. Jonathan Zap, "Foxes and Reptiles: Psychopathy and the Financial Meltdown", Reality Sandwich, captured December 16, 2012, http://www.realitysandwich.com/psychopathy_financial_meltdown

13. Kamran Mofid, Jamshid Damooei and Steve Szeghi, "The World is Revolting Against the US Economic and Business Model: A Call to Action," Global Policy Forum, November 7, 2011, http://www.globalpolicy.org/social-and-economic-policy/the-world-economic-crisis/general-analysis-2/51003-the-world-is-revolting-against-the-us-economic-and-business-model-a-call-to-action.html

14. Matt Taibbi, Griftopia, Spiegel & Grau (September 6, 2011) 70.

15. David Korten, "Is America in Decline? 24 Statistics About The United States Economy That Are Almost Too

Embarrassing To Admit", The Economic Collapse, http://theeconomiccollapseblog.com/archives/is-america-in-decline-24-statistics-about-the-united-states-economy-that-are-almost-too-embarrassing-to-admit

16. Ibid.

Chapter Fifteen

1. Sammy Cahn, Jimmy Van Heusen, (for lyrics and music), Love and Marriage, song first recorded by Frank Sinatra on Capital Records, 1955.

2. Jerome Kern and Johnny Mercer, composers of Two Hearts are Better Than One, song recorded by Frank Sinatra in 1946.

3. Gary Zukav, Spiritual Partnership, (HarperOne, 2010), 8.

4. Jerry McGuire, fictional character played by Tom Cruise in Jerry McGuire, released by TriStar Pictures, 139 minutes, http://en.wikipedia.org/wiki/Jerry_Maguire

5. Gary Zukav, Spiritual Partnership, (HarperOne, 2010) 110.

6. Rodney Dangerfield as quoted in "Quotes from Rodney Dangerfield", Famous Funny Quote, http://famousfunnyquote.blogspot.com/2009/07/quotes-from-rodney-dangerfield.html

Chapter Sixteen

1. Dr. Carol Paris, as quoted in "Single Payer Doctor Carol Paris Packs It Up by Russell Mokhiber", Common Dreams, April 7, 2012, https://www.commondreams.org/headline/2012/04/07-1

2. King James Bible (Cambridge Ed.), Psalm 127:1, http://kingjbible.com/psalms/127.htm

3. Michael Snyder, "29 Amazing Stats Which Prove That The Rich Are Getting Richer And The Poor Are Getting Poorer", The American Dream.com, http://endoftheamericandream.com/archives/29-amazing-stats-which-prove-that-the-rich-are-getting-richer-and-the-poor-are-getting-poorer

4. David Leonhardt, "Why Doctors So Often Get It Wrong," New York Times, February 22, 2006, http://www.nytimes.com/2006/02/22/business/22leonhardt.html?_r=0

5. Marlo Thomas, "What You Don't Know About Cancer – Hope on the Horizon", Huffington Post, April 29, 2012, http://www.huffingtonpost.com/marlo-thomas/hope-in-cancer-research_b_1441357.html

6. Manohar Aich, as quoted in "On Conquering Grinding Poverty And Living A Long Life" by Manik Banerjee, Huffington Post: The Good News, March 18, 2012

7. Michael Snyder, "36 Statistics Which Prove That The American Dream Is Turning Into An Absolute Nightmare For The Middle Class," The American Dream, May 2, 2011, http://endoftheamericandream.com/archives/36-statistics-which-prove-that-the-american-dream-is-turning-into-an-absolute-nightmare-for-the-middle-class.

8. Russell Mokhiber, "Single Payer Doctor Carol Paris Packs It Up," Common Dreams, April 7, 2012, https://www.commondreams.org/headline/2012/04/07-1

9. Maia Szalavitz, "What Does a 400% Increase in Antidepressant Use Really Mean?" Time.com, Health & Family, Oct. 20, 2011, http://healthland.time.com/2011/10/20/what-does-a-400-increase-in-antidepressant-prescribing-really-mean/

10. Thomas Moore, Care of the Soul, (Harper Perennial, Reprint Edition, 1994) 145-46.

Chapter Seventeen

1. Frances Moore Lappe, EcoMind: Changing the Way We Think, to Create the World We Want (Nation Books; First Edition, September 13, 2011) 14.

2. Scott Huler, quoted in Kate Sheppard, "North Carolina Wishes Away Climate Change", Mother Jones, June 1, 2012, http://www.motherjones.com/blue-marble/2012/05/north-carolina-wishes-away-climate-change

3. Arun Gandhi, as quoted in "Arun Gandhi Shares the Mahatma's Message" by Michel W. Potts, India -West (San Leandro, California, Vol. XXVII, No. 13, February 1, 2002) A34, http://en.wikiquote.org/wiki/Mohandas_Karamchand_Gandhi

4. Jonas Salk, quoted in Quonation.com, http://quonation.com/quote/841

5. Noam Chomsky, "Losing' the world: American decline in perspective", TomDispatch.com, http://www.tomdispatch.com/blog/175502/

6. Jack Kaskey, "From USDA Rule Changes to Hasten Modified Crop Approvals", Bloomberg News, February 22, 2012, http://www.bloomberg.com/news/2012-02-22/genetically-modified-crops-will-get-faster-approval-usda-says.html

7. Peter Lehner, "BP Nets $7.7 Billion in Profits, Gulf Fishermen Net Shrimp Without Eyes", Natural ReSource Intelligences Defense Council, February 22, 12, http://readersupportednews.org/opinion2/271-38/10094-bp-nets-77-billion-in-profits-gulf-fishermen-net-shrimp-without-eyes

8. Walter Brasch, The Smirking Chimp, "Pennsylvania Fracking Law Gags Physicians", Reader Supported News, March 22, 2012, http://readersupportednews.org/news-

section2/312-16/10573-pennsylvania-fracking-law-gags-physicians

Chapter Eighteen

1. Mahatma Gandhi, as quoted in Quotations Page, http://www.quotationspage.com/quote/4013.html

2. Dan Froomkin, Paul Bloomenthal, "How The Bank Lobby Owns Washington", Auction 2012 series, Huffington Post, January 30, 2012, http://www.huffingtonpost.com/2012/01/30/auction-2012-banks-lobby-washington_n_1240762.html

Chapter Nineteen

1. George Santayana, quoted from inscription on a plaque at the Auschwitz concentration camp and a subway placard in Germany, Wikipedia, http://en.wikipedia.org/wiki/George_Santayana

2. David Brock and Ari Rabin-Havt, "Media Quotes: The Worst Things Said On Fox News", Democratic Underground, February 23, 2012, http://www.democraticunderground.com/101615914

3. Huffington Post, "Michael Meehan, Berkeley Police Chief, Sent Armed Cop To Reporter's Home At Midnight, Potentially Violated First Amendment", Huffington Post, March 11, 2012, http://www.huffingtonpost.com/2012/03/10/michael-meehan-berkeley-police_n_1336992.html

4. David Sirota, "Forgetting the Past, One Military Movie at a Time", February 24, 2012, truthdig.com, http://www.truthdig.com/report/item/forgetting_the_past_one_military_movie_at_a_time_20120224/

5. Huffington Post, "Chicago Symphony Orchestra Fight: Concert-Goers Brawl During Performance", Huffington Post Chicago, March 11, 2012, http://www.huffingtonpost.com/2012/03/10/chicago-symphony-orchestra-fight_n_1337089.html

6. Dan Kovalik, "Seven Truths Inconvenient to US Foreign Policy", CounterPunch, January 22, 2012, http://readersupportednews.org/news-section2/318-66/9568-focus-seven-truths-inconvenient-to-us-foreign-policy

7. Glenn Greenwald, "End of the Pro-Democracy Pretense", Salon, January 2, 2012, http://www.salon.com/2012/01/02/end_of_the_pro_democracy_pretense/

Chapter Twenty

1. Traditional Gospel Song, Wikipedia, http://en.wikipedia.org/wiki/Old-Time_Religion

2. Buddha, as quoted in Japanese-Buddhism, http://www.japanese-buddhism.com/buddha-quotes.html

3. Edward Estlin Cummings, quoted in Dreams in the Mirror: A Biography of E.E. Cummings, by Richard S. Kennedy (Liveright Publishing Corporation, 2nd edition, October 17, 1994) 456.

4. G. Vincent Runyon, Why I Left The Ministry And Became An Atheist (Superior Books, January 1, 1959).

5. King James Bible (Cambridge Ed.), http://biblehub.com/john/10-30.htm

6. Karen Armstrong, Twelve Steps to a Compassionate Life (Anchor, Reprint edition, December 27, 2011) 55.

7. Karl Marx, Contribution to the Critique of Hegel's Philosophy of Right, Cambridge University Press (August, 1977) 131.

8. King James Bible (Cambridge Ed.), http://bible.cc/ ecclesiastes/1-9.htm

9. Pliny the Elder, Natural History, Book 10, Chapter 1, as quoted in Latin Text & Translations, http://www. perseus.tufts.edu/hopper/text?doc=Perseus%3Atext%3A19 99.02.0137%3Abook%3D10%3Achapter%3D1

Chapter Twenty-One

1. Jim Blascovich and Jeremy Bailenson, Infinite Reality (New York: William Morrow April 5, 2011) 63 – 64.

2. Jason Black, Kieran Downes, Frank Field, Aleksandra Mozdzanowska, Katherine Steel: (Abstract), June 14, 2006, "The Metaphors of Emerging Technologies: Unpacking the disconnects between the "what" and the "how" in the world of "online shopping", DSpace@MIT, http://hdl.handle.net/ 1721.1/33003

3. Author's Interview with Anonymous, April, 2012.

4. Neale Donald Walsch, The Storm Before the Calm (Emnin Books, 2011) 15.

Chapter Twenty-two

1. Todd S. Purdum, One Nation, Under Arms (Vanity Fair, January 2012) 119.

2. Chuck Baldwin, "Can You Imagine This Country?" July 10, 2007, Chuck Baldwin Live, http://www. chuckbaldwinlive.com/c2007/cbarchive_20070710.html

3. Hans Christian Andersen, "Tales, Vol. XVII, Part 3, The Harvard Classics," New York: P.F. Collier & Son, as referenced in Bartleby.com, www.bartleby.com/17/3/

4. Naomi Klein, The Shock Doctrine", Picador; 1st edition (June 24, 2008), 720 pages, page 46, referenced in James LeMoyne, "Testifying to Torture," The New York Times, June 5, 1988.

5. Abby Zimet, "NYPD: Making the Crime Numbers Look Good, Seemingly At Any Cost", Common Dreams, March 10, 2012 https://www.commondreams.org/further/ 2012/03/10 quoting Graham, Rayman. "The NYPD Tapes Confirmed," The Village Voice, March 7, 2012, http://www.villagevoice.com/2012-03-07/news/the-nypd-tapes-confirmed

6. Matthew Warshauer, "Who Wants to Be a Millionaire", ARNet, February 13, 2003, http://www.americansc.org.uk/ Online/American_Dream.htm

7. Epps, Garret, "We the People", Utne Reader -The Nation, May – June 2011, http://www.utne.com/Politics/We-The-People-Constitution-Originalism-Conservative-Politicians.aspx

8. Zukav, Gary, Spiritual Partnership: The Journey to Authentic Power (HarperOne, 1st edition 2010) 237.

9. Patton, General George S., captured October 4, 2013, as quoted in http://rightwingnews.com/quotes/rwns-favorite-george-s-patton-quotes-2

10. Greenwald, Glenn, "Afghanistan and American Imperialism", Guardian UK, 21 March 19, 2012.

11. Michael Snyder, "36 Statistics Which Prove That The American Dream Is Turning Into An Absolute Nightmare For The Middle Class," The American Dream, May 2, 2011, http://endoftheamericandream.com/archives/36-

statistics-which-prove-that-the-american-dream-is-turning-into-an-absolute-nightmare-for-the-middle-class.

12. Krugman, Paul, "How Fares the Dream?", The New York Times, January 15, 2012, http://www.nytimes.com/2012/01/16/opinion/krugman-how-fares-the-dream.html?_r=0

13. Sledge, Matt, "Problems In U.S. Go Far Beyond Dollars", The Huffington Post, February 2, 2012, http://www.huffingtonpost.com/2012/02/02/us-infrastructure-deficit_n_1250886.html

14. Duhigg, Charles and Barboza, David, "In China, Human Costs are Built Into an iPad", New York Times, January 25, 2012 , http://www.nytimes.com/2012/01/26/business/ieconomy-apples-ipad-and-the-human-costs-for-workers-in-china.html?pagewanted=all&_r=0

15. Amnesty International, "Death Penalty 2011: Alarming Levels of Executions in the Few Countries that Kill", Amesty.org, March 27, 2011, http://www.amnesty.org/en/news/death-penalty-2011-alarming-levels-executions-few-countries-kill-2012-03-27

16. Jesse Jackson, "We Have to Choose What Kind of a People We Are", Huffington Post blog, March 13, 2012, http://www.huffingtonpost.com/rev-jesse-jackson/we-have-to-choose-what-ki_b_1341730.html

Chapter 23

1. Hubbard, Barbara Marx, Emergence: The Shift From Ego to Essence (Hampton Roads Publishing; First Edition, 2001) 17.

2. Grace Lee Boggs, "We Need to Grow Our Souls", Common Dreams, March 13, 2012, https://www.commondreams.org/headline/2012/03/13-7

3. Chuck Collins and Pam Rogers, with Joan P. Garner, *Robin Hood Was Right* (W. W. Norton & Company, January 2001) 16.

PART THREE

Chapter 24

1. Adyashanti, *The End of Your World: Uncensored Straight Talk on the Nature of Enlightenment* (Sounds True, 2009) 166, 167.

2. Lehrer, Tom, "National Brotherhood Week" from *That Was the Year That Was*. Track 1, Reprise / Wea Records, 1965, http://www.metrolyrics.com/national-brotherhood-week-lyrics-tom-lehrer.html

3. Evans-Wentz, W.Y, *Tibet's Great Yogi Milarepa: A Biography from the Tibetan*, (Oxford University Press; First Edition, 1928), xiii.

4. Mirabai Starr, translator of "Living Flame of Love" by St. John of the Cross as quoted in Ram Dass, *Be Love Now* (HarperOne; Reprint edition, November 8, 2011) 6-7.

Chapter 25

1. Albert Einstein, quoted in Brainy Quote http://www.brainyquote.com/quotes/quotes/a/alberteins133 991.html

2. Bishop Desmond Tutu, as quoted in *Encyclopedia of Genocide*, Volume 2 (I-Y), (Institute on the Holocaust and Genocide, Jerusalem 1999) ivii.

3. Holy Bible, King James Version, Cambridge Edition, John 10:30, http://bible.cc/john/10-30.htm

4. Holy Bible, King James Version, Cambridge Edition, John 14:12, http://bible.cc/john/14-12.htm

5. Kevin Kelly, quoted in "What is the best definition of Singularity?" Singularity Symposium, http://www. singularitysymposium.com/definition-of-singularity.html, captured 12/20/2012.

6. Pablo Neruda, translated by Alastair Reid, "Keeping Quiet," Extravagaria: A Bilingual Edition (Noonday Press, 2001), 26.

Chapter 26

1. Buddha, quoted in lake orchard studio, December 16, 2010, http://www.lakeorchardstudio.com/2010/12/moment.html

2. Holy Bible, King James Version, Cambridge Edition, John 14:10, http://bible.cc/john/14-10.htm

3. Holy Bible, King James Version, Cambridge Edition, John 10:30, http://bible.cc/john/10-30.htm

4. Abby Zimet, "Solving War Crimes With Wrist Bands: The White Savior Industrial Complex", Common Dreams, March 22, 2012, http://www.commondreams.org/further/2012/03/22-2

Chapter 27

1. Seth Godin, quoted in "Top 50 Social Media Quotes & Social Networking Quotes" by Ryan Park, arrae/network, quote 50, http://adventured.com/about-life-quotes/social-media-quotes-socialnetwork-quotes

Chapter 28

1. Charles Duhigg, The Power of Habit (Random House, New York, February 2012) 273.

Epilogue

1. Night Watch, "The Chinese Dream", finance.townhall.com, March 17, 2013, http://finance.townhall.com/columnists/nightwatch/2013/03/19/the-chinese-dream-n1538023/page/full/

2. Peter Kingsley, Reality (The Golden Sufi Center, California, 2004) 305-306.

3. E.R. Dodds, The Greeks and the Irrational (Berkeley, 1951) 209.

4. Peter Kingsley, Reality (The Golden Sufi Center, California, 2004).